Speculations after Freud

Psychoanalysis has emerged from the intimate, personal experience of therapy into the wider public domain: it has become a cultural term of reference which underpins many disciplines. It has sought to become the dominant language of psychological and social discourse, while trying to remain a separate and institutionally controlled discipline. Owing to this double bind, its own identity is now increasingly in crisis: does it still have a role to play in cultural debate, or must new forms of thinking be developed in its place?

This volume, a collection of essays on the intersections between psychoanalysis, philosophy and cultural studies, asks questions about the future of psychoanalysis. Addressing the dilemmas afflicting contemporary psychoanalysis, *Speculations after Freud* pits together advocates and critics of psychoanalysis in order to challenge its assumptions and its powerful hold on contemporary culture.

Sonu Shamdasani is a researcher on the history and philosophy of psychology. He is Consultant to the Psychoanalytic Forum at the Institute of Contemporary Arts, London, and the editor of Jung's *Seminar on Kundalini Yoga* (forthcoming). **Michael Münchow** is a freelance writer and translator on psychoanalysis and philosophy based in Copenhagen, Denmark.

Speculations after Freud

Psychoanalysis, philosophy and culture

Edited by Sonu Shamdasani
and Michael Münchow

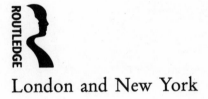

London and New York

First published 1994
by Routledge
11 New Fetter Lane, London EC4P 4EE

Simultaneously published in the USA and Canada
by Routledge
29 West 35th Street, New York, NY 10001

Phototypeset in Garamond by
Intype, London

Printed and bound in Great Britain by
T.J. Press (Padstow) Ltd, Cornwall

Printed on acid free paper

British Library Cataloguing in Publication Data
A catalogue record for this book is available from the British Library.

Library of Congress Cataloging in Publication Data
Speculations after Freud: psychoanalysis, philosophy, and culture/
  edited by Sonu Shamdasani and Michael Münchow.
  p. cm.
Based on papers presented at the conference Speculations: appraising psychoanalysis, philosophy and cultural studies, held Oct. 26–28, 1990.
Includes bibliographical references and index.
1. Psychoanalysis–Philosophy–Congresses. 2. Psychoanalysis and philosophy–
Congresses. 3. Psychoanalysis and culture–Congresses. 4. Freud, Sigmund,
1856–1939–Congresses. I. Shamdasani, Sonu, 1962–. II. Münchow, Michael,
1961–.
BF175.S615 1994
150.19'5–dc20
93–26967
CIP

ISBN 0–415–07655–2 (hbk)
ISBN 0–415–07656–0 (pbk)

Contents

Contributors

Mikkel Borch-Jacobsen is Professor of Romance Languages at the University of Washington, Seattle.

Cornelius Castoriadis is a practising psychoanalyst and Director of Studies at the Ecole des Hautes Etudes, Paris.

James Hillman is the seminal figure behind archetypal psychology and is based in Thompson, Connecticut.

Sarah Kofman is Professor of Philosophy at the University of Paris I, Panthéon-Sorbonne.

David Farrell Krell is Professor of Philosophy at DePaul University, Chicago.

Julia Kristeva is Professor of Linguistics at the University of Paris.

Alphonso Lingis is Professor of Philosophy at Pennsylvania State University.

Nicholas Rand is Professor of French Literature at the University of Wisconsin, Madison.

William Richardson is Professor of Philosophy at Boston College.

Charles E. Scott is Edwin Erle Sparks Professor of Philosophy at Pennsylvania State University.

Gayatri Chakravorty Spivak is Professor of Comparative Literature at the University of Columbia.

Maria Torok is a practising psychoanalyst and theoretician based in Paris.

Preface

Through the preparation of an international conference, the "event" soon detaches itself from the "originators". It momentarily links together a multitude of people, who through participating helped create it and to whom thanks are hence due. We would like to make singular mention of Richard Wells, the former director of the Freud Museum – whose vision for a public programme made available the support and a considerable amount of the limited resources of the Museum. Without these resources the project would never have been realized. The Museum's staff contributed to the organization of the conference – Susan O'Cleary especially, but also Andie Awde, Alex Bento, Paul Cobley, Erica Davies, Keith Davies, Allison Green, Michael Molnar and Ivan Ward. Particular thanks are due to Steve Gans, the consultant to the project, whose lateral thinking played a crucial role in its germination and formulation; Steve Hornibrook, whose early death robbed these debates of what would have been one of their most distinctive voices; Michel Monory and Michel Oriano, successive directors of the Institut Français, who generously made available their facilities together with sponsorship and the assistance of Paola Jojima, Jean-Marc Lanteri and Frédéric Beaufort. Invaluable assistance was also provided by Geoff Bennington, Brion Haworth, Nicholas Harrison, Richard Kearney, Paul Sirett, Tom Waldron, Steve Whitenstall and Sarah Wykes.

The editors and publishers would like to thank Stanford University Press for permission to include Mikkel Borch-Jacobsen's "The alibis of the subject" which appeared in Mikkel Borch-Jacobsen, *The Emotional Tie: Psychoanalysis, Mimesis, and Affect* (1993) and Galilée for permission to publish the English translation of Sarah Kofman's "Il n'y a que le premier pas qui coûte" (1992). Julia Kristeva's "Psychoanalysts in times of distress" first appeared as "Psychanalystes en temps de detresse" in *Lettre Internationale*, no. 21 (Summer 1989).

Each text is preceded by a pre-text and selected bibliography, which introduces the author and sketches the context of their contribution.

M.M. and S.S.

Introduction
The censure of the speculative

Sonu Shamdasani

"What follows is speculation, often far-fetched speculation."
(Freud, *Beyond the Pleasure Principle*)

The genre of an introduction to a collective volume raises the question of the commonality of the papers, beyond a generating event, such as a conference. When the collection purports to be "on" psychoanalysis, the question becomes more charged, as it dovetails into the issue of who, and in whose name, may lay claim to psychoanalysis. Thus it quickly takes on a juridical form, and leads into the thicket of current disputations. Contemporary psychoanalysis is in a state of dissociation due to the multiple claims upon its identity. What follows stages this contestation.

In the case of psychoanalysis, such a situation is hardly a novelty. The policing of identity and the attempt to insure the propriety of its name were articles of its institutional constitution. As an instance, one may cite a discussion in 1908 in the Vienna Psycho-Analytical Society around a proposal to abolish "intellectual communism" in psychoanalysis. Freud, whilst agreeing that each might himself state how he wanted his ideas dealt with, magnanimously waived all rights to his own remarks, making them available for general use.[1] This gesture, allowing and indeed inviting a deregulated purchase upon his ideas, was an essential precondition if they were to enter common parlance and achieve a widespread cultural dissemination. However, it also gave rise to a disturbing and unwelcome spectre. In 1910, in "Observations on 'wild' psycho-analysis", Freud regrettably noted the ineluctable necessity for the International Psycho-Analytical Association, due to the proliferation of "wild" psychoanalysis:

> Neither I myself nor my friends and co-workers find it agreeable to claim . . . a monopoly in this way in the use of medical technique. But in the face of the dangers to patients and to the cause of psycho-analysis which are inherent in the practice that is to be foreseen of a "wild" psycho-analysis, we have no other choice. In the spring of 1910 we founded an International Psycho-Analytical Association . . . in order to be able to repudiate responsibility for what is done by those who do not belong to us and yet call their medical procedure "psycho-analysis".

For as a matter of fact "wild" analysts of this kind do more harm to the cause of psycho-analysis than to individual patients.[2]

These statements may be read as two sides of a cultural double bind, which has been the legacy of psychoanalysis, and bedevilled the possibility of free association and debate. The following year, in the first presidential address at the Weimar conference, the latter principle was already in need of reiteration:

> it seems to me of great importance to expose deviations of opinion to immediate and thorough discussion to forestall any squandering of our strength on pointless side-issues. This possibility, as the events in Vienna have shown, lies not so far afield, inasmuch as the present unbridled ways of psychoanalytic investigation and the multitude of problems that are touched upon encourage changes, as revolutionary as they are unjustified in the principles of neurosis theory that Freud discovered and elaborated through decades of hard work. I believe, vis-à-vis such temptations, that we must never forget that our Association also has the important purpose of discrediting "wild" psychoanalysis and not admitting it to its own ranks.[3]

The association clearly heeded this categorical memorandum, upon whose perpetual remembrance the identity of the "we" rested. One may pause to consider the status of a statute whose installation took the form of an injunction, that could have been forgotten prior to its enunciation, and of an admissions policy constructed in the *post facto* recognition that it was already too late, that the inadmissible had already occurred. The "proper" came after the "improper", and was in part its effect. Within this spectre of "wild" psychoanalysis lurks the fear of the impossibility of legislative control, of ownership, of the enclosure of identity. Otherwise put: that psychoanalysis harbours within itself the possibility of being taken to another destination, deracinated, dispossessed. Imminent history, of course, ironized Jung's proclamation. Hardly had he made it than he fell under its censure, leaving Freud to attempt to reclaim the sole right of enunciative jurisdiction over psychoanalysis, in his epic narrative of its "autogenesis":

> Psychoanalysis is my creation.... I consider myself justified in maintaining that even today no one can know better than I do what psychoanalysis is, how it differs from other ways of investigating the life of the mind, and precisely what could be called psychoanalysis and what would better be described by some other name.[4]

The dramatic rise of revisionistic Freud scholarship in recent decades has laid to rest the "immaculate conception" version of the birth of psychoanalysis through Freud's self-analysis, and revealed the incorporation of psychoanalysis as far more complex than hitherto imagined.[5] If the citable instances of the violent prosecution of the claim to possess the legislative right and tenure of psychoanalysis are innumerable, no less so are the instances of its insufficiency: and it is this latter condition, that the following papers, with their unbridled speculations, attest to.[6]

Introducing such a collection in the Anglo-American context, one meets with a bifurcation. On the one side, one finds psychoanalysis deployed in a devoutly empiricist, clinical temper in the psychotherapeutic profession, and a plethora of reformationist schools, each seeking to orthopaedically develop psychoanalysis. On the other side, one finds an *émigré* psychoanalysis, shaped by the continental reading or appropriation of Freud, installed as a resident alien in other discourses, which has led to novel reconfigurations of psychoanalysis. "Freud", as recent surveys suggest, comes out as the most heavily cited author in social sciences, arts and humanities indices.[7] However, the prestige thus accorded to psychoanalysis in critical discourse has meant that one frequently finds a monolithically conceived psychoanalysis propping up discourses in moments of lapsing, through providing interpretative empowerment – whilst the lapses of psychoanalysis pass unrecognized.

A reader approaching this collection from the first position is likely to initially experience an alienation effect, when faced with such "wild" readings. What is one to make of such a bewildering preference for "theory" and close textual exegesis, seemingly disdainful of the immediacy of the demands of clinical practice and the increasing concerns for professionalization and statutory legislation? Of a blatant disregard for, or lack of consideration of, the more customary obligatory notaries of the profession, such as Klein, Kohut, Kernberg & Co.? Of the advocacy of positions which resemble nothing so much as pathological conditions: loss of self, psychotic fragmentation, manic defence, gender confusion, acting out – and evoke the censure of diagnosis? Of parodic reversals of the traditional categorical maxims of the aims of analysis? Of a view of psychoanalysis as a co-conspirator in the "critique of the subject", at antipodes to more familiar notions of the establishment of the "true self", "ego strength", "identity", etc? And all this, on the surface at least, by way of the same canonical Freudian texts. Clearly, it is the very commonality here that is most disturbing. How can the same primal concepts have such antithetical meaning? The phantasmic doubles of such "speculative aberrations" would seem to veritably belong "in the funhouse".

The traditional gesture from the Anglo-American analytic context has been one of repudiation – often with the simple, tell-tale word – "Lacan" – which so often functions as a synonym for the illegible. This of course does not stop the same name from underwriting similar dictates within another context. Such gestures are girded by the claim to the possession of the "proper" Freud, which would serve to safeguard the futures of psychoanalysis by delimiting in advance the permissible sphere of contestation. The arrogation of such legislative authority necessarily places itself out of court, above the law. Yet the very existence of the interminable multiplications of "new" beginnings and foundations for psychoanalysis, new assumptions of the law, each laying claim to be the sole rightful inheritor of the Freudian estate, would seem to mutually render each of their presumptions untenable.

A constituent premise of this collection would be a resistance to the violent scansion of such totalizations.

These papers attest to an obsessive, compulsive insistence on the name of psychoanalysis, even if one may rightfully ask what, if anything, remains of a supposedly originary conception, "Freud's" for instance. This continued insistence on the name bears the mark of an intended and indeed provocative transformation of psychoanalysis. One may undoubtedly remark that as long as such projects insist upon the utilization of the name, then censure is inevitable. However, they are hardly formulated with the sole intention of inciting short-lived scandals. On the contrary, the insistence on the name is necessitated by the fact that psychoanalysis, for better or worse, has in many respects been the dominant form of psychological intelligibility in the West this century, such that a rearticulation of the latter must in part go by way of the former. Thus the circumscription of the terms by which the former may be debated is not without serious consequences for the latter.

The first step that these papers require would be to risk a momentary suspension of the verities of contemporary practice. For some, it is this move, perceived as cavalierly overriding the exigencies of the suffering and the demand for its alleviation that are daily brought to the therapeutic situation, that provokes censure. If clinicians turn to theory as the safeguard amidst the turmoil and the strain of the clinical encounter, serious tampering with this frame is assumed to threaten the survival of both participants. From another angle, it is precisely because so much potentially rides upon the stakes of this encounter that rigorous questioning is necessitated: such questioning would then be seen not as an avoidance of the call of suffering, but as an attempt to allow it the time of another hearing. A recognition of the necessity of something like psychoanalysis, whilst at the same time recognizing the impoverishment of its means.

To stay with the ambiguity and uncanniness evoked by these readings is to allow such questions to fold back upon psychoanalysis itself. However, this would not be simply to remain in psychoanalysis, as currently conceived, but to attempt to envisage that which it faces, that which it calls forth and that by which it constitutes itself in claiming to respond to. This would restore a provisionality to the decision of/for psychoanalysis, and open the possibility of another response: it was with this hiatus in mind that this project was conceived. Would not the act of articulating and attending to such an interval, prior to the safe assurance of a pregiven interpretation, a predetermined hearing, reveal itself as being far closer to the demands of practice, than had first been supposed? Would this not also restore to contemporary psychoanalysis (if indeed it were possible) the very dimension that has been lacking?

The papers gathered exhibit a noticeable heterogeneity. A linkage could be formed, a posteriori, by regarding each as an instance of a limit negotiation, a brokerage of the *limen* between psychoanalysis and other disciplines. If one of the constituent moves of psychoanalysis was a differentiation from neighbouring disciplines, then these manoeuvres appear as a series of unbe ginnings, or reversals of constitution. As fertile moments of the traversal of the boundaries of psychoanalysis are essayed, it, together with its sur- rounds, are reconceived. This enables the release of issues which no longer sit snugly within a disciplinarian closure of identity. In the process, psycho- analysis reveals an unmasterable exteriority crypted within itself. Issues emerge, or take on forms, that are no longer contained or controlled within it, as by an epistemic safety net. Such a loosening, predictably enough, is not without serious political consequences, as the collapse of the principle of identity brings with it ever more frenzied attempts to shore it up.

This interdisciplinary dispersion gestures towards a relocation of psycho- analysis. That psychoanalysis is not One, cannot be owned, or adequately appropriated. That its heterogeneity renders impossible any pluralist all- encompassing programme, or attempt at unification. Thus the lack of commonality represented here would be indicative less of a lack of cohesive agenda, than a highlighting of the increasingly prevalent cultural (dis)locations of psychoanalysis. One might then consider such readings as less the symptomatic products of a failure of orthopaedics, or of a myopic refusal of the powers of prescriptive vision, than a witness to a capacity of translocation, of alteration, upon which the continued cultural saliency of psychoanalysis perhaps depends.

These papers are above all concerned with the future of psychoanalysis. The stakes are set out with renewed clarity, in a mode that avoids the facile posing of a "for or against" dichotomy. Put one way, the issue turns on whether one can conceive of a transformation of psychoanalysis, in the face of the limit questions raised, such as the following: can it dispense with its hypnoallergic reactions when faced with the enigmatic rapport of the trance? Can its retreat from the political still lead to a restoration of political agency, whether through traditional categories of citizenship or their reconceptualization? Can it suspend its normative regulation of corporality when faced with the theatrics of transsexuality? Can it abandon the therapeutic burden of restoring the certitudes of western selfhood as they falter? Or does the legibility of such profiles spell the end of psychoanalysis?

On such points, the contributors clearly differ – in their sense of the possibilities of psychoanalysis, but also as to where its limits truly lie. For some, the suspicion seems to be growing that the name of Freud is no longer able to guarantee the cheques being drawn on his name, and the recognition of the ruination of psychoanalysis leads to the conclusion that the psychological must be staged through quite other terms. However, this is articulated not by a simple abandonment of psychoanalysis, which would at the same time preserve without challenging the identity of psychoanalysis, through the appeal to an easily attainable elsewhere[8] – but by readings that question the extent to which psychoanalysis has always been ghosted, haunted by "another scene" – and hence that other configurations of the psychological may be envisaged by attending to the Other in the Same. For others, by contrast, not only is a renewal of psychoanalysis possible, but a thus transformed psychoanalysis holds out perhaps the sole means of untying the Gordian knots of contemporary political and cultural life. Within the agonistic contests and lack of consensus staged here, one might nevertheless find the possibility of forms of dialogue rarely encountered in traditional psychoanalytic enclaves.

This collection stems from a conference entitled "Speculations: appraising psychoanalysis, philosophy and cultural studies", which took place on 26–28 October, 1990, under the auspices of the Freud Museum. It posed the question: "Is appraisal of the spectacular theatre of psychoanalysis a possibility – and out of Freud's own home in London?" Skeletally put, shortly after the event, the programme which generated it was liquidated. After losing their posts, the editors proceeded independently with the publication of this volume. If this censure constitutes one mode in which the question of the speculative has all too often been answered, the papers that follow emphatically embody another.

This introduction no doubt betrays the temptation to relay the final papers back to an initial agenda, whilst retrospectively reformulating how it should have been posed in the first place. On both counts, the contributors would be amply justified in contesting the framing of their work. It thus remains to thank them for nevertheless being willing to submit to this double indignity, and for their continued support of this project, despite the abrupt withdrawal of the "official" seal of Freud. For their contributions render otherwise how that inscription is to be read.

NOTES

1 *Minutes of the Vienna Psycho-Analytical Society*, vol. 1: 1906–8, ed. Hermann Nunberg and Ernst Federn (New York: International University Press, 1962), pp. 299–303.

2 S. Freud, *The Standard Edition of the Complete Psychological Works of Sigmund Freud* (hereafter *SE*), ed. J. Strachey (London: Hogarth Press, 1953–74), 11, pp. 226–7.

3 C. G. Jung, *Collected Works*, vol. 18, (London, Routledge & Kegan Paul, 1977) p. 425.

4 S. Freud, *SE*, 14, p. 7.

5 For an up-to-date assortment and assessment of revisionistic Freud scholarship to date, see Toby Gelfand and John Kerr (eds), *Freud and the History of Psychoanalysis* (New Jersey: Analytic Press, 1992).

6 See especially Peter Swales's remarkable uncovering of the illegitimate arrogation of authority to control and manipulate the history of psychoanalysis, through the founding of the Sigmund Freud Archives, in "Freud and the unconscionable: the obstruction of Freud studies, 1946–2113" (forthcoming).

7 Cited by Toby Gelfand in his introduction to *Freud and the History of Psychoanalysis*.

8 The most recent and alarming example is the role played by a rejection of psychoanalysis in the North American epidemic of "Multiple personality disorder", which, judging by the lack of response, has been treated as a negative hallucination by the psychoanalytic community. See Ian Hacking, "Multiple personality disorder and its hosts", *History of the Human Sciences*, vol. 5, no. 2 (1992); Ruth Leys, "The Real Miss Beauchamp: gender and the subject of limitation", in Judith Butler and Joan Scott (eds), *Feminists Theorize the Political* (New York: Routledge, 1992) and Mikkel Borch-Jacobsen, "Pour introduire la personnalité multiple", in *Importance de l'hypnose*, ed. Isabelle Stenghers (Paris, 1993). Related issues are also taken up in my "Automatic writing and the discovery of the Unconscious", *Spring: A Journal of Archetype and Culture*, vol. 54 (1993) and my introduction to the reissue of Théodore Flournoy, *From India to the Planet Mars: A Case of Multiple Personality with Imaginary Languages* (Princeton: Princeton University Press, 1994).

1 Psychoanalysis and politics

Cornelius Castoriadis

Cornelius Castoriadis is a practising psychoanalyst. From 1979 he has been Director of Studies at the Ecole des Hautes Etudes. He initially gained recognition for his political activities which led him to co-found the group and journal "Socialisme ou Barbarie". A central thrust of his work has been "the project of autonomy", a struggle to overcome heteronomous structures of power both at a political and a psychological level. Two fundamentals are crucial in his work: the radical imagination of the singular human psyche and the imaginary institution of society. By arguing for the irreducible creative power of the singular human psyche, Castoriadis seeks to expose and undo any discourse, political or psychological, which professes that the singular human being may be exhaustively explained away by a thought-system outside it. Second, Castoriadis posits that the very fact that societies institute themselves cannot be explained in terms of anything outside this act. This thought firmly resists the heteronomous derivation of the structure of society from any metaphysical, theological or mythological realm.

In the present article, Castoriadis challenges the traditional pessimistic assessment of Freud's politics. He complements the famous Freudian maxim, "Where id was, there ego shall be" with the formulation, "Where I (Ego) am (is), That (Id) should/ought also to emerge". He also discusses the three "impossibles", as judged by Freud: politics, pedagogy and psychoanalysis. How does one convey autonomy? If autonomy is already in place then it does not need to be established; if it is conveyed, how can it then be autonomous and independent of the process of implementation? The answer is to be found in a new conception of psychoanalysis as a *practico-poetical* activity which takes into account the potential autonomy of the other and helps him/her to actualize it. In particular, psychoanalysis performs a negotiating task between the radical imagination of the subject and the imaginary institution of society, elements of which the individual has internalized as part of the formation of the ego. Psychoanalysis helps in creating self-reflexivity while refraining from positing itself as the legislator of human desire. Castoriadis shows the interdependence of psychoanalysis, pedagogy and politics in the impossible, i.e., non-given, project of autonomy.

SELECT BIBLIOGRAPHY

Castoriadis, C., *Crossroads in the Labyrinth*, tr. Martin H. Ryle and Kate Soper, Brighton: Harvester Press and Cambridge, Mass.: MIT Press, 1984.
—— *The Imaginary Institution of Society*, tr. Kathleen Blamey, Cambridge: Polity Press and Cambridge, Mass.: MIT Press, 1987.
—— *Philosophy, Politics, Autonomy*, tr. David A. Curtis, Oxford and New York: Oxford University Press, 1991.
—— *Political and Social Writings*, 3rd edn, tr. David A. Curtis, Minneapolis: University of Minnesota Press, 1988–93.

* * *

Discussions about the relation between psychoanalysis and politics have usually focused, in a one-sided way, on isolated formulations of Freud, or on his excursions and incursions into the philosophy of society and of history (*Civilization and its Discontents, The Future of an Illusion, Moses and Monotheism*). "Pessimistic" or even "reactionary" conclusions regarding the implications of psychoanalysis in terms of the projects of social and political transformation have almost always been drawn from these writings. Psychoanalysts, to the – insignificant – extent that they express an opinion on these matters, have shown a lazy and suspect readiness to satisfy themselves with these "conclusions". For this to be possible, it has been necessary to neglect or keep silent about other writings (e.g. *Totem and Taboo*) and other formulations of Freud, to which I have drawn attention elsewhere.[1] Moreover, and more seriously, some substantive questions, much more important than Freud's "opinions", have thereby been covered up. What is the signification of psychoanalysis itself, as theory and as practice? What are its implications, certainly not all of them fully explored, to say the least, in Freud's own writings? Has psychoanalysis nothing to do with the western emancipatory movement? Is the work directed towards the knowledge of the unconscious and the transformation of the human subject wholly unrelated to the question of freedom and the questions of philosophy? Would psychoanalysis itself have been possible outside the social-historical conditions achieved in Europe? Can the knowledge of the unconscious teach us nothing as regards the socialization of the individual, and, as a consequence, the institutions of society? Why should the practical perspective adopted by psychoanalysis in the sphere of the individual automatically become void when passing over to the collective sphere? One must recognize that these questions are seldom, if ever, raised, and never in a satisfactory manner. In what follows I summarize and enlarge on the conclusions of twenty-five years' work.[2]

I shall take as my starting point a remark of Freud's which I consider to be profound and true. He said twice that psychoanalysis, pedagogy and politics were the three impossible professions.[3] He did not explain why he took them to be impossible, a term which must be taken literally as well as *cum grano salis*, since, after all, he created psychoanalysis and practised it. We can reflect usefully on his use of this term, "impossible". He did not say that these professions were extremely difficult, as, for instance, are those of a brain surgeon, a concert pianist or Himalayan Sherpa. He said: impossible. Why? Certainly not because they have to do with that most intractable of all materials, the human being. Generals, salesmen and prostitutes deal with the same material, and we would not pronounce their professions impossible.

We can, of course, think of one strong reason why psychoanalysis and pedagogy, at least, may verge on the impossible; this would be that both have as their object the changing of human beings. Things, however, are not that simple. A behaviourist psychiatrist, a pedagogue like the father of President Schreber, the wardens of a Nazi or Stalinist concentration camp, the agents of Minilove and especially O'Brien himself: they all act in order to change human beings – and often succeed.

In all these cases, the aim of the activity is fully determined in the mind of the agent: it is to eradicate from a patient's mind and soul any trace of personal thinking and willing. The agent uses determinate means and he is supposed to be in full control of these and of the process in general. (That he may fail and that the reasons for such a failure would not be accidental is another matter.) Finally, means and ends are, in these cases, supposed to stand in a rational, identitary-ensemblist relation. Given the conditions (including whatever knowledge the agent may possess), given his aims and given what he knows or thinks he knows about the patient, he acts, or ought to act, in the most rationally efficient way. (His knowledge may, of course, include knowledge of deep psychological processes – as in Bruno Bettelheim's analysis of the rationale for the treatment of prisoners in Nazi camps: the main method of such a treatment was a breaking-up of the self-image of the prisoner, the demolition of his identificatory bearings. Orwell saw this with clarity and profundity in *Nineteen eighty-four*.)

If we now consider psychoanalysis, we see that none of this applies. Despite discussions of the aims and ends, or even end, of analysis, the objective the analyst is trying to reach is not definable in determinate and specific terms. O'Brien reached his objective when Winston Smith not only confessed what he was required to confess, but admitted to himself that he really loved Big Brother. This is a clearly describable and definable subjective state. Nothing similar can be said about the end of an analysis. (I only consider here what I beg permission to call the "full" – not ideal – analytical process. Certainly, the nature of the case may often lead the analyst to limit his ambitions.)

Freud, as is well known, has repeatedly returned to the question of the end and ends of analysis, giving various, apparently different definitions of it. I will consider here one of the last he gave, for I think it is the most comprehensive, the most pregnant and the most risky. It is the famous "*Wo Es war, soll Ich werden*" – "Where That was, I should/ought to become [and not 'be']".

I have discussed and commented at length on this formulation elsewhere,[4] and I shall now only sum up my conclusions. If, as Freud's formulation unfortunately seems to imply when considered within the sequence of his text, we take the sentence to mean that the *That*, the *Id*, *Es*, has to be eliminated, conquered by the *Ich*, the *Ego*, the *I*, dried up and reclaimed like the Zuider Zee, then we propose to ourselves both an impossible and a monstrous objective.[5] Impossible, of course, since there can be no human being whose unconscious is conquered by the conscious, whose drives are fully permeated and controlled by rational considerations, who has stopped fantasizing and dreaming. Monstrous, because reaching such a state would entail killing what makes us human. This is not rationality, but the uncontrolled and uncontrollable continuous surge of creative radical imagination in and through the flux of representations, affects and desires. Indeed, one of the objects of analysis is to free this flux from the repression to which it is usually subjected by an Ego which is a rigid and essentially social construct. This is why I propose that Freud's sentence be completed with: "*Wo Ich bin, soll auch Es auftauchen*" – "Where I (Ego) am (is), That (Id) should/ought also to emerge".

The object of analysis is not to eliminate one psychical *Instanz* ("agency" or "instance") to the benefit of another. It is to alter the relation between *Instanzen* – and to do that it has to alter one of them essentially: the I, the Ego or the conscious. The Ego is altered by taking in the contents of the unconscious, by reflecting on them and by becoming able to choose lucidly the impulses and ideas it will attempt to enact. In other words, the Ego has to become a self-reflexive subjectivity, capable of deliberation and will. The aim of analysis is not saintliness; as Kant said, nobody is ever a saint. The point is important, because analysis is thereby explicitly opposed to all ethics based on condemnation of desire and therefore on guilt. I want to kill you – or rape you – but I will not. Contrast this with Matthew 5, 27–8:

> Ye have heard that it was said by them of old time, Thou shalt not commit adultery. But I say unto you that whosoever looketh on a woman to lust after her hath committed adultery with her already in his heart.

How could analysis ever forget the cardinal fact upon which it is based: that we start out life looking on a woman "to lust after her", that this desire can never be eliminated, and, most importantly, that without it we would not become human beings, nay, we would not even survive?

The altered relation between *Instanzen* can thus be described as repression replaced by recognition of unconscious contents and reflection on them: inhibition, impulsive avoidance or acting out give way to lucid deliberation. The importance of this does not lie in the elimination of psychical conflict; nobody ever assured us that we are entitled to a conflict-less inner life. It lies in the instauration of a self-reflecting and deliberating subjectivity which has not become a pseudo-rational and socially "adapted" machine, but on the contrary has recognized and freed the radical imagin-ation at the core of the psyche.

I insisted on translating Freud's *werden* by "become" and not "be", because the subjectivity I am attempting to describe is essentially a process, not a state reached once and for all. This is why we can elucidate the aim of analysis, but cannot strictly define it. What I call the project of auton-omy on the level of the singular human being is the transformation of the subject so that he or she can enter this process; this is consubstantial with the aim of psychoanalysis.

This aim cannot be reached, nor even approached, without the self-activity of the patient: remembering, repeating, working through. The patient is the main agent of the psychoanalytical process.

Here we do not have means separated from ends. The various aspects of the analytical setting are not its means; rather they are conditions for its unfolding. The process itself is analytical in so far as it is always both means and ends. Free associations, for instance, are not just a means; as they unfold they express and realize the patient's developing capacity to free his flux of representations and thereby also recognize his affects and desires. The flux of associations, punctuated by the analyst's interpretations, brings into action the reflexive activity of the patient: he reflects himself and reflects upon himself, he re-turns to the material and takes it up again.

Thus psychoanalysis is not a technique, nor is it correct even to speak of psychoanalytic technique. Psychoanalysis is rather a practical/poetical activity where both participants are agents and where the patient is the main agent of the development of his own self-activity. I call it poetical because it is creative: its outcome is, or ought to be, the self-alteration of the analysand, that is, strictly speaking, the appearance of another being. I call it practical, because I call praxis that lucid activity whose object is human autonomy, an activity which can only be reached by means of this same autonomy.

From this perspective, things are similar regarding pedagogy. Pedagogy starts at age zero and no one knows when it ends. The aim of pedagogy (or *paideia*) – I am of course speaking normatively – is to help the newborn hopeful and dreadful monster to become a human being, to help this bundle of drives and imagination become an *anthropos*. I here take the term human being, *anthropos*, to mean an autonomous being in the sense indicated above; we may say, as well, remembering Aristotle, a being with the capacity to govern and be governed.

Pedagogy has at every age to develop the self-activity of the subject by using, so to speak, this very self-activity. The point of pedagogy is not to teach particular things, but to develop in the subject the capacity to learn: learn to learn, learn to discover, learn to invent.

This, of course, pedagogy cannot do without teaching certain things, any more than an analysis can progress without the analyst's interpretations. But like these interpretations, what is taught must always be considered a stepping-stone, not just for the possibility of additional teaching, but for the development of the learning, discovering, inventing capacities of the child. Pedagogy has necessarily to teach things, and in this respect many excesses of certain modern pedagogues have to be condemned. But two main principles remain: (1) Any educational process which does not aim at developing to the maximum the self-activity of the pupils is wrong. (2) Any educational system which cannot reasonably answer the question of the pupils, "Why should we learn that?", is faulty.

I cannot enter further into the vast subject of the relations between psychoanalysis and pedagogy. But one misunderstanding must be dispelled. Psychoanalysis does not postulate an intrinsically "good" human being; nor does it believe – like Reich, Marcuse or some French ideologists of "desire" – that we have only to let desires and drives express themselves for universal happiness to follow. The result in such a case would rather be universal murder. For psychoanalysis as, indeed, for common sense and for thinkers from Plato and Aristotle to Diderot, the adult has internalized a huge number of externally imposed constraints which go to form an integral part of his psyche. From the psychoanalytic point of view, this human being has renounced omnipotence, has accepted that words do not mean what he wants them to mean, has recognized the existence of other people whose desires most of the time oppose his own, and so on. From the social-historical point of view, the adult has internalized virtually the whole of the existing institution of society and more specifically, the imaginary significations which in each particular society organize the human and non-human worlds and give them meaning.

Pedagogy, in terms of psychoanalysis, consists of a nurturing of the newborn, bringing it to the state described above, with the minimal inhibition of its radical imagination, and the maximum development of its reflexivity. But, from a social-historical point of view, pedagogy must bring the child up to internalize, and therefore to accept fully, the existing institutions, whatever these may be. Clearly, we have reached an apparent antinomy, and a deep and difficult question. This brings us to politics and to the project of autonomy as a necessarily social, and not simply individual, project. I shall come to this presently.

Let me, however, initially return to the Freudian "impossible" with which I started. The impossibility of psychoanalysis and pedagogy lies in the fact that they both attempt to help in creating autonomy for their subjects by using an autonomy which does not yet exist. This appears to be a logical impossibility within the usual identitary-ensemblist logic. To be sure, human reality exceeds this logic. But the impossibility also appears, especially in the case of pedagogy, to lie in the attempt to produce auton-omous human beings within a heteronomous society, and beyond that, in the paradoxical situation of educating human beings to autonomy while – or in spite of – teaching them to absorb and internalize existing institutions.

The solution to this riddle is the "impossible" task of politics – all the more impossible since it must also lean on a not yet existing autonomy in order to bring its own type of autonomy into being. To this we now turn.

Psychoanalysis aims at helping the individual to become autonomous, that is, capable of self-reflexive activity and deliberation. In this respect, it belongs fully to the great social-historical stream and struggle for auton-omy, the emancipatory project to which democracy and philosophy also belong. But, as I have suggested, psychoanalysis as well as pedagogy also always faces the question of the existing institutions of society. This is directly apparent for pedagogy. For psychoanalysis, the encounter with the existing institutions is the encounter with the concrete Ego of the patient. This Ego is largely a social fabrication; it is designed to function in a given social setting and to preserve, continue and reproduce this setting, that is, the institutions which created it. These institutions are thus maintained not so much through violence and explicit coercion as through their internalization by the individuals in whose fabrication they par-ticipate.

Institutions and social imaginary significations are creations of the radical social instituting imaginary. This imaginary is the creative capacity of the anonymous collectivity, clearly manifest, for example, in the creation and evolution of language, family forms, mores, ideas, etc. The collectivity can only exist as instituted. Its institutions are always its own creation, but usually, once created, they appear to the collectivity as given (by ancestors, gods, God, nature, reason, the laws of history, the workings of competition, etc.); they become fixed, rigid and worshipped.

There is always in institutions a central, strong and effective element of, as well as instruments for, self-perpetuation (what we would call in psychoanalysis repetition), and the main one of these instruments is, as stated previously, the fabrication of conformable individuals. Such a state of society I call heteronomous; the *heteros*, the other who gave the law is no one but the instituting society itself which, for very deep reasons, has to disguise this fact. I call autonomous a society which not only knows explicitly that it has created its own laws, but has instituted itself so as to free its radical imaginary and enable itself to alter its institutions through a collective, self-reflexive and deliberate activity. And I call politics the lucid activity whose object is the institution of an autonomous society and the decisions about collective endeavours. It is immediately obvious that the project of an autonomous society becomes meaningless if it is not, at the same time, the project of bringing forth autonomous individuals, and vice versa.

There is indeed an illuminating analogy, but by no means an identity or "structural" homology, between the questions and the tasks which the project of autonomy faces in the individual and in the social fields. In the heteronomous case, the rigid structure of the institution and the disguising of the radical, instituting social imaginary correspond to the rigidity of the socially fabricated individual and the repression of the psyche's radical imagination. In terms of the project of autonomy, we have defined the aims of psychoanalysis and pedagogy as, first, the instauration of another type of relation between the reflexive subject (of will and of thought) and his unconscious, that is, his radical imagination and, second, the freeing of his capacity to make and do things, to form an open project for his life and to work with that project. We can similarly define the aims of politics as, first, the instauration of another type of relation between the instituting and the instituted society, between the given laws and the reflexive and deliberating activity of the body politic and, second, the freeing of the collective creativity, enabling it to form collective projects and to work with them. The essential link between these two aims of politics is found in pedagogy, education, *paideia*: for how could there be a reflexive collectivity without reflexive individuals? An autonomous society, as a self-instituting and self-governing collectivity, presupposes the development of the capacity of all its members to participate in its reflexive and deliberative activities. Democracy in the full sense can be defined as the regime of collective reflexivity; everything else can be shown to follow from this. And there can be no democracy without democratic individuals, and vice versa. This is also one of the paradoxical aspects of the "impossibility" of politics.

One can show even more clearly the intimate solidarity between the individual and the social dimension of the project of autonomy. The socialization of the psyche, even its sheer survival, requires that it recognizes and accepts the unfulfillability of its nuclear, primeval desires. In heteronomous societies this has been achieved not by the interdiction of acts, but by the interdiction of thoughts, by blocking the representative flux, by silencing radical imagination, as if society were applying, in reverse, the ways of the unconscious. To the omnipotence of unconscious thought, society replies by attempting to bring about the full impotence of this thought, and ultimately of thought *tout court*, as the only means to limit the acts. Forbidding to think has thus appeared as the only way to forbid the acting. This goes much further than the "severe and cruel superego" of Freud; history shows that it has actually entailed a mutilation of the radical imagination. We want autonomous individuals, that is, individuals capable of self-reflexive activity. But, unless we are to enter into an endless repetition, the contents and the objects of this activity, even the development of its means and methods, must be supplied by the soul's radical imagination. This is the source of the contribution of the individual to social-historical creation. And this is why a non-mutilating education, a true *paideia*, is of paramount importance.

I turn now to what I have called the riddle of politics. An autonomous society entails autonomous individuals. Individuals become what they are by absorbing and internalizing institutions; in a sense, they are the main concrete embodiment of these institutions. This internalization, we know, is anything but superficial: modes of thought and of action, norms and values and ultimately the very identity of the individual as a social being, all depend upon it. In a heteronomous society, the internalization of the laws, in the widest sense of the term, would be useless if it were not accompanied by the internalization of the supreme law or meta-law, "Thou shalt not put the laws into question". But the meta-law in an autonomous society can only be, "You shall obey the law – but you may put it into question. You may raise the question of the justice of the law, or of its appropriateness." (I shall not here enter into the formal clauses that may or should accompany this meta-law.)

We can now formulate the answer to our riddle, which is at the same time the first object of a politics of autonomy, of a democratic politics; this is to help the collectivity create the institutions which, when internalized by the individuals, will not limit, but rather enlarge, their capacity for becoming autonomous. It is clear that from this formulation, together with the principle of equality implicit in the plural "individuals", one can derive the main rules for a fully democratic institution of society, one incorporating, for instance, human rights and the equal, effective possibility of participation in all forms of power.

I shall not elaborate these points further since they are beyond the scope of our present discussion, except to comment on my expression above: the first object of a politics of autonomy. It is first, because it is the presupposition of all the rest and, in the long run, contains all the rest. There are, of course, other objects which are not exactly secondary. One such is the creation of specific institutions corresponding to the above maxim and specifying it in the given circumstances. Another is actual self-government. And a final one is proposals and decisions pertaining to collective works and endeavours. Autonomy is not just an end in itself: we want autonomy for its own sake, but also in order to be able and free to do things. The disincarnated ratiocinating political philosophy of our times always forgets this. A politics of autonomy must participate in all this; it is neither the psychoanalyst, nor the pedagogue, nor the conscious-ness of society, but it is an essential dimension of the latter's self-reflexivity. As such, it has to act on human beings, positing them as autonomous, to help them achieve their autonomy, without ever forgetting that the ultimate source of historical creativity is the radical imaginary of the anonymous collectivity. We can thus understand why politics is an "impossible pro-fession" like psychoanalysis and pedagogy, and perhaps even impossibly more impossible than these, given the nature and the dimensions of its partner and its task.

I shall end with some remarks on the most important question of all, which is common to psychoanalysis and to politics.

Social institutions hold sway over individuals because they fabricate and mould them; they do so completely in traditional cultures, and still to an important degree in our liberal societies. These institutions are internalized by the individual throughout his life. What is of decisive importance in this is the internalization of social imaginary significations. Society tears the singular human being from the closed universe of the psychical monad, forces it to enter into the harsh world of reality, but offers to it, in exchange, meaning. In the real world created by each society, things make sense, life and (usually) death have a meaning which, for the individual, is the subjective face of the social imaginary significations.

This *Sinngebung*, or rather *Sinnschöpfung*, is the crucial and hard point. Psychoanalysis does not teach a meaning for life. It can only help the patient to find, invent and create for himself such a meaning. There is no question of defining it in advance and in a universal way. On one of his more discouraged days, Freud wrote that analysis does not bring happiness, but can only transform neurotic misery into common, banal unhappiness. In this, I find him over-pessimistic. As such, analysis does not bring happiness, but in bringing neurotic misery to an end it helps the patient to form his own project for life.

But this does not exhaust the question. Why does analysis often fail or become interminable? In one of his last works, "Analysis terminable and interminable" from 1937, Freud invokes many reasons for this and ends by pointing to what he calls the "bedrock", the repudiation of femininity, which takes the form of penis envy in women and of the refusal of the passive or feminine attitude towards another male in men. He also mentions the aggressive-destructive drive and the death wish. It seems to me that death indeed plays a paramount role in this problem, but not exactly as Freud saw it.

An interminable analysis is essentially characterized by repetition. It is like neurosis, but at a higher level; it is repetition redoubled. Why this repetition? Cutting short a long story, we can say that repetition in the sense relevant here is the small change of death; it is the way in which the patient defends himself against the reality of wholesale death. The reason analysis fails or becomes interminable is, first, the incapacity of the patient – and of the analyst working with him – to accept the death of what he was and is in order for him to become another person (Freud knew this well, though he described it in different terms). The second reason is more important; it is the incapacity of the patient – and in this he is of necessity alone – to accept the reality of effective, total and complete death. Death is the ultimate rock against which an analysis can run aground.

Life, as we all know, entails the continuously suspended precariousness of meaning, precariousness of cathected objects, precariousness of cathected activities. But death is, as we also know, the meaninglessness of meaning. Our time is not time. Our time is not the time. Our time is no time.

Analysis, or maturity, is not achieved unless and until the person has become able to live on the edge of the abyss, within this ultimate double bind: live as a mortal, live as if you were immortal. (*"Eph' oson endechetai athanatizein"*, wrote Aristotle in the *Nichomachean Ethics.*)

These legendary banalities, as Jules Laforgue would say, find a fundamental analogy on the social and thus also on the political level. Heteronomous societies accomplish a *Sinnschöpfung* for everyone, forcing upon all its internalization. And they institute real or symbolic representations of a perennial meaning and an imaginary immortality in which everyone is supposed to participate in various ways. This can be the myth of the perennity of an instituted artifact – the King, the State, the Nation, the Party – with which everyone can, *tant bien que mal*, identify himself.

I think that an autonomous society would have none of this – on the public level, I mean – and that one of the main difficulties, if not perhaps, *the* difficulty facing the project of autonomy is the difficulty encountered by human beings in accepting, *sans phrase*, the mortality of the individual, of the collectivity and even of their works.

Hobbes was right, though for the wrong reasons. Fear of death is indeed the mainstay of institutions. Not the fear of being killed by the next man, but the justified fear that everything, even meaning, will dissolve.

Nobody, of course, can "solve" this problem. Any solution to it, if there is one, will only emerge on the way to a new social-historical creation, and to a corresponding alteration of the human being and his attitude toward life and death.

Meanwhile, it would certainly be useful to reflect upon the partial answers given to this problem by the two societies in which the project of autonomy was created and pursued, i.e., the Greek and the western. One cannot help being struck by the enormous differences in their answers and relate these differences to other essential aspects of the two attempts to create a democratic society. But this is a huge theme which has to be left for another time.

NOTES

1 See Cornelius Castoriadis, "Epilegomena to a theory of the soul" (1968), in *Crossroads in the Labyrinth* (Brighton: Harvester Press and Cambridge, Mass.: MIT Press, 1984).

2 See the first part, "Psyche", in Castoriadis, *Crossroads in the Labyrinth*, pp. 3–115; also *The Imaginary Institution of Society* (1964–54, 1975) (Cambridge: Polity Press and Cambridge, Mass.: MIT Press, 1987), pp. 102–7 and the whole of Chapter VI.

3 In "Analysis terminable and interminable" (1937), in *The Standard Edition of the Complete Psychological Works of Sigmund Freud* (hereafter *SE*), ed. J. Strachey (London: Hogarth Press, 1953–74), 23, p. 248 and, before that in "Preface

to Aichorn's *Wayward Youth*" (1925), *SE* 19, p. 273, where it is taken to be a traditional *bon mot*. Freud in fact talks about "government" (*Regierung*), not politics. But, for reasons that will become apparent shortly, traditional "government" does not present the problems discussed here.

4 See Castoriadis, *The Imaginary Institution of Society* and *Crossroads in the Labyrinth*, references as above. Freud's phrase is in the *New Introductory Lectures on Psychoanalysis* (1933), *SE* 22, p. 80, where it is translated as "Where id was, there ego shall be". Elsewhere, and very frequently, Freud talks about "taming of the drives", *Bändigung*.

5 Freud, of course, knew this perfectly well as many formulations in "Analysis terminable and interminable" show.

2 Psychoanalysts in times of distress

Julia Kristeva

Julia Kristeva is one of the most prominent writers of cultural theory in France and Professor of Linguistics at the University of Paris. Originally trained as a structuralist linguist, she took on a semiologist agenda for cultural studies and has contributed to such diverse fields as linguistics, semiotics, feminism, politics, art history, religious studies and psycho-analysis. Her challenge to the structuralist supremacy of language, or the "symbolic" in Lacanian psychoanalytic discourse, has been to argue for signifying agencies prior to language. Her most original contributions lie in her attempts to restore access to these prelinguistic, "semiotic" levels of experience through analyses of poetic styles, works of art, religion and politics and more recently through her own psychoanalytic practice.

In this essay, Kristeva situates psychoanalysis within its current confron-tations with both the neurological sciences and a general cultural indifference towards psychological life. She demonstrates the psychoanalytic access to a signifying process, prior to linguistic meaning, pertaining to the psycho-logical drives. The sense of this process may be recovered in the highly individualized analytic transference situation through psychoanalytic work that is attentive to the indices or traces which the drives may leave, for instance, in the inflection of the voice of the analysand. This task is an interpretative work of art, a *poiesis* which is shown to apply to the vast areas of suffering *not* reachable by psycho-pharmacology. Kristeva illustrates her theorization through reference to two concrete cases, one of which involves a close collaboration between psychoanalytic and pharmacological therapy.

SELECT BIBLIOGRAPHY

Kristeva, Julia, *Desire in Language: A Semiotic Approach to Literature and Art*, ed. Leon S. Roudiez, tr. Thomas Gora, Alice Jardine and Leon S. Roudiez, Oxford: Basil Blackwell, 1980.
—— *Powers of Horror: An Essay on Abjection*, tr. Leon S. Roudiez, New York: Columbia University Press, 1982.
—— *The Kristeva Reader*, ed. Toril Moi, Oxford: Basil Blackwell, 1986.

—— *In the Beginning Was Love: Psychoanalysis and Faith*, tr. Arthur
Goldhammer, New York: Columbia University Press, 1988.
—— *Black Sun: Depression and Melancholia*, tr. Leon S. Roudiez, New
York: Columbia University Press, 1989.
—— *Language the Unknown: An Initiation into Linguistics*, tr. Anne
Meuck, London: Harvester Wheatsheaf, 1989.
—— *Strangers to Ourselves*, tr. Leon S. Roudiez, London: Harvester
Wheatsheaf, 1991.

* * *

What good are psychoanalysts at a time of distress oblivious to itself? I
imagine a huge city with houses of glass and steel, reaching the sky,
reflecting both the sky, itself and you. People cultivate their image, hurried
and made up in the extreme, covered in gold, pearls, pure leather. In the
streets, on every corner, the filth piles up and drugs accompany the slumber
or rage of the outcasts . . .

This city could be New York. It resembles any big city of tomorrow,
ours . . .

What does one do there? One thing only: buying and selling commodities or images (it all amounts to the same thing), for these are flat symbols
without depth. . . . Those who can or who try to preserve a life which
neutralizes the luxury as well as the horror will have to contrive an
"interior", a secret garden, a homely hearth or simply and more
ambitiously: a psychological life.

Yet that is where the drama commences. This interior life which the
West has constructed, at least since Plotinus, did, from the beginning of
the Christian era, transform the face-to-face of Narcissus with his image,
into the joining of hands in prayer. This interior life, having consolidated
itself through the spiritual itinerary, as well as through the carnival of the
Middle Ages, and having surfaced as the fragile ego of Montaigne,
the passions of Diderot, the meditations of Hegel or of Kant, this life
reaches its completion and comes to a close in the psychological drama,
the psycho-drama. Plotinus has degenerated into . . . Dallas. In fact, those
who inhabit the city of steel do not lack inner drama, as serious, depressive,
neurotic or psychotic as the Freudian unconscious would have it. By
escaping the surface of performance, one falls into the trap of psychology.
Psychoanalysis thus has its work cut out. For it is precisely from this
compressed space of psychological ill-being that Freudian psychoanalysis
attempts to draw us.

To speak the language of the city, taken as an image of modernity –
which necessarily implies counting social history among the factors of
organization and permanence of psychic life – psychoanalysis transforms
money into time, and the feeling of unhappiness, that it recognizes, into
speech before another. An unheard-of metamorphosis which runs contrary

to mercantile economy and its bordering neurosis, and which gives sense to psychosis. For, from this prison of the soul which at least two thousand years of inner experience has built up, psychoanalysis seizes upon the naive vulnerability in order to make an opening in it, and make the polyphony of our motives resonate.

Better than anyone else, Proust sums up what becomes, or will become, the psyche – which according to Freud, is *not* a soul. "The sick feel closer to their soul." Or further,

> For even if we have the sensation of being always enveloped in, surrounded by our own soul, still it does not seem a fixed and immovable prison; rather do we seem to be borne away with it, and perpetually struggling to pass beyond it, to break out into the world, with a perpetual discouragement as we hear endlessly, all around us, that unvarying sound which is no echo from without, but the resonance of a vibration from within.[1]

A permanence of the psychic system and a sonorous leak from the enclosure: Freud gives us a first technique for working this sound and this leak, a technique which we shall develop in due course. From our empathy with mental illness, from our proximity to illness, we learn to traverse the psyche – without end. The psychic may be the place where the somatic symptom as well as the delirious projection are elaborated and hence clear themselves up: the psychic is our protection, on the condition that one does not remain enclosed within it, but that one *shifts* it through an *act of language* into sublimation, into an act of thought, of interpretation, of relational transformation.... Elsewhere I pose the question of the "psychic" as a *verbal act*, that which is neither a way towards action nor a psychological rumination in the imaginary crypt, but a mark of union between this inevitable or necessary rumination and its elaboration, verbal to begin with.

Thus this aggravation of psychological illness that characterizes the modern world, this "soap opera" which appears as the necessary reverse of the society of performance and stress could be a call for psychoanalysis. "Give us the meaning of our inner disaster, relieve us from it!", the psychological disarray seems to say, this *alter ego* of the society of display.

The stake of psychoanalysis is therefore to transform this prison of the soul which the West has built as a means of survival and protection and which now proves a disaster: this stake is therapeutic and at the same time ethical and, incidentally, political. If, however, there really is an implicit call for the psychoanalytic operation to assert itself and grow, then this call is full of traps. I am not thinking of the ever-present danger of transforming psychoanalysis into a normalization which will guide the wounds of the psychic system towards social success. This notably American degradation of the cure is known and denounced, and even if it remains a threat, fighting it is rather a task of the past towards which the present ought to be attentive.

Two great confrontations await psychoanalysis of tomorrow with respect to the problems of organization and permanence of the psychic system. The first is its competition with the neurosciences: "The cocktail or the word!", which is now the question of to be or not to be. The second is the test to which psychoanalysis is subjected by the desire *not to know*, which converges with the apparent ease offered by pharmacology, and which characterizes the negative narcissism (as André Green said) of modern man.

THE DRAMATURGY OF THE DRIVES

One could summarize the analytical position schematically in the following way: there is an unconscious psychic life which obeys the determinations and constraints that are knowable and modifiable through interpretation within the transferential relation. Some of these determinations and constraints are of the biological order; the modern advances of neurobiology and of pharmacology allow one to influence the behaviour and to modify *fragments* of the psychic life. The link between the analytic cure and these interventions is more acute today than ever, and it requires the attention of the analyst in a different way in each concrete situation.

From a logical point of view, the assault by the neurosciences does not destroy psychoanalysis, but invites one to resume and reactualize the Freudian notion of the drive: the hinge between *soma* and *psyche*, biology and representation. The drive is the ultimate level of organization and permanence reached by listening and Freudian theory, which is to say: the analytic construction (or if one prefers: the imagination). In other words, what we understand from biology is . . . drive: energy, if you like, but always a "carrier of meaning", a "relation" with someone else, be it even with myself. Through this double nature (biological and energetic-semiotic), the drive is already also structure. From the source (organ) to the aim (satisfaction), its strength or weakness plots the constraints under which the most tenacious relations inscribe themselves. Most tenacious, because the most archaic (ontogenetically and phylogenetically speaking) and most discordant with regard to linguistic expression. It is within this frame of drives that an ego with its relation to an object will gradually mould itself. Even if it is true that the structure of the subject builds itself precisely from different positions of the ego *vis-à-vis* the different modalities of the object (I insist after all on this plurality of the selves and of the types of objects that take shape in the gap between drive and language), the Freudian analyst would not forget that this subjective structure is loaded with the fate of the drives and their double nature (biology *and non*-linguistic representation). The phantasm, for instance, can be understood as the result of the irruption of the drive into the serene logic of judgment

– the latter finding itself modified to the point of hallucination or delirium. Thus the phantasm comes to remind us in its own way that drive and, by inference, affect are not only a myth, but a factor of organization and permanence which fundamentally moulds the activity of thinking (of judgment and of speech). Similarly with affective dullness, denial of the object, the listless speech of the depressed, only to take examples that I shall develop further on. Having observed that depression *disavows* the meaning of discourse, which is to carry Eros towards the object, we infer that the destructive drive (the death drive, if one prefers) renders impossible the ties which guarantee the separation between ego and object. Instead this drive sets up the melancholic subject, the negative Narcissus, the absolute master, not of an object but of a mortified *thing* forever lost.

To sum up: taking seriously the "myth" of the drive and setting out from an *imaginary deployment* which restores the logic of the drive, one is led, in fact, to an opening, this time of the constraint of language which, of course, in the last analysis determines our quality as speaking beings. One is brought to understand by this factor of organization and permanence, which is discourse, not only multiple meanings and hidden assumptions or logical presuppositions, but also the very dislocation of the capacity for words: a dislocation (schizophrenic or melancholic . . . the figures vary) which appears from then on as the privileged witness to the *sense of the drive*, thus adding itself to the *meaning of speech*. After its linguistic phase and while being attentive, by way of its Freudian heritage, to the drive (and more attentive than before due to the pressure from the neurosciences), today's psychoanalysis and no doubt that of tomorrow will decipher the dramaturgy of the drives beyond it, *the meaning of language* where the *sense of the drive* disguises itself. Indications of this sense of the drive may be translinguistic: the voice, for instance, its intensities and its rhythms often carry the secret eroticism of the depressed who has cut his linguistic ties with the other, but who has nevertheless buried the affect in the obscure code of his vocalization where the analyst will seek a desire not quite as dead as that . . .

Thus one arrives at the factors of organization and permanence which are the immediate object of analytic interpretation, in so far as they are dependent on the relation to the other and are accomplished in language. In the light of what has just been recalled concerning the primacy of the destiny of drives, these signifying constraints seem to constitute a complex and heterogeneous organization whose formation begins from the earliest age of the subject and, developing through its history, determines its symbolic destiny.

POLYPHONY, INTERFERENCES

Following the development of linguistics and of the human sciences in the 1960s, the notion of *structure* in psychoanalysis, owing essentially to Lacan,

has allowed one to think with greater precision than hitherto the organization of this symbolic destiny – or this "being of language" – which
presides over the psychic life. Surely it should come as no surprise to
Freudians that a discourse or a symptom related to us in confidence could
be envisaged as a virtual unity, of which the elements do not make sense
except within the relation (or the relations) which they entertain within
this unity, such as in the relation which the speaking subject entertains
with his or her interlocutor, and in particular with the analyst. In addition,
Freudian practice had revealed that this web of signifying relations which
characterizes a symptom, a discourse, a transference, a subject, while being
a *theoretical construction*, none the less remains the one and only *reality*
in which the psychic life realizes itself, comes to know itself, and a fortiori
the only reality from which the analyst, on whom someone has made a
demand by addressing himself to her, can possibly act in order to modify
it. Three questions seem to arise from this situation in the analytical
domain. Is the destiny of the speaking being reducible to speech and
language, or should even other *systems of representation* be taken into
consideration in order to think this being's logical particularities and/or in
order to reach the very psychic level, on which sense reveals itself to the
subject? What features of *interpretative speech* can enter into resonance
with the symbolic destiny of the subject in order to reach as far as his
biological substrate and modify it? If this power of the analytical cure
exists, how does one think its limits and its ethics?

To answer the first question, the development of semiology has led to
the conception of different signifying systems (iconic code, musical code,
etc.) that are irreducible to language (the latter being envisaged as a structure or a grammar, a language or a discourse, a statement or an utterance).
This has shaken "linguistic imperialism". Concurrently, a return to Freud,
and in particular to the Freudian concept of *representation*, takes into
account a plurality of psychic representatives: thing-representation, word-
representation, representation of drive, representation of affect. The ensuing
result is a "laminated" model of the psychic signifying process with hetero-
genous *traces* and *signs*. The analyst is bound to take this polyphony into
consideration in order to hear the discourse addressed to her at these
different linguistic and translinguistic levels (voice, gesture, etc.) and also
to tune in to the one among them which makes sense in the transference,
here and now.

According to the ideal hypothesis, the interpretative silence ought to
make the different structures of sense reverberate as far as the consciousness
of the subject. More directly and more frequently, it is the analytic *interpretation* which locates the various expressions of ill-being (linguistic or
translinguistic) and restores them to the subject. How? By naming the
familial determinants which in the history of sexual development have led
to this symptom or that structure. But often and above all by finding an
adequate formulation which, in mobilizing the affects of the analyst and

her own series of psychic representations (words, things, drives), expresses itself in elliptical, metaphorical or condensed terms. A real *poiesis* of interpretation enters into play here, comprising the musicality of the voice as well as tropes and including the "argumentative" description of mental functioning. Being the ultimate reality of transference and counter-transference, this *poiesis* crosses conscious listening and addresses itself to unconscious psychic representations of the patient, notably those of the drive, of which one may suppose that they adjoin the neuronal flux proper to subcortical "electric" or "humoral" systems. The footbridge which connects, or the hiatus which separates the unconscious representatives from the neurobiological register are perhaps infinite, perhaps non-existent; but while theories and experiments discuss their exact relation, the interpretative speech, in this way structured in linguistic and translinguistic polyphony, performs its psycho-somatic effects.

Thus understood, the violence of analytic interpretation cannot but grip us, and the very request that the patient addresses to us, authorizing us to effect it, seems to be a slender justification: this very request, is that not an integral part of the symptom as much as the beginning of its overcoming? The ethics of psychoanalysis might thus rest on two exigencies proper to the western rationality to which it pertains. On the one hand, the maintenance of *one* sense, of *one* truth, valid and demonstrable in a given situation: this is the "normative" side of psychoanalysis, the "norm" being dictated by the state of analytic theory and the place which the actual analyst takes in it. On the other hand, the maintenance of a respect (in the guise of freedom) for the desire and for the *jouissance* of the patient, which makes it appropriate or not to welcome our interpretation (the structure of the patient manifesting itself precisely in his specific resistance to our interpretation); a respect which at the same time implicates the validity of this very interpretation and also unveils the *jouissance* of the analyst under the cover of the "truth" of her constructive interpretation. No other discourse in the history of western rationality reaches this aspiration to balance truth and *jouissance*, authorized and implicated by *jouissance*: an equilibrium which by virtue of itself guarantees its own vitality, which is to say the immanence of death (discourse of knowledge) and of the resurrection (discourse of desire). The place of psychoanalysis consequently remains disturbing to the social contract which Freud maintained was founded on an act of killing. By not being content with remaining the dead father of knowledge but, this being understood and assumed, by disclosing himself in addition as a subject of affect, desire or *jouissance*, the analyst denounces colleges and academies, but produces instead the restructuring effects in the psychic system of the other.

Different types of psychic representations are directed towards language, although they are irreducible to its grammatical and logical structure or to the bipolarity of transference and counter-transference within which the interpretative discourse takes place. These types of representations lead one to consider each concrete analytic situation as a specific microcosm. And this in such a way that even if psychiatric notions of "structures" (hysterical, obsessional, schizophrenic, paranoid, etc.) may serve as initial and rudimentary marks for analytic work, these structures do not hold out against a micro-analysis attentive to the heterogeneity and polyvalence of psychic representatives. More and more, we are led to think of inter-ferences of structures, or "limit states" which, while being new clinical facts bringing attention to the evolution of subjectivity and psychic states, possess above all the advantage of fundamentally putting into question the validity of the classical nosographies. Thus the apparent abstraction of psychoanalysis, attentive to linguistic and translinguistic expression of psy-chic determinants, leads in fact to an *optimal individualization of the treatment*. Each treatment becomes an idiolect, a work of art and the pro-visional putting into place of a new theoretical creation within the Freudian continent. One may, consequently, ask oneself what the distinguishing marks of these discourses are with regard to Freud's thought, and where one passes the boundary between fidelity, innovation, dissidence. . . . The history of the analytic movement and above all the ecumenical reality of doctrines (Freudian, Kleinian, Winnicottian, Lacanian, etc.) indicate that beyond the misunderstandings and the impasses, Freud did open up a track to which innovators of all strands are compelled to refer if they persist in laying claim to psychoanalysis. A narrow track where, on the one hand, sexual experience is obstinate towards language – resulting in repression as well as an ensuing necessity for interpreting through language the marks of the unconscious revealing themselves in it, but, on the other hand, a track where the erotization of language in the transference permits the signification of sexual experience, leading to relief from the symptom, a parallel to a greater power of the signifying capacities of the subject (this last in no way prejudging his adaptability, viability, normalization – does one need to stress it?)

Two examples of analytic treatment provide evidence for the above remarks and signal two typical obstacles to analytic speech.

DEPRESSION

A young woman 30 years of age, Florence, complaining of strong bouts of manic-depression, came to see me after a tentative analysis with a colleague, broken off because of having aggravated, according to the patient, the intensity and frequency of the cycles. Having consulted a psychiatrist prior to seeing me, Florence was on Imipramine, and since her previous analyst could not accept pursuing the analysis under these conditions, we initially undertook a psychotherapy. In the course of this, being continually under Imipramine, Florence wanted to lie down: after some months she gave up the anti-depressants and her analysis continued without medication. . . . Florence confirmed that Imipramine reduced her excessive anxiety and allowed her to approach through speech the dramatic situations from her childhood and her present life without falling into the states of serious depression which she had known on several occasions. The anxiety threshold being apparently quite low for this patient, her stabilization through the pharmacological treatment favoured the binding of the drives and their representatives with the word-representations. Yet, so it seemed to me, a certain distance of the speech of the patient ensued (in relation to the drive and to myself) from these chemical interventions which appeared necessary to me, although provisional. However, I saw in these interventions another benefit adding itself to the binding that they favoured between the drives and the words: the introduction of a third party between us (the medicine, the psychiatrist) began to mould the manic excitement (Florence was not omnipotent, nor was I: there was a third, but also a different reality), and this allowed us to approach both her narcissism and its projection into the exaggerated idealism to which Florence wanted to consecrate me. Thus, with a modified anxiety threshold, we approached more easily the manic-depressive mechanisms Florence had put into place in order to face loss and separation. A new object relation established itself between me and her, less catastrophic, less a threat of the unbearable danger of annihilation in the case of real or imaginary separation. Once this new object relation – which is also a new structure of the subject – had been consolidated, Florence went off Imipramine. She tried from then on to rely solely on the new symbolic and imaginary web which we had constructed with the "regional" help of Imipramine and so no longer lean against chemistry but rather exclusively on the psychic representatives which we had reworked and whose disintegration threatened her much less.

During the period of the analysis under Imipramine, I had the feeling that the intensities of the drives were levelled but the discourse was "anaesthetized". This impression essentially issues from the fact that under these conditions, Florence was able to dream dreams relating to states of anxiety hitherto unrepresentable: the anxiety of being devoured and swallowed by her mother and conversely of devouring and swallowing her mother; but my impression also issues from the fact that, while they were all dreamt and reported (which is already a considerable psychic effort in relation to the previous depressive muteness, the "white death" of the depressed internal signifier), these dreams were accompanied on the part of Florence by a feeling of distance and defensive incomprehension. Now, in the second phase of the analysis, we were able to recapture and analyse these same dreams.

First dream: a dream of an anthropophagic wedding feast. The wedding resembles the wedding photo of her parents. In the dream, the guests devour their own limbs and heads; the scene takes place on the staircase of my house.

Second dream: Florence vomits after sexual intercourse: it is the head of her mother which falls into the basin. This dream preceded by a short while the moment when she became pregnant.

How did we resume these dreams? Having become a mother in the course of the analysis and continuing her treatment without recourse to medicine, Florence had developed another symptom: the fear of her phantasms of killing her daughter. Tirelessly, she kept repeating to me how these phantasms inhabited her, haunting and emaciating; how she did not really feel capable of carrying out the act, but how this phantasmatic rumination was exhausting for her.

I said, "Assassin – basin – assimilate" [*Assassine – bassine – assimiler*]. Within this very condensed interpretation according to a tragic or grotesque poetics, Florence managed to recover the sense of the drive and the symbolic signification of these two past dreams and to link them to her present anxiety. The longing to assassinate her daughter is the return of the longing to take and assimilate (devour) Imipramine, although to begin with it is the head and the parts (breast and basin) of her mother (the cannibalistic dream) which she is aware of having spat out into a basin (the dream of vomiting) so as to leave space for her child (being pregnant, making her own pelvis [*bassin*] inhabited). The sense of the drive in these dreams previously worked in her psychic system by pushing back the depressive symptoms, if only, for instance, by the formation of the reported dreams which substituted themselves for the melancholic muteness. But this sense of the drive did not accede to the signification of speech. My interpretations did not provoke associations. It now became a symbolic signification, an elaboration.

"Assassin – basin – assimilate." The "internal vibration", so Proust would say, for it is thus that I consider my interpretation, had resonated from the unspeakable but agonizing and depressing representatives of the drive to the verbal explicitation which the patient, helped by the indications of my interpretation, had been able to make for herself: an explicitation of the structure of her depression and of its manic opposite. It is not her daughter that Florence wants to kill. She wants to rid herself of the image of the girl that she is herself, an assassinating-cannibalistic girl that she believes herself to be, assimilating-devouring-vomiting her mother in order to avenge her infantile paralysis (immobility of her pelvis) which had seriously handicapped her during her early childhood and removed her from her mother (one often over-invests orality in order to recapture an object which escapes a failing motoricity).

My word-play, inscribed within the dynamics of the transference and the explicative-argumentative work which we had done, is the result of an empathy with this economy of the drives: of an identification with the narcissistic wound, the motoric difficulties, the oral voracity and with the manic attempts to avenge herself through devouring-expulsion of the depressive *thing* for which there are not yet linguistic *signs*, but merely the echoing carriers of the intensities of the drives. In reintroducing, by my interpretation, this economy of the drives into the divested language of the assassin (Florence wants to kill, but she feels detached, as if at a distance from the nevertheless obsessive desire), I revitalize language at the same time as the transference, but also the analysand herself by recalling the time and the history of an archaic phantasm of devouring and its function as compensating the narcissistic wound provoked by the failing motoricity.

From this fragment of analysis, I would like to draw out some points which seem essential, in my view, for psychoanalysis today and – why not – for tomorrow:

(1) The interference of pharmacology whose impact to me seems bound to develop in two directions. First, more and more patients will get a mixed treatment (pharmacological and psychoanalytical), which will necessitate an exact appreciation of the effects of the drugs and the interaction with the transference. Second, informing the public is imperative in order to demonstrate the enormous field of psychic illnesses *not targeted by pharmacology*, and which reactualize the necessity for psychoanalytic treatment in the strict sense: that is to say, of a still finer analysis of the psychic apparatus in transference and its ability to translate drives into words.

(2) The "signifier of death" of the depressed speech appeared straight away to the listening of the analyst in the *denial of the signifier* by the patient ("devitalized" speech, slowed down, divested, monotonous or accelerated, but effaced, "nothing") and in the devalorization of language as vector of the transference.

(3) Nevertheless, the desire and the determinants of the symptom which did not succeed in being signified in speech seem to have left their code or their sense in the preverbal register (voice, intonation) or in the homophony which makes room for the play of the signifier, for an echoing.

(4) Analytic interpretation could become for a while the accomplice of "regression" and of "holding" by making itself the echo of that other sense while rendering itself essentially a mark of union towards the mentalization and conscious formulations of the initial trauma and of the ensuing desires, in a language for the other.

(5) The depression seems to be organized according to a relation with the other who is not separated from the depressed subject, but remains under its ascendancy as its *thing*: unnameable and mortified (one finds this symbolic reunion again with the paradise not lost in the "marriage of suicide"). Thus this specific object relation is certainly coded in the "content" but also in the "form" of the depressed discourse: the object relation *and* the structure of the discourse are in the same way determinants (factors of organization and permanence) of the depression. Consequently, analytic intervention has or should have a bearing (by its signification and by its form) on these two factors of permanence of the psychic system of the subject (the *object* and the *discourse*).

PERVERSION

Common, real and particularly resistant to analysis, perversion interests me here for the following reasons:

(1) The narcissistic satisfaction through a partial object which characterizes perversion has as an equivalent a fetishistic discourse: exhibitionism. This discourse is acquainted with everything and does not really want to know anything.

(2) The overvaluation of speech functions as a resistance to analysis: *affects* are split from the *discourse* which relates the perverse phantasm, and this isolation continues even when the phantasm is communicated to the analyst with the unconscious intention of including it in the sado-masochistic economy of the patient.

(3) It may consequently prove necessary to make the image and the representations of the perverse act appear as *possibles* within the transference; such an actualization of the perverse scenario during the treatment mobilizes the intensities of the preverbal representatives of the affect or of the drive and constitutes a precondition for their "translation" into interpretative speech.

Didier came into analysis complaining about his inability to have satisfying sexual relations. It very quickly became clear that his sexuality was voyeuristic and exhibitionistic, masturbatory with the sado-masochistic scenarios provoking a maximum of pleasure besides those peeps at a distance. Didier did painting for himself. He had never exhibited, except for his mother when she was alive. Since the death of his "public", the mother's apartment had been closed and Didier no longer dared to touch it nor to see it, or sell it. His discourse on the couch was voluble. He knew everything and expected nothing from me: masturbatory speech of an exorbitant infantile power; he just spoke of his rituals as if he were reading the script of a director who in a cool state puts on display the actions of other people, of the actors whom he overlooks at a distance. I had the feeling, or the counter-transferential conviction, that the secret of Didier lay in his mother's apartment, but also in a *secret discourse* which encrypted the drives and the affects, and did not allow them to appear in his speech. The speech of this patient was cut off from affects. His affects were invisible in his speech. I also accepted seeing Didier's works: collages of cut-up posters with colours covering them or smeared across them, with white surfaces. The voice of Didier became excited and more alive. His discourse about the canvases, which he unrolled before me, lying on the couch, or of which he gave me a sample photograph so that I could follow his explicit exposé, was always a neutral discourse, technical, aesthetic. It was up to me to supply the perverse meaning to this display: from these severed limbs, from these faecal matters. I had allowed Didier a certain perverse acting-out during the treatment, showing his canvases, and I grafted onto this demonstration the discourse of non-perversion lacking in it. He accepted this perverse phantasm – his or mine? – and with his phantasmatic capacity thus unbolted, Didier's phantasmagoria began to be replaced, little by little, by his enactments which the phantasmagoria had not completely eliminated, but in relation to which he no longer feels an exhausting dependence, for he was able to integrate them, work them through his discourse into a new and more complex psychic structure.

The factor of organization and permanence with respect to perversion would be a relation to the other reduced to being an agent of the sado-masochistic pleasure of the subject who thus consolidates his omnipotence. The ensuing discourse, while having all the logical and grammatical characteristics of normative speech, nevertheless has no heuristic or communicative value, for the unconscious sense, which it transports beyond its appearances, resides in the neutralization of the other (the analyst) and in her reduction to a fetishized object of perverse megalomania. To enter into the play of this unconscious determination presupposes a dismantling of the fetishized speech. An investment of the scenario-*image*, but also of the *act* as a truly "real language" of the pervert. Only subsequently could it be possible to give back to speech (and to the relation to the other) its polyvalent, heuristic and communicative dimension where the complexity of the subject (and not the "cut-offness") deploys itself at the end of the analytic process.

SPEAKING A HISTORY

To the extent that the putting into place of the transference depends on the desire to know, to know *oneself*, and to transform *oneself* with a view to getting better, one is allowed to ask oneself if such a subjective disposition is not historically determined. From the ethical demand of the Jewish God to the trinitarian mystery of the Christian subjectivity and as far as the "What do I know?" of Montaigne, whose reduplicated ego already in many respects prefigures that of Freud, the forms vary of this subjective desire for the other and for truth, on which one could build western history and psychoanalysis itself, like on an infinite appropriation of the memory for a new history of the sick subject and its symptoms. On the other hand, the gratification of the narcissistic misery which accompanies the modern crisis of values seems rather to run counter to such a psychic interestedness without which no subjective mutation could be envisaged.

Psychoanalysis situates itself at the counter-current of this modern comfort which signals the end, not of History, but of the possibility of *speaking a history*: comfort and end where one, however, nevertheless senses the saturation as well as the criticism and rejection.

Yet, analytic technique cannot ignore this *narcissistic coil* and this *decline in the desire to know*: it has to recognize them, to go along with them and only afterwards to try to surpass them, moving towards this new form of self-knowledge which Freud inaugurated by integrating the "illness" into the very bosom of the psychic system and making of psychic life an interminable construction-destruction. The analytic approach to depression and perversion, among other "modern" symptoms, could be considered as an example of the extension of the analytic field as far as the frontiers where it encounters the greatest resistances.

Even today and more still tomorrow, psychoanalysis seems to me to be this art – I admit: this artifice – which allows men and women of the modern city, so sleek, haughty, paying and payable, to preserve a life, in so far as it is true for the speaking subject that life awakens and wanes away with and from the psychic life, where speech is the axis of a heterogeneous dynamic. With psychoanalysis, Freud not only opens a refuge from the society of display and consumption. By recognizing and integrating the logic of monetary exchange, Freudian psychoanalysis subverts the alienating city so as to allow for a metamorphosis. If not, what could then truly change between the crystal of the silver-plated towers, the implacable banality of the banks and a destiny programmed as far as the genetic code? For the above reasons, psychoanalysis could perhaps tomorrow be one of the rare places preserved for change and surprise, that is: for a life. It will take into account the factors of psychic permanence (from biology to drives and to language), but it will also go along with those who wish to change them; for, being faithful to the scepticism of Freud and nevertheless also attentive to the plasticity of psychic discourse, we maintain that this modification is possible.

Translated by Michael Münchow

NOTES

1 Marcel Proust, *Remembrance of Things Past, 1: Swann's Way*, tr. C. K. Scott Moncrieff (Harmondsworth: Penguin, 1989).

3 "Man is by nature a political animal" or: patient as citizen

James Hillman

James Hillman is the leading thinker in the Jungian tradition and the seminal figure behind the archetypal psychology, which has realigned depth psychology with the artistic and cultural imagination. The leitmotif of his work has been the imagination, and he has conceived of the task of psychology as above all redressing its repression in contemporary society. From the outset, Hillman has been mainly concerned with the ends of contemporary analysis. With *Suicide and the Soul*, he challenged the medical model of psychotherapy and separated analysis of soul from medical therapeutics. In *The Myth of Analysis*, he argued that analysis has been wedded to an inherently misogynistic and Apollonic cast, through which the feminine and the Dionysian could only appear as neurotic. Such critiques were accompanied by a radical re-visioning of analysis as an aesthetic and imaginative endeavour. Recently, in "Oedipus revisited," he suggested that the very attempt to reform analysis still remains blindly oedipal in the heroically self-centred and truth-seeking cast of its rhetoric, and is to little avail, as it continues to neglect the call of the suffering of the polis. Subsequently, after practising as an analyst for thirty years, Hillman terminated his practice. Most recently in *We've had a Hundred Years of Psychotherapy and the World's Getting Worse*, he argues that the individualism of contemporary analysis needs to be abandoned, and a notion of selfhood, as founded in and through community, developed in its place.

In the following paper he contends that the current practice of analysis impedes, rather than facilitates, political change, by turning citizens into patients. He maintains that the three prevalent symptoms which afflict clinicians today: sexual acting out, schedule addiction and narcolepsy – could be re-visioned not as symptoms of individuals, but of analysis itself, as variations of its attempt to put an end to itself.

SELECT BIBLIOGRAPHY

Hillman, James *The Myth of Analysis: Three Essays in Archetypal Psychology*, Evanston: Northwestern University Press, 1972.

—— *Re-Visioning Psychology*, New York and London: Harper & Row, 1975.

—— *Suicide and the Soul*, Dallas: Spring Publications, 1978.

—— *The Dream and the Underworld*, New York and London: Harper & Row, 1979.

—— *Healing Fiction*, Barrytown: Station Hill, 1983.

—— *Interviews*, Dallas: Spring Publications, 1983.

—— and Kerényi, K., *Oedipus Variations: Studies in Literature and Psychoanalysis*, Dallas: Spring Publications, 1991.

—— and Ventura, M., *We've had a Hundred Years of Psychotherapy and the World's Getting Worse*, San Francisco: Harper, 1992.

* * *

There is nothing for it but to summon help from the Witch – the Witch metapsychology. Without metapsychological speculation and theorizing – I had almost said "phantasy" – we shall not get a step further.

Freud[1]

The theory of the instincts is, as it were, our mythology. The instincts are mythical beings, superb in their indefiniteness.

Freud[2]

For many years I have been engaged in the selection, teaching, analysing and judging of candidates in training for the profession of analytical psychotherapy. That term "analytical psychotherapy", is meant here to be neutral, covering psychoanalysts of the Freudian persuasion, individual psychologists of the Adlerian, analytical psychologists of the Jungian and others who follow Reich, Horney, Winnicott, Balint, Klein, *et al.*

In the intense examination of these candidates from their first application and interviews through supervision sessions and case reports an outstanding omission occurs, an omission in our methods of inquisitional scrutiny that I came to recognize only in the last years when my own metapsychological speculations bewitched me toward the world.

The omission? We never inquired into the political life, history, opinions and activities of the candidates, nor was the political life of the patient whose case was being supervised and reported in great detail ever brought into discussion.

Religion, yes. Economic level, of course; earning power is certainly not neglected. Family history, work, ethnic roots, emotion, ideals, of course; dreams, memories and sexual *frissons* with great finesse; even films, literature, gardening, automobiles, theatre, art, pop music – but no politics. To what party did the patient belong, if any; what political engagement in the community; what leanings in regard to the daily issues – left, right? What causes and concerns is the patient now engaged with, how do politics play a role in family fights? What was the political history of the family: labour, anarchistic, Marxist, socialist, landed conservative, red white and blue, i.e., redneck, white skin and blue collar, knee-jerk liberal, shopkeeper individualist, parlour pink, blackshirt fascist, protester ... in other words, how and in what manner to what extent was the patient a citizen.

If we concede that a major aspect of our lives is not only social, that is, not only enmeshed in the web of a class and a style, an economic strata and a favoured language, and if we concede that the social context affects attitudes, moods, reflections, or what we call psychological consciousness, is all this not true as well for the political? How and why had it been omitted?

Omission, whatever its reason, is a lacuna in consciousness, indicating, I suppose we here in a Freudian context all agree, a repression. Or, to put it more vigorously: this lacuna indicates the presence of denial, a defence mechanism against the political, keeping analytical psychotherapy immune from infection by the body politic, *au dessus de la mêlée.*

Though my thrust is to condemn this absence, else I would not have felt it enough to have written a paper about it, I shall try to back off and neutrally inquire: what is its necessity? Let's take the defence as a symptom, as essential and necessary to the *Sache*, and let us ask what does the absence of the political serve? What is the presence in the absence?

I suggest we read the defence as an immunological defence, a shield to keep analytical psychotherapy from invasion by the passions of the passing parade, inviolate, so that the psycho-patho-phenomena of the individual may bud, bloom and flourish in dream and mood, fantasy and feeling, projection, symbolization, association and transference, within the confines of the consulting room, its *temenos*, its hermetic vessel. As the work must be kept immune from too much metapsychological reading, too much gossip, social encounters, family members, the easy commerce of usual life – so it must be kept safe from politics.

The political, in other words, is only one of the infections and invasions against which therapy sets up its immunological defence. We do not see professionally members of our own or of the same family. We do not see the lovers of our patients or their husbands, wives, children. We do not work with our friends; we do not attend seminars, performances or exhibitions of our patients, nor do they come to ours. This is the new discipline of immunity called professional ethics, unimagined by Freud. We do not engage in the patient's lives in any way; only their psyches. The lines are defined, strictly disciplined and nowadays, policed. The thickness of these barriers attest to the importance given to the fantasy of a complete separation of life and reflection, of exterior and interior, of person as patient and person as citizen.

Clearly here the metapsychological Witch is at work, for these barriers, separations and defences, this system of immunization conceals anthropological and ontological assumptions about the nature of human being and the nature of being itself:

1 that human being and being itself can be sectioned;
2 that the conscious will can maintain these divisions without seepage;
3 that segmentation favours psychological awareness;
4 that the psychological and the political can be conceived as two distinct discourses;
5 or, to put it as an extreme contradiction so as to be most clear: the political is not psychological and the psychological is not political.

Most probably analytical therapy wants to remain within the confines of its territory as prurient mystics of the interior. That could be our discipline and our job: the inquisitional pursuit in reflective quiet of individual dream, fantasy, mood, image. The investigation and understanding of the individual person. Yes, this is an endeavour, but is it therapy of soul? Does it make the unconscious conscious, as Freud set our task? For that we must go where the soul is sick and where the unconscious most darkly and thickly reigns: the *polis*. For the unconscious does not stand still. That's what the word implies. Where is this unconscious today; certainly not in childhood, family, sexuality, symptomatic anomalies, feelings, relationships, arcane symbols – that stuff is on every talk-show, in every self-help manual. What was once "the unconscious" appearing as a slip of the tongue is now on the tip of the tongue. Where we are least able, however, most suffer from, and anesthetize against, i.e., repress, with ear-plugs, door-bolts and alcohol, with electronics, hi-fi, coffee and shopping is the world out there, the polis. We remove psyche from it and we are unconscious in regard to it; the polis is the unconscious. We have become superconscious patients and analysts, very aware and very subtle interiorized individuals, and very unconscious citizens.

INDIVIDUALISM AS DISEASE

The patient cannot, definitely not, by definition not, become citizen so long as the model of the psyche which therapeutic analysis serves remains fixed where it is. This model locates psyche either as intrapersonal (within the human subject) or interpersonal (between subjects in relationships, transference, group dynamics and family systems). Soul is not in the world of things like trees, rocks, cars and ashtrays, nor is it in the world of systems like education, finance, party politics, language and technology. Even if today more and more physical and institutional phenomena are spoken of as "sick", we yet locate psychopathology in the human individual.

Of course culture critics, like Szasz or Illich or Foucault can show the absurdities of this isolating location and the relativity of the word "sick" depending altogether on a cultural definition. Yet, they do not go further out on the limb to conclude that if the definition of psychopathology resides in the culture, then psyche itself may be defined to reside there as well.

No, we have not drawn that conclusion and remain dedicated to individualism. We still restrict psychopathology to the human person and therefore psyche, too, belongs ontologically to the human subject. Analytical psychotherapy continues to argue that if nature or culture show sickness, this is because of human actions: we are its cause. So, cure the human first; everyone in analysis – architects, politicians, teachers, businessmen – and then the world will get better.

This hasn't worked, won't work, because the model is faulty. It leaves soul out of the world – things are soulless and the individual human must carry with the should of his shoulder the substantiating burden of soul, reanimating by his and her personal projective breath what the theory declares by definition dead.

The death of the world soul was articulated by the French, Jesuit-educated, bachelor-soldier-gentleman, Descartes, who called it *res extensa*. Out there, as well as everything in this room including our bodies, is just dead matter. Descartes, if not the 1500 years of Christianity before him, killed off the world, turning it into a soulless mass, a littered field. Descartes and the Christians invented litter and pollution, and shopping, too. Of course, M. Descartes was confirmed by a European consortium including Mr Newton and Herr Kant – this despite Plato and Plotinus and Ficino, and the Romantics for whom the great God Pan was never dead, and especially Spinoza whose God and world were one substance, that is, whose world was utterly and completely ensouled, spirited, divinized – or in our measly secular language, libidinally cathected. Let us remember this bit of philosophical history, usually called Descartes-bashing. Let it remind us that analytical psychotherapists are indeed French Freudians, that is, Cartesians. So long as we regard the world external to therapy and the individual as the only possible place of consciousness, we may be practising with the tools of Freud, but what we practice is the theory of Descartes. And the soul can't get out of analysis until it can get out of Cartesianism and, allow me to add, Christianism.

Now Freud does try to get out. (I venture to say that his insistence upon his Jewishness was part of his attempt to free himself from the Cartesian-Christian *Weltbild*. But that is just an aside.) Freud tries to escape from individualism by appealing to the universality of the Oedipal theory; by grounding the libido in a biological substrate; by widening eros to a cosmic principle beyond the erogenous zones of the skin; by descending to archaic depths like the primal horde, the primordial id, *thanatos*, nirvana, entropy. These metaphysical bewitchments imagine collective forces beyond the individual.

Yet, if we look closely at his 1922 paper, "The libido theory", we see he blocks his own escape. Immediately following the paragraph on narcissism, he refutes Jung's broader collective view of libido and then refutes Trotter's herd instinct which "impels individuals to come together into larger communities". "Psychoanalysis", says Freud there, "finds itself in contradiction to this view. Even if the social instinct is innate, it may . . . be traced back to . . . the childhood of the individual. . . ."³ Or, as he says in 1921 on the herd instinct:"Let us venture, then, to correct Trotter's pronouncement that man is a herd animal and assert that he is rather a horde animal, an individual creature in a horde led by a chief."⁴

I think his escape route can be found in that same 1922 encyclopedia article ("The libido theory") where he describes "object libido". This, as you all recall, is the libido that flows out to objects and absorbs libido back from objects. You also know well the corollary idea that "the pathogenic process as witnessed in dementia praecox is the withdrawal of the libido from objects"⁵ in such a manner that the ego itself becomes an object of the libido, or, that narcissistic state in which one is in love with oneself.

If mourning is that feeling which recognizes the death of the object, that psychic condition which bespeaks an object libido no longer cathected to the world, then are we not in mourning all of the time? And is not the ideology of consumerism, which runs the economy of the West and broke through the Berlin Wall, in other words, shopping – our major leisure-time activity according to social statistics – that symptomatic compromise which compulsively mourns object loss by concretely attempting to recathect. Because the Wicked Witch of western metapsychology has declared the world dead, only I, *res cogitans*, am. Of course I live alternately, even concurrently, both omnipotence and mourning. Of course I am depressed, the major syndrome presenting itself in western medical practices, and of course I feel *Weltschmerz*, and of course Sophia, as the Gnostics and alchemists said, laments. Congenital chronic depression and the manic defences against it, including that manic defence called hope for salvation and redemption, are the price we continue to pay for the death of Pan and the pagan world soul.

Some recent American social and ecological psychology – of course without mention of pagan gods or an *anima mundi* – has been subverting psychotherapy by revealing its foundations in nineteenth-century, liberal, humanistic individualism. I am referring to works by Sandel, Bellah, Cahoone, Wicker and especially Sampson, whom I shall be quoting. (As you can begin to feel, there is already a social and ecological psychology in my move: I am replying to France from America, even more, privileging my own viewpoint, not deconstructing at all but arguing, positing, just like an old-fashioned modernist.)

I quote now Sampson: "There are no subjects who can be defined apart from the world; persons are constituted in and through their attachments, connections, and relationships."⁶ A Cartesian *res cogitans*, detached, unencumbered, free to choose, self-owning and self-defining (making up one's "own mind"), prior to community and its government and for whom community and its government exist presents the modernist fantasy of individualism that is by definition anomic, long before *anomie* was discovered by Durkheim as a sociological phenomenon. The strong individual with a strong ego, able to cope and manage and handle problems as an independent entity endowed with freedoms to speak, think, worship, assemble, travel, print, own land and will it to descendants; whose communal life is not inherent but derives from social contract freely entered into else life would be brutish and short, and whose reason is independent of any context; this individual whom analytical psychotherapy attempts to shore up with its notions of self-determining ego development is simply an anachronism. It is a view of human nature reaching its apogee in the western nineteenth century, the political context of Freud's time and place. In fact, the theory of the person that continues to dominate analytical psychotherapy is itself a sociological or ecological reflection of a particular psychological climate which also saw the apogee of colonialism, industrialism, capitalism, etc.

From this ecological, or political if you prefer, point of view our theories of the person who is the patient and the practice of understanding the person apart from political context in which I the person is embedded and by which I the person is constituted can only further the delusion of a transcendental subject, a subject transcendent to community, requiring a guarantor for my isolated subjectivity, a transcendent original self or God. This ultimately unknowable and non-phenomenal guarantor is either a neurotic fiction or an omnipotence fantasy which urges each therapeutic analysis towards an unreachable and utopic goal. Moreover, this elaborate fantasy of individualism repeats not merely the splendid isolation of the colonial administrator, the captain of industry and the continental academic in his ivory tower; it also reconstructs in the consulting room the theological God of monotheism, anomic, transcendent, omniscient, omnipotent. Because we do not practice politics, we practice religion. Of course, Freud and Jung had to tackle religion again and again, and Lacan had to state that if religion wins, psychoanalysis is doomed. Religion, by which I mean our western monotheistic God-apart-from-world, will always threaten analytical psychotherapy since the *anthropos*, the patient, is created precisely in the image of that God.

These critics, or theorists, and I again quote Sampson, say that the endeavour of psychotherapy to understand the individual, and then, on that model apply what is revealed by analytical investigation to the body politic – in the manner of the Freudian left and Norman O. Brown – is delusional because there is no longer that individual. The paradigm has shifted. So that Sampson can say: "Quite simply, understanding the individual as individual is no longer relevant to understanding human life."[7] Chaos, anarchy, decentralization, networking, ecology, deconstruction – dehumanizing existential protagorean man as measure of all things – will force the latent citizen from his hiding place as patient to make a run for it, driven by object libido toward a new refuge among the community of soul in the world.

Let us go back for a moment to Aristotle's sentence: "man is by nature a political animal" (*anthropos phusei politikon zoon*). Let us expand upon the four terms.

1 *Anthropos*: not merely man, but mankind, human being, and the completely realized human being, since form and *telos* imply each other, for the formal cause provides the image toward which, for the sake of which, for the actualization of which, humankind is. We not only are political animals by nature; we are most complete and actualized as political animals.

2 *Phusei*: the basic stuff and structure, the original substance, the essence, the nature, the reality of human kind, is political.

3 *Politikon*: from *polis*, the city, and citadel. The word polis means in its etymological roots and cognates: throng, crowd, runny, connected for instance with *palude* (swamp), pour, flow, fill, fill up, flood, overflow, swim, an innately plural meaning, poly, many, as in the Latin cognate *pleo-plere, plenus, plerus, plebs, plus, plural*. Polis, therefore, less as institutions, governments, civic affairs than as a more, a throng, a community, the *demos* (Dionysos is said to have been the favourite divinity of the *demos*).

4 *Zoon*: the animal force of life, an organic vitality, an *élan vital*, any individual person. *Zoe* was one of the main words associated with Dionysos.

PATIENT AS CITIZEN

What would it be like were we to imagine the patient as citizen? What then would be the nature of therapeutic discourse? Can we imagine a therapy session, an interview with a new candidate, a case supervision within the polis of Athene, rather than under the tutelage of Oedipus and his *heuriskein* or figuring out, his blind drive to "know thyself", *gnothi seauton*.

I am suggesting that we can imagine a post-analytic therapy, a post-self-centered therapy that dissolves those identities which recent deconstructionism has shown to be problem-ridden if not invalid; identities such as gender, family role, historical continuity of the person, even the subjectivity of ego. If identity can be dissolved, with it goes those isolating individualisms of therapeutic language such as unity, centredness, wholeness, integration and especially that intensely reflective substantive mythologem or bewitching God-term, Self.

For this term, Self, is the last redoubt of all substantialism and all identity. It has yet to experience its own identity crisis. Wherever it appears

– and sometimes in disguise of person and personality, individual and individuality, it assumes itself as carrier of reflexive consciousness – which is of course its primary meaning. In that word is the mirror. And its earliest compound meanings in English (late medieval) as selfsame and self-willed point directly to the term as carrier of identity. In other words, the attack on subjective identity needs a further displacement of the basic supporting idea of all analytical psychotherapy, the idea of self.

Suppose we were no longer to imagine Self as a homeostatic interior dynamics of a biological organism, or as the moral spark of an unknowable transcendent, or as the simply given, reflexive activity of consciousness, or as the *auton*, or autonomy (self-willed and selfsame) of any distinctly defined system. Suppose we were to recognize, see through, bracket out and then discard these favourite notions of self. One reason for the discard being that none of these favourite notions require external relations; no necessity for an outer, an other, even an echo. They can be imagined wholly for themselves, and so one can know oneself wholly by and with oneself, in the gaze of self-reflective *inspectio*, as Descartes called it. As fundamentally self-reflectively self-satisfied, they require the outer and other only for narcissistic supplies, as transitional objects, as flat glassy mirrors, in order to "have experiences" like going through fusion and separation, envy, authority problems, castration feelings and so on.

Instead let us imagine another definition, neither biological, theological, psychological or ontological – instead political. Self as the interiorization of community.

Then to ask in a therapeutic session about the political is to ask about Self. Then to pursue self-development requires community pursuits. Then to turn for confirmation of one's self-steering course – am I on track or off; am I repressing; am I centred – one looks less to the dynamics of psyche or to the voices and visions of transcendent epiphanies than to the actual community of one's actual life. Then the pursuit of insight necessitates an objective correlative, the place where insight arises, the community, rather than the transference.

I don't want to literalize community as the actual politics of neighbourhood, or any of the myriad political levels of engagement. Rather, I am intending toward Alfred Adler's *Gemeinschaftsgefühl*, a social feeling that fictionalizes many goals, many literal political activities, as retorts for the feeling, where object libido can be intensified, differentiated, manifested. Throughout one imagines oneself as citizen where discourse about self and the reading of this self and its actions is conceived always within a context of *Gemeinschaftsgefühl*.

If Self and its draw toward reflective interiority refers not to an immanent soul-spark of a transcendent God, or to a germ, seed, truth, centre or core of will-power, but rather is constituted of communal contingencies, then the draw toward interiority must at the same time be a draw toward exteriority, toward the contingencies of the actual ecological field – where

I am placed, with whom I am, what is happening with my animals, my food, my furniture, what the toaster and newspaper and refrigerator purr do in the field I am in. To find myself I must turn to them, visibles and invisibles. Then to work on the unconscious, to foster my growth, my self-understanding and to cure my illness, I will no longer drift into dream, walk solitary in nature, shut myself off to meditate, to analyse or recall my childhood, expecting something inside my skull or skin to reveal itself and guide me. Instead I turn to what is simply there, my rooms and their trash, my acquaintances and their reactions, my neighbours and their concerns, for this presents my self, for it is of them I am constituted. Interiorization of community means taking in, noticing, attending to what actually engages me and enrages me. The environment is now the mirror and insight is now outrage.

Emotions remain dominant. But no longer are they conceived to be literally interior, only within my physiology, in the deep id, older brain, neurovegetative recesses, hormonal secretions. Instead, an emotion may be imagined as a "divine influx" as William Blake said, "afforded" by the world in J. J. Gibson's sense, as "affecting presences" as Robert Armstrong called them, revealing "importance" in Whitehead's sense, carried by objects, scenes and situations as their "physiognomic character" in the manner of classic Gestalt psychology. An emotion now becomes a field of signification and value, affecting me to move out, *ex movere*, of self-enclosure.

As mourning would no longer be interiorized as depression and treated as an inner state independent of the object losses in the world soul, so rage will not be regarded as a private condition of aggression or hostility inside my individualized self-responsible personality. Instead, rage presents a primal outrage over an actual situation. I am affected by its presence, by the presence of the enraging. In Wallace Steven's words: "The lion roars at the enraging desert / Reddens the sand with his red-colored noise".[8] So, too, shame will not be interiorized as guilt and attached to an imaginary structure called ego or self and owned by it, but shame will reflect specific "falls", i.e., sins of omission and commission that the I, as human, carry as I walk through the world. Nor will fear – that supreme emotion for acknowledging the power of the object – be converted to objectless anxiety and considered wholly intrapsychically. Nor, finally, will desire that reaches as far as the heart can fathom and lifts repression from the world's face disclosing its desirability – desire as the response to the radiance of the world – nor will this be stuffed into the closet of personal needs.

For patient to become citizen, analytical psychotherapy can hardly do more at first than return to the world the emotions which call the patient to the world. By following the innate extraversion of emotion, its fascination with the object and its libidinously sticky attachment to the other, the patient's involvement changes from self to object. Yet, all the while an interiorizing is going on, making more subtle and sophisticated the emotional field, attending to the world's need for soul and the soul's need for a world beyond itself. For the world calls to the libido from the face of every object. It lures and screams and terrifies, to which we remain deaf, defended by our immune system that declares these calls to be projections because emotions have been locked up inside.

THERAPY AS SYMPTOM

In these last pages let us focus again upon the practice of analysis. "Clinical practice" as the professionals like to call it.

In the circle of my hermeneutic colleagues, more and more I hear three sorts of complaints: the first, "I believe I have a slight narcolepsy; I fall asleep, doze off in the middle of the hour". The second; "I wish I really could cut down. I'm doing twenty-five, thirty-five or forty-five hours a week and it's too much". The third – this complaint is not spoken directly – refers to sexual compulsions, indiscretions between analyst and patient, ethics committees, testimony, investigations, denunciations for what is called "acting out in the sexual sphere".

What is the psyche doing in these three afflictions that occur in therapy, to therapy, perhaps because of therapy? One thing is clear: in all three symptoms some desire wants to put an end to analysis. Let us take the third one first, the sexual compulsion.

Quite clearly the consciousness and the conscience of the analyst knows that breaking the rule of erotic restraint not only ends analysis as such, but also may well end the analyst's career as analyst. None the less, the acting out, as it is called, occurs in more cases than are officially reported or admitted. There are many interpretations of this symptom. Let me attempt a reading of the sexualized compulsion in terms of the "object libido".

The other person in the room – patient or analyst – embodies the only human possibility within an analysis to whom object libido can flow. The person in the other chair represents cure of the analytic narcissism simply by being there as an other. Moreover, the patient for the analyst and the analyst for the patient become such compelling objects because they have also been tabooed by the analytical rules as libidinal possibilities. Analyst and patient may not act their desire for each other. The narcissism of the situation – that libido is turned to the ego and not to the world (except world as other person in the other chair) – makes them absolutely necessary to each other, while the taboo sets them absolutely outside of each other. The outside object, however, is also inside analysis. So patient for analyst and analyst for patient becomes the symbolic mode of ending analysis by means of falling in love.

Of course, the persons are often torn by the love dilemma of the narcissistic patient: "cure by love" in preference to "cure by analysis".[9] We must ask, however, whether this neurotic choice, as Freud calls it, arises from the narcissism of the patient and of the analyst or whether it arises from the narcissism of the analytical situation. After all, the fantasy of an opposition between love and analysis occurs within the prior fantasy of cure which has brought the persons together in the first place. The erotic compulsion besetting both persons is a symptom not of their ethical fallibility or of their vulnerability to personal repressions. Rather it is a symptom of therapy.

It is therapy generating its own symptom to which neither patient nor analyst are immune because therapy's isolated narcissistic individualism cannot confine the instinctual drive of object libido which appears in the guise of the disease, erotic obsession, a disease which seeks to cure the persons of the more fundamental disease, therapy itself.

The second of our three conditions, narcolepsy or falling asleep, like falling in love, also puts closure to analysis as a prolonged hovering over the case exposed, closure to consciousness itself as it is defined by "attention", "wakefulness", "cortical activation", "apperceptive alertness", "continuity of awareness". The psyche absents itself from the analytical activity; in fact, it enters the state of the dream, the primary condition requiring analysis. Falling asleep, like falling in love, is the fall from self-control; the subject utterly displaced back into the Zuider Zee. Curiously, like falling in love, the overpowering drowsiness occurs only in the analytical session, not at home, not watching the telly, not driving the car, not during other conversations, lectures, committee meetings. The narcolepsy is a "therapeugenic" symptom, as if therapy in the person of the analyst was not merely deconstructing itself but was hell-bent on destruction of consciousness.

The language of the second complaint – "I wish I could cut down, do less, get away more, rearrange my schedule but I haven't been able to" takes us into the realms of addiction. The addiction to my schedule, that is to the regular hours for seeing patients each week, each month, even years in advance, literalizes and substantiates time into exact blocks in an appointment book. To mislay or lose the agenda is utterly disorienting: one has become agenda-dependent, even looking forward to September or January each year for the newly-bound blank, fresh schedule book.

Although I have set this schedule myself, I am not its master. I have become the slave of analytical time. Schedule as Robot, Golem, Till Eulenspiegel, Frankenstein. Desire attempts to break free. Desire imagines libidinal objects other than analytical hours, but the schedule does not allow it. "I must check my schedule." I have become dependent upon the autonomy of substantiated time. Schedule as other overrides my will. I see little difference between substance dependency like alcohol and drugs and substantiation dependency like time-slots and schedules. Both declare the defeat of independent individualism. I am bound over to an objectification, which is what the object libido desires, reaches towards. But the obscure objects of desire which bind me to the world and make me co-dependent with its desirability – we so desperately need each other – remain unfulfilled and the object libido compromised when the objects are not the things of an animated world, but are its substitute: alcohol, drugs, tobacco, love object, shopping for bargains, schedule.

None the less, we know from Freud that every symptom has its *telos*. As compromise, a symptom intends to cure the condition in which the symptom originates. The symptoms I have just sketched threaten individualism right into its citadel, the double-door closed keep of the analytical chamber. These three symptoms – erotic compulsion, narcolepsy and schedule addiction – attest to a breakdown in the model of analytical psychotherapy, that model which supposes itself immune to movements, not only of the world, but movements of the object libido reaching for the world, movements too often theoretically distorted by and therefore clinically disguised as projection and acting out.

So, as often in the past, I am again reading the pathologizing (this time the pathologizing going on in therapy itself) as a necessary falling apart (this time a breakdown of its immune system), a disclosing of its liberal humanist notion of self-determination, a crack in its Christianized personalized skin-bounded soul, and a return of the object libido from the inherently agoraphobic apolitical self-enclosed individualism of therapy to the animation of the world soul, the *anima mundi*, whose claim on the patient as political animal is prior to the claim of therapy.

When analysis can recognize that citizen takes priority over patient, then analysis can revert its differentiated subtle attention to that ground against which Jung and Freud limned individuality: the collective, the herd instinct, the primal horde, that throng and flood of the polis and the call of the *agora*. Then, no longer would our motto be Apollonic and Oedipal, ΓΝΩΘΙ ΣΕΑΥΤΩΝ, know thyself; no longer, *cogito ergo sum*, but *convivo ergo sum*, – freely translated: "I party, am of a party, and therefore am."

NOTES

1 S. Freud (1937), "Analysis terminable and interminable", *Collected Papers V* (London: Hogarth, 1950), p. 326.

2 S. Freud (1933), "Anxiety and the instinctual life – Lecture XXXII", in *New Introductory Lectures on Psycho-Analysis*, tr. W. J. H. Sprott (London: Hogarth, 1950), p. 124.

3 S. Freud (1922) "Two encyclopedia articles: the libido theory", *Collected Papers V*, (London: Hogarth, 1950), p. 134.

4 S. Freud (1922), *Group Psychology and the Analysis of the Ego*, tr. J. Strachey (London: Hogarth, 1948), p. 89.

5 Freud, "The libido theory", p. 133.

6 Edward Sampson, "The challenge of social change for psychology: globalization and psychology's theory of the person", *American Psychologist*, vol. 44, no. 6 (June 1989), 918.

7 Ibid., 916. See also Edward Sampson, "The decentralization of identity: toward a revised concept of personal and social order", *American Psychologist*, vol. 40, no. 11 (November 1985) and "The debate on individualism: indigenous psy-

chologies of the individual and their role in personal and societal functioning", *American Psychologist*, vol. 43, no. 1 (January 1988).

8 Wallace Stevens, "Notes toward a supreme fiction", in *The Collected Poems of Wallace Stevens* (New York: Knopf, 1978), p. 384.

9 S. Freud, "On narcissism: an introduction", *Collected Papers IV* (London: Hogarth), p. 59.

4 Psychoanalysis in left field and fieldworking

Examples to fit the title

Gayatri Chakravorty Spivak

Gayatri Chakravorty Spivak is Avalon Foundation Professor in the Humanities at Columbia University. Her translation of and introduction to Derrida's *Of Grammatology* has been important in the dissemination of deconstruction in the English-speaking world. She has been described as a feminist Marxist deconstructivist, and in this context as "the ethno-cultural agenda", reading psychoanalysis from the so-called margins. Her work has been concerned with the cultural politics of knowledge.

In this paper, she is concerned with the question of the relation between the limits of the subject of psychoanalysis. She particularly addresses the question as to whether psychoanalysis can foster social agency in a world of decolonization and migrancy. She considers the situation in which a "post-colonial" psychoanalysis finds itself, with particular reference to the heritage of British and French Imperialism and the contemporary US.

Through an extended analogy between psychoanalysis and baseball, she draws out the modes in which psychoanalysis has attempted to extend its provenance. In contrast to Hillman, she comes to a qualified affirmation of the possibilities of psychoanalysis. She argues that it attempts at least to engage the "sub-individual zones of sense making" and the ethic of responsibility; by contrast with analytic philosophy, which takes the "mental theatre" of the subject as a given.

SELECT BIBLIOGRAPHY

Spivak, Gayatri Chakravorty, *In Other Worlds*, New York and London: Routledge, 1987.
—— *The Post-Colonial Critic: Interviews, Strategies, Dialogues*, ed. Sarah Harasym, New York and London: Routledge, 1990.
—— Outside in the Teaching Machine, New York and London: Routledge, 1993.

* * *

I am very well aware that in dealing so autocratically and arbitrarily with [psychoanalytic] tradition – bringing it up to confirm my views when it suits me and unhesitatingly rejecting it when it contradicts me – I am exposing myself to serious methodological criticism and weakening the convincing force of my arguments. But this is the only way in which one can treat material of which one knows definitely that its trustworthiness has been severely impaired by the distorting influence of tendentious purposes.

(Sigmund Freud, *Moses and Monotheism*)

CRICKET AND BASEBALL

I have long wanted to make Grace Kelly's daughter's motto in life my own: "Never explain. Never complain!" I seem never to be able to bring it off. I begin again with explanations and complaints.

Explanations and complaints are exactly not promises and excuses, which are structural performatives, whose uttering is their performance. In a certain sense a promise can never quite be kept or broken (although this does not concern the performance of the promise, its utterance), even as, *mutatis mutandis*, an excuse can never quite be false or true. Explanations and complaints inevitably arise in the rifts and fault lines of this structural (non)necessity of and in promises and excuses. They invoke a future present, and they invariably evoke a past present in order to dissimulate the fact that a performative is structurally (though not necessarily "in fact") free of the burden of the future.

It is quite possible that Caroline or Stephanie (I forget which, my source is *People* magazine) was attempting to protect the performative, profoundly dependent upon social convention. This has something like a relationship with the explaints and complanations – absolution by accusing knowledge – that I was invited to utter at the Conference whose papers comprise this anthology. These are the emergent social conventions of the politically correct conference. Why else was I there, a non-practising, non-psychoanalyst, not-scholar of psychoanalysis, among psychoanalysts? Since explanations and complaints, promises and excuses, and all the portmanteau phenomena in between – not to mention the construction of portmanteau words – are in the domain of the psychoanalytic everyday, it gives me pleasure to speak of them by way of opening.

If I am the ethno-cultural agenda, the representative of the "Cultural Studies" mentioned in the Conference Description, why did I accept the invitation? A large part of the reason (although not the entire reason) was that the compulsion to offer ethno-cultural complanations or explaints is produced both by the demand for them as well as the absence of such demands in different ways.

Let me give you in a few words the nature of these explaints and complanations, banal alas, but "true", easy to mouth or even to know, but hard to learn. Ex-colonials cannot protect the contemporary performatives because for them the performatives are always infelicitous, always more and less than a citation or iteration (making other in quoting).[1] Many of us assiduously deny this in the performance even as we are vigorous in its constatation. But the fact is that even this is no special privilege, simply a more embarrassingly visible or noticeable example of the nature of all performatives. When we make promises or excuses, for curing or not wanting to be cured – to give a vulgar example recognizable at least by someone who has been a client if not a practitioner of psychoanalysis – can *we* perform conventions laid down according to Hebraic and Hellenic stories? No, but nor can the jewgreek or greekjew, fully, felicitously, for intention must inhabit pre- and post-existing conventions to utter the performative; and intention – what knows this better than transference – is always differantially contaminated, never identical with itself, always almost catching up. Yet can *we* not claim a special privilege by the fact of serving as the embarrassingly visible; for the difference in degree, in the name of a difference in kind? Probably not, except probably by tearing a hole in theory, and uttering the embarrassing, the easy to say but hard to learn responsibility, to utter which we were invited in the first place: because you tried to cast us in *your* mould, because your special task was to be universal and to universalize, and we did not come out *quite* like you, your universalizing conventions will not produce promises and excuses for us; our decrepitude is not that we have broken promises and offered false excuses, but that we cannot get an intention-convention fit in that language. We *know* no one can. But since we are teaching the best of you this lesson by being abundantly noticeable, how about letting us off the hook of having to? (Institutional psychoanalysis, for all its subtleties, is one of these languages, producing performatives.) Do we offer this explaint? Can we? Should we? The answer is an uneasy "no". How about those to whom these universalizing idioms have been available only notionally, only as guarantees unimaginable by them, established by extremely remote controlling apparatuses? What will they have if not this? Museumized or pre-capitalist shamanism? In the context of the construction of a rational subject for academic freedom within the university, I have suggested an (ab)use of the Enlightenment. Can one propose the same thing about psychoanalysis? I cannot imagine a world without the University. Can I imagine one without psychoanalysis? How could I, an outsider to this gathering of psychoanalysts and philosophers of psychoanalysis, on the ethno-cultural agenda, have any appropriate word to offer, on behalf of "Cultural Studies", that would not be trivial?

To grapple with this problem, I had originally thought to take the example of a metropolitan game that gave the colonized an entry into the metropolitan soul: cricket and *Beyond A Boundary* being the obvious exhibits.[2] India's own Ashis Nandy has also written on cricket.[3] Nandy is a social psychologist who has regularly berated disciplinary psychologists in India for dully and belatedly following the metropolis. Yet I cannot feel the constitutive weight of psychoanalysis upon everyday urban (and even to some extent rural) existence (albeit more and more male as it trickles toward the bottom) in India as I can of cricket. And I dare say the case would not be wildly different in Jamaica.

In trying to find a situational imperative that would permit me to respond to the invitation, then, I turned from my place of citizenship to my source of income, the United States, from cricket to baseball.[4] Before going on with the questions of the status of psychoanalysis as constitutive for the hybrid as opposed to the post-colonial subject, however, let me linger for a moment on the two games as ports of entry into "civilizational competence".

In "Cricket and national culture in the writings of C. L. R. James", Neil Lazarus writes:

> To begin an essay, intended for publication in the United States, on the subject of C. L. R. James and cricket is inevitably to feel oneself under the shadow of an objection. The problem is that while James is unthinkable without cricket, cricket is unintelligible to most Americans ... External facts would seem to support this conclusion: when James's classic autobiography *Beyond a Boundary* (1963) was issued in an American edition in 1984, for instance, it failed miserably despite the positive reviews that attended its publication.[5]

It is not just that cricket is generally unknown to the US left-inclined culturalist reading public. Lazarus makes the further point that it is "unintelligible". I have not the impertinence to summarize the subtle argument of *Beyond* here, especially since our subject is not cricket, but psychoanalysis, another sort of game. Yet it must be said that the unintelligibility of cricket to the US intelligentsia as well as "sporting" public – notice how the British connotation of that word is unavailable (as it attaches to the word) in standard American English – may have something like a relationship with the difference in the "imperialist spirit" of the two "nations" – to the extent that the items within quotation marks are generalizable.

My generalizations will remain well within the imaginable extent of their reach: as both James and Nandy argue, in their different ways, the male colonial subject does not "become" the British national subject by learning the rules of cricket "by heart". They advance, rather, into the intimacy that provides the adjective in Nandy's felicitous phrase for "the colonizer": "the intimate enemy".[6] (I have repeatedly written of the process, less felicitously, as "epistemic violation".) But the American "nation" – in spite of its vaguely northwestern European dominant imaginary – draws its credit from its historical negotiability through migrancy. Whatever the publicity-value of Italian or Filipino baseball teams, baseball is "American", while cricket is "colonial". Somewhat against the grain of *his* argument, let me quote Nandy, half as an example of *my* argument: "Cricket is not a synecdoche in the culture of its origin; it is so only in some of the cultures which have adopted it."⁷ An international brotherhood of what today is politely called the Commonwealth could perhaps be established in terms of an internalizing of cricket but is not, today, possible in baseball. Many assimilated colonials think that this is something essentially good about the British and something essentially rather embarrassing and vulgar about the Americans. "It seems history is to blame."⁸ The work of neo-colonialism does not require that kind of intimate relationship which becomes a dirty secret, the hallmark of territorial imperialism (which we are told, was economically a losing proposition from the very start). It may not be simply by chance that the contrast can be rather strongly felt between *Beyond a Boundary* (1963) and Robert Coover's *Universal Baseball Association* (1967). The mood of the central characters (resolutely male) in *Beyond* and *Tao* is that of the "wild anthropologist" reversing the role of the native informant; that of the third-person hero of *Universal* is nationalistic in the strictest sense, an autistic (pre-)supposition of the dominant idiom of "nation" that is absolutely (and "cultural" "relativism" has not helped here) ignorant of idioms nationally constitutive elsewhere, where national is world (as in World Series) is universal.

It is in this latter problematic, of baseball rather than cricket, that I have found the first part of my title. Another word before I explain a bit further.

The traffic in "Cultural Studies" between the United States and various parts of Asia now has a strong "made-in-America" flavour. The earlier Birmingham model drew its strength from the British-style inimical intimacy and its real first source of strength seems to us outsiders to have been Black Britain. The impulse for the somewhat mercurial US "Cultural Studies", with its uneasy comradeship with liberal multiculturalism, as I have argued elsewhere, comes from the New Immigrants who began entering the United States when Lyndon Johnson changed the Immigration Laws in 1965.⁹ This is, of course, to create a simple narrative out of immense complexity.¹⁰ But it may be said with some justice that this style of "Cultural Studies" makes of the various Asias and Africas a colourful cluster of "national origins" where a rhetorical version of psychoanalysis – with its "anthropological origin", and "religious origin", and its story of "subject-construction" – can find a field. (In the post-Soviet era, the field will expand with a more complicated politics, haunted by the politically computed difference between refugee and migrant.) It is as if the autistic "nationalism" of baseball should now want to transform "the rest of the world" to its own rules by rewriting it as "national origin". I have often quoted Gramsci to describe this, and now I quote myself quoting Gramsci:

> Necessarily without a detailed awareness of the rich history of African-American struggle, Gramsci was somewhat off the mark when he presented the following "hypothesis" for "verification:" "1. that American expansionism should use American negroes as its agents in the conquest

of the African market and the extension of American civilisation." If, however, these words are applied to new immigrant intellectuals and their countries of national origin, the words seem particularly apposite today. The partners are, of course, "Cultural Studies," liberal multi-culturalism, and post-fordist transnational capitalism.[11]

It is apparently easier to "become American" than British; that is the seduction. You psych out your master by the vaccination of cricket; you catch the American dream by playing ball. A male story, although it seems not without interest – of "historical moment" and "national character" – that women claim baseball as they never have bothered to claim cricket.

But why "in left field"? "The left field" is the back part of the left side of the baseball diamond. In the context of the configuration of today's global culture this is how it might turn out if an immigrant academic chose to make sense of things in terms of the imperial/national sport of the United States. "Psychoanalysis in left field." The full expression can also be "Psychoanalysis *out* in left field".

Like most metaphors from games, the actual play is rather more interesting than the figurative use. Indeed, within all its shifting discontinuous frames, the work or play of psychoanalysis is, just in this way, on another register of long- and short-term responsibility than its use as political or cultural figure, although the two uses cannot always be conveniently polarized. The so-called figurative uses are also, of course, working games and we sometimes call them cultural politics rather than "Cultural Studies", which is itself a game of academic work of varying cultural politics. And so on, indefinitely. I am quite aware (I think) that, speaking about psycho-analysis at a conference, I might have been slightly more in my own game than the psychoanalytic performers were in theirs. That said, let me move back in or step out into the question of "the left field" in baseball.

The figurative meaning of "out in left field" or "in left field" (or indeed, "way out in left field", where the usefulness of "left field" almost drops out) is, although never simply (since the situational and rule-bound "reasons" remain to be thought out) "way-out" in the sense of not there, without a clue, seriously irrelevant, missing the point, even crazy. If one looks at the structure and performance of the game, a value-judgment depends on who is being talked about, and the "who" is written in (at least) the uneven weave of intention, reflex, "chance", that all moments of rule-governed games require.

If you (and basically we are talking about a homo-socially defined situation) are a hitter, and you want to outwit the fielder by putting him "way out in left field", as it were, you hit deeply and cautiously so that the ball flies overhead, or you pretend to hit that way so that the fielder is way out in left field, while you hit close; either way you score a home run fast.

We are, then, speaking of the hitter – the agent – rather than the fielder, the reactor or reagent, who is, interestingly, the hero of the figure. (It is as if the figurative use is itself rehearsing the secondariness of figure to truth; and the truth of psychoanalysis is in the responsible *tête-à-tête*, as the truth of baseball is in the playing-field. More about this toward the end of the essay.)

I have already mentioned that the dominant form is male. Add to that the fact that we are necessarily considering the right-handed hitter. If it is the figure that gives us a clue to the figure–truth hierarchy staged in the figuring of truth, the roles of the hitter–fielder shift abysmally when psychoanalysis is in left field. And the question that we have not asked at all so far – who pitches? Which side is he on? – has something like a relationship with the question foreclosed by *all* ethno-cultural agendas: who decolonizes? Whatever it is, it's not, for me, cricket, although it is, of course, uncanny. And, for me, judge it as you will, psychoanalysis in left field cannot *only* mean psychoanalysis being distant from the scene of action. Psychoanalysis out in left field cannot *only* mean psychoanalysis up the creek without a paddle. Psychoanalysis *way out* in left field cannot *only* mean utterly absorbed in its own system, out of touch with the *découpage* or contextual cut that makes it work.

For academics whose desire is to keep the scandal of the real North–South wound or cut open, the "metapsychological" is not only "philosophical" and "anthropo-religious" in addition to dynamic/topological/economic but also "ethico-political", waiting to be "set to work", in another way.[12] This exigency is not necessarily removed by insisting that "Psychoanalysis is *really* materialist", "Psychoanalysis is *really* historical", and straining for evidence from within some narrative of selective northwestern European philosophy or history. The dazzling results produced by some of my friends by these efforts are indeed way out in left field in that limited sense: so utterly absorbed in one's own system that one is quite out of touch with the *découpage* or contextual cut that makes it work, a massive begging of the question, proving it works by assuming first that it does.

What draws "Americans" like me to the action in that space, however errant, in the hinterland of the left side of the baseball diamond is a bit more complicated. Let us dare to err there. If we simply strive to fit baseball in the field with psychoanalysis in the clinic at this stage, the analogy might short-circuit. Errant, I will first consider a few far-flung examples in terms of the analogy. I will let you draw the conclusions. On the way to my own conclusion, I will construct a counter-point of moves strained to establish parallels breaking down the number of active players and the continuity of the field of play, haphazardly, as hazard happens, following chance by choice: explaints, therefore, and complanations.

INDIA

Let me, then, propose this question: given radical iterability, how have the right-handed hitters in India dealt with the pitcher they perceived to be the scientific dominant discourse of psychoanalysis?

The majority of practising psychoanalysts (and, *mutatis mutandis*, psychologists and clinical psychiatrists) who accept "psychoanalysis" as a science, learn its practice professionally (still as a version of abyssal responsibility, responses being drawn from both sides, the main effort being to keep the innings going as long as necesary, permitted or possible) and publish accordingly. Their offerings are to be found, say, in the pages of *Samiksa* (the journal of the Indian Psychoanalytic Institute) or *The Journal of the Indian Psychological Association*. They are, strictly speaking, fielders out in left field without a clue, playing psychoanalysis like cricket, where knowledge of the rules of the (wrong) game produces the inability to perceive the depth of the play. For this reader, one of the most telling examples of this phonomenon is a Research Note such as "Adaptation of Kundu's neurotic personality inventory in Bengali", supplied by a conscientious woman psychologist, "the work done under the guidance of Dr. S. Chatterjee, Head, Psychometry Unit (RTS) & Dr. (Miss) M. Mukherjee, Indian Statistical Institute, Calcutta".[13]

There is also a fairly large number of attempts, through the anthropologico-religious connections of psychoanalysis, to interpret "Hindu psychology", mythology and epic in terms of a general psychoanalytic lexicon. One of the most interesting examples is no doubt Sudhir Kakar's "Tantra and Tantric healing", which acknowledges the Tantra system as an instrument for psychoanalysing (albeit not for Psychoanalysis) rather than a cultural oddity.[14] Since, however, this instrument is clearly "unscientific" and assumes a credulous clientele, the cultural-political problem of blocking access to modernity that anthropological benevolence merely compounds has not been avoided even by such a conscientious effort.

Most of the efforts are less bold. What does strike one is the absence of a noticeable feminist impulse in this particular line of work.[15] When considering the *Mahābhārata*, for example, Indian psychologist/psychoanalysts do not notice that, in the recited table of contents in the first episode of the epic (put there as an oral mnemonic of the great narrative for the singer, *pace* Lyotard's appropriation of the short tale for postmodern legitimation), it is obsessively repeated that the male transgression for which the devastating defeat – the *mythos* of the epic – atones was to have brought Princess Draupadi into the Royal Assembly in her bloodied garment, when, in menstruation, she was in her "female nature" or *strīdharma*. If regulative psycho-biographies are historical rather than (or as well as) archetypal, should one consider this as significantly different from the Moses-Totem-(narcissus-)Oedipus story rather than consider "Indians" as persistent deviations from the ideal subject of the admittedly impossible psychoanalytic narrative? Should feminist psychoanalysts in "India" intervene on a different ground? Should that ground include the detail that, in the earliest version of the story, it is Nature that intervenes to lament the transgression rather than man intervening to protect her honour? Should it include the fact that tradition has suppressed her unanswerable question of/as woman as property, posed precisely to the deliberately unreproductive patriarch? How far should one intervene inductively? Was Freud ultimately deductive or did he, at a certain point, also start begging the question? Remember those curious statements in "Narcissism" and "Femininity" about unavoidable assumptions and *idées fixes*?[16] Can rules of a game be "true"? and so on.

When considering the *Rāmāyana*, Indian psychologist/psychoanalysts do not seem to have noticed that, like the historically pre-Oedipal male Cadmeans rememorated at the opening of *Oedipus the King* (a male martial collectivity for which there is, incidentally, an episodic parallel in Indic epic), the future Queen Sita is found in the plough's furrow, in a chthonic representation of the primal scene under her (foster-) father's control. Her (foster-)father's name is simply "Father" (*Janaka*): etymologically, "he who engenders". One of Sita's epithet/proper names is, therefore *Jānaki* ("of the Father"; or, of course, Janaka's daughter). The feminine gender of *janaka* as a common noun in Sanskrit – *janani* (mother) – is bypassed in this birth, these namings. *Jānaki* is not a common noun. At the end of the epic, when asked to undergo the trial by fire to test her faithfulness, Sita refuses, calls upon the earth, which splits and takes her back. If regulative psycho-biographies are also historical, how should feminists intervene in that the culturally sanctioned feminine role-model fixes on Sita's devotion to her husband rather than on her arche-teleological a-partness from the circuit of marriage and, indeed, monogamy? (It is her husband's brother who succeeds to the throne; her own twin sons play almost no role in the story.) How can such interventions hope to undo the perennial possibility of political mobilization in the name of "Hinduism" in post-coloniality? Should we forget that the blind Oedipus' final speech (which breaks the decorum of Greek tragedy by taking place on stage) is addressed to marriage, as the institution that coded his life as transgression? And, of course, all those other questions as well. Can it be that we are looking here at a different (rather than deviant) game, open still to intervention and the carving out of a practice that is responsible by volleying responses rather than imposing an alien "science?"

Freud has foreclosed this by situating matriarchal polytheisms in the prehistory of mankind, even as he dismisses the rationalistic element in Eastern religions as ancestor-worship. By this he is able to claim the parricide story as the beginning of human history.[17] But do feminists have time to intervene on this level, to make the repressed return? Only in so far as this presupposition is shared by the colonized culture, it would seem. Or, to be more precise, as it enters the presuppositional baggage of the educators. I will later make some suggestions about the constitution of the "masses" whose mobilization defeats decolonization. In this context, it is well to remember that the polytheist description is vigorously contested, in different ways, by both "fundamentalist" and enlightened Hindus.

In "Figures for the 'Unconscious' ", Kumkum Sangari points out that, in two novels written by two Indians thirty years apart (under the regime of cricket and baseball, respectively – and the differences remain to be worked out), an Indian cultural unconscious seems to be situated in the figure of the tribal (aboriginal or indigenous) woman.[18] The politics of this configuration emerges in the economy, in both cases, of two women: a tamed and a wild. The wild one is, of course, the tribal. The tamed is the modern Indian woman, emancipated Hindu rather than tribal; measuring the distance between an imitative modern ego and a rich historico-cultural unconscious. Denial of access to modernity as woman's virtue is played out here by Indian men. Criticizing both male writers, Sangari warns against dehistoricizing, romanticizing and thus disempowering the autochthonous tribal.

Sangari herself points out, in agreement with some of the discussants of the paper, that she is not really engaging with the rich Freudian concept-metaphor of the Unconscious. If I understand her right (and I am not sure of this, since she is highly critical of my way of thinking), she is engaging with the implicit conflation of the Unconscious with a primitivist golden-ageist view of history, often advanced in colonial and post-colonial societies in the interest of patriarchal consolidation. She most astutely notices that the author of the second book has taken a degree in anthropology in the US. If Dutt internalizes the spirit of Kipling and Rider Haggard, Joshi is into the Universal Baseball Association. He, the intellectual finished in the US (as in a finishing-school) – an ally of the well-placed New Immigrant – pitches to the right-handed hitter stateside, the apostle of the New Cultural Studies. The hitter drops one into short left field. The fielder – way back up against the wall of the former colony – flounders, remembering cricket, and produces more documentation of a merely premodern cultural wealth. The hitter makes a home run, securing national origin, universalizing the game, producing the new multicultural America, where Indian is a prefix with a past and an American future, to produce, on cue, complanations and explaints. America is, ideologically and by the logic of cultural relativism, in favour of fundamentalism.[19] Thus by a move of the Joshi type, the chasm of contradiction between the Women's Movement, indeed all resistance, in the former colonies and the substance of Cultural Studies widens further. If one wants to pick up this lack of play, between resistance in the South and "knowledge" in the North, the focus will have to shift; from the staging of Culture to the staging of Development. And the pertinent discipline is not psychoanalytic cultural critique, but, perhaps, a wild psychoanalysis of International Affairs.

As I have pointed out, Sangari's excellent piece is not, strictly speaking, psychoanalytic. But perhaps it does not seem relevant to engage in feminist psychoanalytic intervention in the theatre ("play" has allowed me to slip from field to stage) I have described. The more important field of intervention seems outside this theatre: to dehegemonize and reinscribe the secular Enlightenment. My own concentration on psychoanalysis has thinned of late for this very reason. I sit, after all, in the bleachers of the stadium.

UNICULTURALISM

No one spoke *as* an American at the Conference. Yet the game was baseball. Let me offer an explaint.

Universal Baseball Association was published in 1967, in the full flush of the Vietnam War, the best moment perhaps for a satirical novel that gives full utterance to the unchallenged baseball spirit, the American Imaginary, unencumbered yet by liberal multiculturalism. Here is J. Henry Waugh, an Underground Man in the line of Walter Mitty, fantasizer of the Association, watching a kid through the window of the corner drugstore playing an "unrealistic" baseball game on a pinball machine. The sight of the inadequate representation is "sufficient to produce the necessary transgression", of moving from the particular to the universal: " 'The Great American Game,' it said across the top, between the gleaming girls ..." I think the Nephew of psychoanalysis would have made something of that placing between the gleaming girls, the purloined title.[20] There is no time to consider this here, but the conclusion of this section will pick up the track. Let us continue quoting:

> Well, it was. American baseball, by luck, trial and error, and since the famous playing rules council of 1889, had struck on an almost perfect balance between offense and defense, and it was that balance, in fact, that and the accountability – the beauty of the record system which found a place to keep forever each least action – that had led Henry to baseball as his final great project.[21]

It was that almost perfect balance between offence and defence and that accountability that had led Henry to baseball as his final great project. Eight years later, Professor Kristeva, a European uniculturalist, seriously rather than through political satire, exhorted us to listen again "to the *Stabat Mater* ... [for] Christianity is doubtless the most refined symbolic construct in which femininity ... is focused on *Maternality*".[22] Here is her version of the perfect balance between offence and defence. Offence: "Christianity, it is true, finds its calling in the displacement of that bio-maternal determinism through the postulate that immortality is mainly that of the name of the Father." Defence, next sentence: "But it does not succeed in imposing *its* symbolic revolution without relying on the feminine representation of an immortal biology."[23] Between the gleaming girls, the great game of balancing the symbolic and biological, the defensive and the offensive, in a system of accountability.

Admittedly, Professor Kristeva's systems seem sometimes as brilliantly wild and self-contained as J. Henry Waugh's Association. But even psycho-analysis at its stodgiest – in the offices of "awful American shrinks" who are clearly not up to the Lacanian analysts' offer of nothingness by being nothing – gives us a self-contained system that seems to be, paradoxically, a general form of equivalence. Thinking about that other supposedly uni-versal game – Capital – I recall that the original title of our session had been "Politics and its players". I move by sheer inertia into that dreary argument, trivially yet murderously true, that, if psychoanalysis is part of "modernization" in its special sense of making accessible to Eurocentric subject-constitution by default, it has quietly displaced itself into the pro-ject of "development". (One of the demands of Bhopal activists must needs be, and is, money for psychiatric rehabilitation of the survivors.)

Psychoanalytic formalism of the subject, with an informed exchange of cultural currency, can be used to evaluate everyone. There seems to be no reason why it cannot produce a greater and greater range of cultural descriptives. Nobody ever worries any more about the status of the implicit validity claims in these exercises. Why should we assume humans beings are this way singly or collectively when we are ostensibly proving that they are? This move in the game, the prime move in the biggest game in town, is called (once again) begging the question. Who calls the emperor's new clothes? Who would be so unsporting and so embarrassingly boring as to suggest that there is no adequate and intrinsic virtue in hitting the ball with the bat and pursuing the consequences? What is *hors jeu*, outside the game? How can we trace the game back within a boundary inside the diamond in the clinic? We are moving toward the second half of my title: "and field-working". But not yet.

However brilliant its discourse, this particular unacknowledged suppo-sition is to us as irritating as is that question-begging that I mentioned earlier. It clearly makes no difference to the players. At best they'll say, "But you have nothing better to offer". If you take away the general form, are we to legitimize ourselves by local barter and basket-weaving? I retreat: it's all true. And yet ridiculously imitating now the sublime final Foucault, I whinge. "I am not looking for an alternative." Friendly Americans uni-versalizing Foucault tried to push him into saying that he was offering "an attractive and plausible alternative... for recent liberation movements". "I am not looking for an alternative", said Foucault.[24]

Because we are served by the extreme substitutability of psychoanalytic discourse in many mental theatres, we must acknowledge the usefulness of psychoanalysis in its own house, in the analytic situation. I cannot imagine a world without psychoanalysis; though I know many who can.

How does the new multiculturalist culture-working American deal with that latter group? At the Conference, Professor Alphonso Lingis, a man of impeccable politics, gave us an example that was all the more instructive because of his obvious personal goodwill. Although the passage has not been included in his contribution to this anthology (my own contribution is considerably changed), I should like to refer to it briefly.

In that original talk Professor Lingis gave an account of transvestite theatre for the American in the Asia-Pacific, and a subsequent encounter with a bisexual boy. Under neo-colonialism, the liberal American who talks about the wonder of the pagan world-soul but wants to get in touch with the boy from the hills still universalizes from a particular case. Of course, the relationship between the US and the rim is still somewhat different from that with the other Asias, so this too is situation-specific, and would not fit, for example, a West Asian trip.

The first thing to remember, is that, in this sort of account, the American is on holiday. Professor Lingis knew enough not to say "we". That would have been the old style. "It is a muggy tropical evening", his account began, "*one* gets horny". It is not just that the "one" is male, but it is also that "one" does not live there. It is not a "muggy *tropical* evening" for the normal person in that society. It is a "muggy *evening*". And if you live and work there, then in fact you might (I am not even talking about you as a woman yet) toward evening be returning home by bus. I am not even talking about the people dying on the streets, but just people of our kind going to work returning by bus. You might feel you want perhaps to snooze a bit. And if you are indeed a woman who has been working in the telephone exchange let's say, you come back by bus and you groan that you have to put the meal on the table. It is not "a muggy tropical evening when one gets horny". A tiny set of changes but much more crucial than any talk of cultural difference.

At the Conference, Dr James Hillman offered us post-analysis in the place of post-modernism. He seemed to be speaking as an unreconstructed modernist. As such he trivializingly constructed deconstruction as something that has done some mischief that can be corrected by his modernist post-analysis. He is in the broadly Habermasian tradition, vividly staged in *The Philosophical Discourse of Modernity*.[25] Here again, J. Henry Waugh is a powerful and useful figure. The Habermasian's imaginary construct of Derrida is much like Waugh's fantasy of Casey, a mythic player of base-ball.[26] The Universal Baseball Association must be protected from Casey. Here is Waugh, almost giving in:

Casey, in his writings, has spoken of a "rising above the rules," an abandonment of all conceptualizations, including score-keepers, umpires, Gods in any dress, in the heat of total mystic immersion in that essence that includes God and him equally. Of course, some say he never wrote it, it's all apocryphal, inventions of Monday and his Universalists, distorted by redactions without number, but no matter, the idea itself remains. What it leads to, though, is inaction, a terrible passivity: Casey on the mound shaking Flynn off, waiting – but who is playing Casey today? . . . The idea excites him. A rising above. Yes, why not? . . . It doesn't matter: death is a relative idea, truth absolute! . . . Impulsively, he walks out there, to the mound, not because it's a rule of the game, but because he feels drawn.[27]

But the game protects him beyond any mere attraction of "the mound". " '[You] *love* this game, don't you?' " asks the star pitcher of his fantasy. "It's just what it is." The self-identical. By the end of the book the heliotropic prick has usurped the place of the clit, which had merely glimmered in the false light of the pinball machine. "Damon holds the baseball up between them. It is hard and white and alive in the sun . . . 'Hang loose,' he says, and pulling down his mask, trots back behind home plate."[28] The defeat of the mad philosopher who would destroy the game does not disturb the man's world. Universalist presuppositions remain undisturbed in post-analysis.

ARABS AND JEWS

Is a deconstructive conference different?

A Colloquium entitled *Entre psychanalyse et Islam* took place at the Collège International de Philosophie in Paris in 1989, in the heart of deconstruction country. There are many interesting papers to be found in its Proceedings. I will begin with the lead piece by Abdelkébir Khatibi.[29]

The most moving thing about "Frontières" is Khatibi's deconstructive embrace of Freud. According to Khatibi, Freud tried to desacralize the notion of the Jews as a "chosen people" by putting it at the door of the personality of Moses the Man. It caught on because it spoke to the "archaic heritage" of the Jewish people that followed the path of a group pathology. Moses was an Egyptian, and Christ a murderer in this retelling, says Khatibi. Islam, lacking a murder, gets one sentence in this long retelling. It is no more than an "abbreviated repetition of the Jewish" religion.[30] Freud exiles the error, argues Khatibi. In a brilliant move, Khatibi describes the double revelation of Mohammed, the first intelligible only to Khadija, his senior wife, as from the start "lettered". Since the revelation is illegible to Mohammed, the holder of the proper name, no Father's son, but his grandfather's ward, a Bedouin's nurseling, Mohammed "sacrifices his signature". This is the lettered version of the murder (even as circumcision is a lettered version of castration)[31] in the historically youngest religion of the Book, "the lost Book".[32] Khatibi transforms the historical pathology of Islam to a negative cryptonymy – the encrypting of the sacrificed signature as something that cannot be avowed. Thus Islam consolidates the difference at the origin of monotheisms: "The unicity of Allah and of the Arabic language marks this frontier, in the Islamic imaginary, [as] the founding signature, the emblem."[33] This is in the spirit of Freud's inquiry into his own religion, but against Freud's history-bound dismissal of Islam. When Khatibi himself breaks the transparency of the Prophet's proper name by reading his elder brother's name under it as a hypogram, one cannot help thinking that the Prophet of psychoanalysis figures there somewhere. The Franco-Maghrebin male cultural worker produces rather a robust and affirmative case of the explaint, the complanation. If you want to move this into the playing fields, it is like two teams that have had ups and downs in the history of the game and in the current configuration are no longer in the same league. It's the same game; they are peoples of the Book. There have been misunderstandings. It's time to play ball. In spite of the real differences, it's more in-house than universal.

Khatibi is not himself a practising analyst, of course. Yet in the end he gives us a good generalization: "It is not a question of psychoanalysing Islam or of Islamizing psychoanalysis and even less of Judaizing or Hinduizing it, but rather exercising it as a frontier position in the language and exercise of a profession."[34] Do we have an example of the exercise of this frontier position? Let us briefly consider two other players in the volume – both, in a certain way, outsiders to the topic of the issue, but both insiders in that they are practitioners: Daniel Sibony, a Jewish Franco-Maghrebin, and Martine Medejel, a Gauloise married to a Moroccan. Here the lines of negotiation between major and minor league can be plotted more easily.

These practising analysts have shifted the lines from two Peoples of the Book to an opposition which reflects the vicissitudes of the long losing streak of the by-now lesser team: Arab against French. And indeed they both speak of problems of migrancy. They are both what outsiders recognize as "French" Freudians to the extent that they take it for granted that all origins are a play of traces, that "to have one's origin as lost is still to *have* it".[35] Both want to draw a lesson for psychiatric responsibility from this paradoxical conviction. Sibony offers the narrative of an Arab migrant boy's aphonia and his "cure", as a case where Sibony, on the abyssal seesaw of transference/responsibility – in this case with a child who would not respond – was witness to the emergence of French speech parasitically to a conversation between Sibony and the boy's mother about, among other things, the lack of coverage for circumcision by French Social Security:

> Perhaps that is the essential thing in certain therapeutic acts: to make a graft of the origin to liberate the subject, so that he [*sic*] may, like a swimmer touch bottom, not to remain there but to make a fresh start [*donner l'impulsion* makes a good pun in French] to get back up to the surface . . . in other languages.[36]

This, for Sibony, is the "*original* 'circumcision' ". The boy says, in French, "c'est fini".[37]

From her loss of control over the proper naming of her son, Medejel draws her lesson from/of *différance* as a weaving lesson:

Having many first names may open the work of the letter, undo and redo [*déjouer et rejouer*] the point of division in the name. Divide and tie [*lier* gives a wonderful pun with kinship inscription in French]. Retie if necessary. This possible slippage of the conflict of signatures is then the opening of a space for the emergence of the subject, of which Lacan speaks when he says "it cannot do anything but always name itself unknowingly, and not knowing by which name."[38]

As I have already suggested, we are here on the register of adjusting the record between two teams, even perhaps renegotiating rules. Within such intimacy, we can notice certain differentiations in the larger focus of global left-field play. Let us tabulate.

Sibony is the well-placed male migrant helping cure the problems of underclass migrants. His hold on the Frenchness of French society may be minimally more secure because of his Jewishness, although there are plenty of historical ironies behind this claim. Medejel's problems with choosing an Arabic first name if she converts and of the different status of the first name of her Moroccan son from the first name (marking mother-love) for a French son is not a typical one. Yet in both cases what is secure is French, as a language or a "culture". Sibony seems not to care that the so-called culture of origin has a different mode of existence today, elsewhere. It is not simply his *past* and the *past* of his patients. He seems to ignore that the cutting of the graft is also the death of the host, the loss of a language, that if the "country of origin" is considered as *alibi* but not *in illo tempore*, circumcision is not sublating a prehistoric castration in these cases. Because of the history of imperialism, there is no likelihood that Medejel's retying of the mother–son knot will result in a loss of French for the Moroccan son. (That loss is more likely with an Anglophone marriage for a Frenchwoman, but the other problem – between psychoanalysis and Islam – is not likely to arise there.) Indeed, the problem here is not just Islam but the apparent subordination of a woman from a dominant culture. If Sibony's graft kills the host, Medejel's position as the subject of retying the knot in the division between first and last names might be absurdly enviable or simply absurd for a North African woman living in France. But psychoanalysis at work is like Ernesto Cardenal's God, who must save Marilyn Monroe with the same Grace that abounds for the destroyed children of Latin America, winning games when apparently it is only form that matters.[39]

But a student of cultural politics can lodge an explaint and at once advance a complanation. Why does a too-quick graft of the origin in the Eurocentric migration kill the host culture? When the notion of the origin as a field of the play of traces becomes too much of a received idea, such questions cannot be asked. Let us go slower here.

As many have pointed out, Freud thought of himself, among many other things, as rewriting Kant. One of the marks of this Freudian auto-bio-graphy shows in the name "sublimation".

In Kant's "Analytic of the sublime",[40] the ungraspable grandeur of awe-some natural phenomena is sublim-ated (named "sublime") in order, in fact, to validate the sublimity of the moral will. This surreptitious validation is a two-step: pain at not being able to grasp grand Nature, followed by pleasure at reassurance of being human, not only natural, in other words, having a moral will.

The philosophical connection between this and Freud's thinking of "sub-limation" can easily be seen. *Es kommt darauf an*, to keep it alive in the responsibility-work of psychoanalysis.[41] Here is the philosophical connec-tion, spelled out by a non-specialist; fine-tune it, you who know.

Until *Beyond the Pleasure Principle*[42] put a frame around the *mythos* of psychoanalysis, the conflict which was seen to constitute the subject's history was the discrepancy between the ungraspable natural necessity of the instincts and the contingent grasping reach of the drives, themselves unevenly appropriate for coupling with "the external world". The vali-dation of the sublimity of the moral will comes through the deflection of these by sublimation, which connects the conflict to responsibilities relating to the cultural universal.

In the philosophical field, Derrida long ago offered a supplement to this two-step of validation. When in the throes of philosophical sublimation (so to speak), the philosopher wishes to universalize (entailing always a causeless cause), she should "trace" it, inscribe it in the textuality within which the particular subliming moment arose:

> I have indicated a way out of the closure of this framework via the "trace", which is no more an effect than it has a cause [although we must "rationalize" each "(con)text" thus, the Kantian Sublime being a possible theorization from this which is offered as a universal model], but which in and of itself [since it is *this* situation, *this* trace, *this* rationally computed effect of *that* rationally established cause, all impossible localizations stopping the train of the differantiating present], outside its text [commonly subordinated as *con*-text], is not sufficient to operate the transgression necessary [for universalization].[43]

A few pages later the young philosopher (this was written twenty-five years ago, today the Derridean discourse of responsibility is rather more complicated, but then we are putting *Beyond the Pleasure Principle* out of court for this discussion) gives us a rule: "The *practice* of a language or of a code supposing" – observe the precise distinction between a theoretical presupposition and a practical supposition here – "a play of forms without a determined and invariable substance, and also supposing *in the practice of this play*" – not *free* play, *this* play is indistinguishable from work, as in the hinges of a tool having play – "a retention and protention of differences" – not presupposing an undifferentiated origin (retention) or end (protention) – "must be ... the regular [*réglé*, in French the implication of a "rule of thumb", an invariable practical situation(trace)-specific rule rather than a universal law] erasure" – crossing out by invoking the situation, yet keeping visible the generalizable element – "of the archi-, ... this latter executing a critical labour on everything ... that maintained metaphysical presuppositions incompatible with the motif of *différance*."[44]

When "origin-as-play-of-traces" becomes a formula, then the persistence of this effortful rule, *whenever* the "metaphysical" urge to validate the moral will takes over, is lost. In spite of the error in David B. Allison's earlier translation, Derrida is not here offering a "system" but a "rule".[45] We are speaking of a game at play, a practice at work. However complicated the manoeuvre, the persistence of this double gesture remains the abyssal responsibility of deconstruction, its "setting-to-work".

Let us now return to the moment when its formulaic citation becomes most evident in Daniel Sibony's account. Speaking of the problem of migrants, Sibony is able to make a nice distinction between structure (division-at-the-origin) and case – Law and trace:

> But things start going wrong because that origin [necessarily lost, but still an origin], is *handed down* (the object of desire is nothing but the object of transmission ...) *by beings of flesh and blood* who are themselves entangled in and with it.[46]

Let us consider the limit of this capacity to distinguish.

As the Franco-Jewish analyst, Sibony can share a sense of exile with the Austro-Jewish father of psychoanalysis and tell comparable stories of his schoolroom experiences.[47] The little analysand in his Franco-Arab mother's arms, tied to him by the authoritative event and male bond of circumcision, is thus distanced from him not only by class, but also by "race" (that inaccurate term). Sibony may be North African but he is not "Arab" (that inaccurate term) quite like the little boy.

That distance asserts itself in the suspension of Sibony's capacity to distinguish between chronological priority – belonging to situation or "trace" – and the graphic of origin – belonging to the motif of *différance*, here travestied into something like a logical presupposition. He conflates "historical" time and the impossible temporality of origins. When he recalls his own schooldays in the Maghreb, he "remembers" that the Muslim "scholar seemed not to know that the sacrifice of Ismael, which he read as a 'radical' event, was an interesting modulation of its original version, called the sacrifice of Isaac and written 15 centuries earlier".[48] Unable to use or set-to-work the best of his "theory", Sibony is unable to cross out yet keep visible his tie with the universalizing Father who is the Subject of Science. He falls through this gap as the migrant boy learns to speak French.[49] Let us recall a similar invocation of "fifteen hundred years" in Freud, lamenting the historical loss of Judaism:

The triumph of Christianity was a fresh victory for the priests of Amun over Akhenaten's god after an interval of fifteen hundred years and on a wider stage. And yet in the history of religion – that is, as regards the return of the repressed – Christianity was an advance and from that time on the Jewish religion was to some extent a fossil.[50]

Christianity is here linked to the neurotic development of an originally repressed "unrestricted polytheism".[51] And the best of Judaism, its sense of being "chosen", ostensibly related to the Man Moses, is now linked back to the understandable self-concept of a great Imperialism, for the first time conceiving "the sublime abstraction" of monotheism in Aten, the sun worshipped not "as a material object" but as a "symbol":[52] "In Egypt, so far as we can understand, monotheism grew up as a by-product of imperialism: . . . Where did [the] tiny and powerless [Jewish] nation [*sic*] find the arrogance to declare itself the favourite child of the great Lord?"[53] It is because Moses was an imperial Egyptian, worshipper of Aten, who, after

> the death of Akhenaten and the abolition of his religion . . . could remain in Egypt only as an outlaw . . . . Perhaps as governor of the frontier province he had come in contact with a Semitic tribe which had immigrated into it a few generations earlier. . . . He chose them as his people and tried to realize his ideals in them.[54]

Arrived at Mount Sinai, and obliged to worship the violent Yahweh, god among many rival gods, the Jews remembered Egypt, and their good governor, and constructed the myth of "the chosen people" from the culture of that remembered imperialism. Freud the dispassionate and unbelieving analyst helps them to remember further:

> It may encourage us to enquire whether the religion of Moses brought the people nothing else besides an enhancement of their self-esteem owing to their consciousness of having been chosen. . . . That religion also brought the Jews a far grander conception of God, or, as we might put it more modestly, the conception of a grander God . . . for an unbeliever this is not entirely self-evident; but we may perhaps make it easier to understand if we point to the sense of superiority felt by a Briton in a foreign country which has been made insecure owing to an insurrection – a feeling that is completely absent in a citizen of any small continental state. For the Briton counts on the fact that his Government will send along a warship if a hair of his head is hurt, and that the rebels understand that very well – whereas the small state possesses no warship at all. Thus, pride in the greatness of the British Empire has a root as well in the consciousness of the greater security – the protection – enjoyed by the individual Briton. This may resemble the conception of a grand God. And, since one can scarcely claim to assist

God in the administration of the world, the pride in God's greatness fuses with the pride in being chosen by him.[55]

"Cricket is an Indian game accidentally discovered by the English."[56] Transcendental imperialism by this Freudian account is a Jewish game accidentally practised by the British.

Persecuted by the Nazis, arrived at last in "lovely, free, magnanimous England", "a welcome guest at last" in the last year of his life, Freud "traces" Judaism.[57] But at least in the "dispassionate" overarching argument he offers the history of individual psychopathology as an analogy for the history of religion. In the spirit of that argument, it may be asked, where has that itinerary arrived in 1989? I will let the reader conclude. But I may, I hope, be forgiven if I find Sibony's conscientious ecumenicism less convincing than Khatibi's anguish.

FRENCH CRICKET

I am not altogether uninterested in alternatives, after all, for it makes of necessity a virtue, of iterability a strength. I propose French cricket. It is a game that was played in my childhood on the streets of Calcutta. The rules had been modified, although observed with a ferocity that had subverted the gentlemanliness of the game. The number of players was flexible, dependent upon the number available, although always divided neatly into two. Since props could not be afforded either, the wickets were stable, usually subtropical trees. (Indeed, this was what required the greatest and subtlest modifications, but cricket it was.)[58]

As I was the sole representative of the ethno-cultural agenda at the Conference, so was I the only girl on a loosely constituted French cricket "team" in my childhood. And it is on that biography of the subversion of tokenism that I turn to look, out the fourth corner of the cricket–baseball–France triangle.

And I spot a major player of renown, Assia Djebar of Algeria.[59] In her "Forbidden gaze, severed sound", she outlines the scenario:

> Throughout the nineteenth century, the battles were lost one after the other, further and further to the south of the Algerian territories. The heroes have not yet stopped biting the dust. In that *geste*, women's looks and voices continue to be perceived from a distance, from the other side of the frontier [no longer only between the two teams of Psychoanalysis and Islam, as in *Intersignes*] that should separate us from death, if not from victory.
>
> [Colonial discourse:] But for those born in the age of submission, feudals or proletarians, sons or lovers, the scene remains, the watching women haven't moved, and it is with a retrospective fear that men began to dream that look.

This does not congeal into a project of restoring history or giving voice, neither of which is to be relinquished, of course. This particular striving articulates itself in a desire necessarily for an unsatisfied desire:

> [Post-coloniality:] Thus, while outside an entire society partitions itself into the duality of the vanquished and the victorious, the autochthons and the invaders, in the harem, *reduced to a shack or a cave*, the dialogue has become almost definitively blocked. If only one could cathect [*investir*] that single spectator body that remains, encircle it more and more tightly in order to forget the defeat![60]

Far from universalizing, here the reader of history – the author of the book – is, as in most cases of reading narrative for ethical instantiation, in the "analysand"-position, her ability to "do the right thing" on her own, her propriety, crossed out, although of course visible. If only one could . . . is the mode.

Within this stricture, she reoccupies the graphic that was narrativized by Freud, from the male perspective, as "castration". (To borrow Melanie Klein's word, this was the narrative that was "permissible" for Freud.[61] And no amount of penis-phallus finessing will allow us to escape the narrative. For every element in a narrative, as we literary critics well know – and indeed *all* readers "know" – does not have to be "real". A narrative is made up of signifiers. To borrow Derrida's phrase, even if we read phallus for penis, there is no escaping the "transcendental signified".)[62]

And indeed, in terms of my running argument, we can ask, what have women been permitted to know?

> Men have always known (in this special way [via the "archaic heritage"]) that they once possessed a primal father and killed him. . . . There must have been something present in the ignorant masses, too, which was akin to the knowledge of the few and went half way to meet it when it was uttered. . . . The genesis of monotheism could not do without these occurrences.[63]

This is the permitted narrative of castration sublated into circumcision that still seems to work for the migrant boy. For women only the unsubstantiated memory of mut(ilat)ing.

Djebar narrativizes that graphic as "severed sound". The oral-historical songs of Kabyle-Jewish-Muslim women, keeping track of the North African history of the region, has been lost to women through the "Arabization" of Algeria to construct a binary opposition to French Imperialism.[64]

This situational or textual "tracing" of the graphic of being cut off, colonized women being cut off from women as agents of historical narrative, is of course precisely that, a "trace", not a bid to take over the universalizing narrative of castration, not because the latter is correct, but because universalizing is a symptom. Yet it is still the graphic of the cut.

(There goes my analogy. It was still cricket – French cricket, where, for us children in Calcutta – in our text – French was, as in James McPherson's story, simply a catachrestic name for something other than English.[65] Notice that it won't fit Djebar so snugly.)

In that it "is" a "trace", it must be taken to be the mark of an absent presence, even if mistakenly. That supposed presence – a lost object – produces a feminism that is rather different from the project of winning back the "forbidden gaze" from men's "scopic exclusivity".[66]

That battle is fought on a different terrain, making dangerous alliances with white men – Delacroix, Picasso – in order to rewrite their text:

> These women of Algiers – who have remained motionless in Delacroix's painting since 1832 – if it was possible yesterday to see in their fixity the nostalgic expression of happiness or of the softness of submission, today their desperate bitterness is what must strike our most sensitive nerve.[67]

In quite another context, the defensive assertion – "psychoanalytic theory is thus appropriated here as a political weapon" – shows up women's solidarity on this difficult terrain.[68] As Djebar points out, given that entry on that terrain presupposes all kinds of alliances with the master-system, every victory is a warning there.[69]

Here is another bit of French cricket, from the early work of another renowned woman, Doris Lessing, "Rhodesian" transplant in England. Let us consider how she reoccupies "the uncanny".

Freud describes the layman's attitude to psychoanalysis in this way:

> The uncanny effect of epilepsy and of madness has the same origin. The layman sees in them the expression [*Äußerung*] of forces hitherto unsuspected in his fellow-men, but at the same time he senses their trace [*spüren*] in remote corners of his own being.... Indeed, I should not be surprised to hear that psychoanalysis, which is concerned with laying bare these hidden forces, has itself become uncanny to many people for that very reason.[70]

Here is "layman" Martha, the central character of *The Four-Gated City* (a well-known Jungian archetype), after a protracted session of "responsible" analysis, with Lynda, the madwoman in the book, out on a walk on the familiar street outside her residence. (In this already too-long essay, I cannot burden the reader with the textual analyses these passages demand):

> The day was fresh and the world newly painted.... She stood facing up, up, until her eyes seemed absorbed in the crystalline substance of the sky with blocks of clouds like snowbanks, she seemed to be streaming out through her eyes into the skies, but then sounds came into her, they were vibrations of feet on pavement, and she looked down again at an extraordinarily hideous creature who stood watching her.[71]

After a long description of this experience of the uncanny – the familiar rendered strange – Martha is made to feel pain, "in a way she had never known pain, an affliction of shameful grief":

> What an extraordinary race, or near-race of half, uncompleted creatures. There they were, all soft like pale slugs, or dark slugs, with their limp flabby flesh, with hair sprouting from it, and the things like hooves on their feet, and wads or fells of hair on the tops of their heads. There they were all around her, with their roundish bony faces that had flaps of flesh sticking out on either side, then the protuberance in the middle, with the air vents in it, and the eyes, tinted-jelly eyes which had a swivelling movement that gave them a life of their own, so that they were like creatures on their own account, minuscule twin animals living in the flesh of the face, but these organs, the eyes, had a look which contradicted their function, which was to see, to observe, for as she passed pair after pair of eyes, they looked half drugged, or half asleep, dull, as if the creatures had been hypnotised or poisoned, for these people walked their fouled and disgusting streets full of ordure and bits of refuse and paper as if they were not conscious of their existence here, were somewhere else: and they were somewhere else, for only one in a hundred of these semi-animals could have said "I am here, now, noticing what is around me".[72]

I include Lessing because this is a consideration of the metropolis, of the master race at home. This dystopia (indeed the uncanny may be the secret of dystopias) is rewritten at the end of the narrative in a mode that can lead to utopias, a sanctioning of the "present" that is counter to the compulsion to repeat a longing for when-I-was-not-yet and when-I-will-be-no-longer of which Freud's narrative makes the uncanny a sign, a reminder, even a trace if we attend to the German verb translated as "perceive": "whatever reminds us of this inner 'compulsion to repeat' [probably inherent in the very nature of instincts – . . . powerful enough to overrule the pleasure principle] is perceived [*verspüren wir*] as uncanny".[73] Freud refers us to *Beyond the Pleasure Principle*, and we realize that the compulsion is to repeat the trace of the stasis of death that surrounds our little island of pleasure.

Lessing's main narrative ends with a reinscription of that ocean of death as a "present" space that exceeds the subject, precisely as attention to a repetition: "She thought, with the dove's voices of her solitude: Where? But *where*. How? Who? No, but *where*, where. . . . Then silence and the birth of a repetition: *Where*? Here. Here? Here, where else, you fool, where else has it been, ever".[74]

The rememoration of the "present" as space is the possibility of the utopian imperative of no-(particular)-place, the metropolitan project that can supplement the post-colonial attempt at the impossible cathexis of place-bound history as the lost time of the spectator.

This, too, is French cricket. The same motif of a repressed longing, the compulsion to repeat, but modified into a Quest for the common space of globality as utopia. One does not want to be too systematic – where is my grammatological crossbow and eraser? – but certainly for the white ex-"Rhodesian" post-Marxist there is a greater "permission" to offer a universal narrative. And Lessing does cross out. By now Martha Quest (*spüren*) has her husband's name, Hesse. And the utopia in *Four-Gated City*, the only unepigraphed section in the book, is in the "science fiction" (that splendid oxymoron) mode, and its title is "Appendix", at least as a reminder that an attempt is being made here to "trace" the universal. Does it work? We must learn to read. French cricket is pretty desperately dependent upon the here and now and that is its only link with the "responsible" part of psychoanalysis, not its filing-cabinet know-it-all repository of rules.

The language of this analysis is *echt* French cricket, bits and pieces from many healing practices. As per the robust model of responsibility, both learn. Can real people do this? How could one know, literature merely figures the impossibility of a perfect psychoanalysis.[75] The Martha–Lynda thing begins to work when telepathy is released between them. Is it real telepathy? The authorial voice gives us no guarantee. It is only Martha who thinks she can hear Lynda's mind inside her own and feels sure hers is going over. Does that mean Martha is mad too? Yet is it not a truism to say that "terminable" analyses, se-curing people within "permissible" narratives, in principle (though of course not always in fact) decides situationally what it is not to be mad? And is not telepathy the perfect model of successful transference, responsibility flowing both ways, both sides responding and accountable? Was Freud mad when he speculated on telepathy? Is that why Ernest Jones suppressed those speculations?[76]

By herself, battered Lynda knows only the compulsion to repeat and the attendant fear of the uncanny. The two women together push the compulsion over into the openness of utopia. The utopian appendix – strictly the future anterior – is about a widely dispersed idiot-savant group of telepathic children already being diagnosed and organized by system-bound benefactors trying to put back together a world devastated by nuclear holocaust by the public use of reason.

What is being reoccupied by these two players is the graphic of the uncanny and castration; the uncanny as "the entrance to the old *Heim* [home] of all human beings [*Menschenkindes* – literally human children], to the place where each one of us lived once upon a time and in the beginning".[77] Upon exiting this home, only half of us inscribed that home in terms of a constitutive error – misrecognition of sexual difference as castration – that is underived because a recognition at that stage cannot be theorized within the male model: to misrecognize sexual difference as

a particular and quite special penis that had a great significance [*eine große Bedeutung*] in early childhood but had later been lost . . . the woman's (the mother's) phallus [*Phallus*] that the little boy once believed in and – we know why [*wir wissen warum*] – does not want to give up.[78]

If this is the narrative that is permissible in gendering, it will engender spectacular complications in figuring out the woman as anything but reactive in her agency.[79]

But suppose we assumed sexual difference at the origin, and the womb not as a place where we all once lived but a place where we all came from with nothing but a potential for articulating differences and nothing but one signifier to work with – one primary object that gives us plus (desire and need) as well as minus (loss and refusal). Even as a programme of artificial intelligence begins to construct a system of differences with nothing but a binary, the ego (nothing but a *differente Beziehung*) begins to construct a system of qualities that will bear all the quantities that will be permissible in the graphing of a life upon the *socius*.[80] Nothing of Freud's best – the theory of the unconscious, of the drives and their strategies – is disturbed here. But, for the sexually differented subject, biology is inscribed as the already differentiated field of the signifier, rather than the taboo of anti-essentialism. That part of psychoanalysis that, even in its ruins, still has the intention of taking seriously the sub-individual zone of sense-making, playing by the rules of subjecting to restore social agency, and that part of deconstruction which must work at the bond between intentional subjectivity and responsibility, find a haven here.[81] This is Melanie Klein, another major player in my field of French cricket, read against the grain, particularly though not only against the grain of her readers, who fetishize the object rather than the relationship, fetishize the mother rather than the human child as assigned and sign-making.

In the grip of his narrative, Freud is way out in left field. The ball is flying high overhead. He is foiled again and again by the most valuable right-handed hitter of all time, as long as the game is baseball, the ferocious two-fisted red-blooded Phallus. Lacan could not exit the game, for he had not quit the application – based on that originary underived error of cognizance, of sexual difference.

The lost object still focuses us, but French cricket puts trace-quotes around lost, freshly each time, or some times. Where the field of agency is considered, the stricture of responsibility to the trace of the other is called Reparation to the Primary (or lost?) object. We cannot all be men, but we have all had a primary object which we could not but recognize as our only signifier, in sexual difference, plus as well as minus.

Institutional psychoanalysis establishes the originary error of the boy as formula. It becomes a fetish for the originary fetish, a rationalized substitute that will keep that narrative as dominant.

Gramsci remarked that we are all intellectuals, small i, the head is a part of the body.[82] Some of us cannot and some of us do not want to be (the line is blurred) institutional intellectuals. In the same way some of us cannot (the line is blurred) and some of us do not want to be mothers, but in so far as the primary object is only permitted to be narrativized as something like a breast, we are all mothers' children. As such we reoccupy the place of the agent in analysis, even as for tracking the subject we turn, again and again, to the science fiction of the unconscious, held by the analyst as the institutional Mother or Father. Entry into the other side of sexual difference by masquerade is another aspect of agency. In the text of the subject, masquerade is indistinguishable from its impossible antonym. I cannot imagine a world without psychoanalysis, at least as an item on the roll of techniques for reading narrative as ethical instantiation. Yet how much I have to assume Europe in order to understand the brilliance of that exposition! But yet again, if we are going to assume Europe, we must remember that, in the broader global context nothing can be gained from analytical philosophy in the area of ethics because it assumes the mental theatre of the subject as given.

Because of this general character of psychoanalysis, there will be attempts to use the unconscious as another name for ideology (Althusser), as repository of the narrative of reference (Jameson), as an analogue for the flow of capital (the early Lyotard), as model for the value-form (Goux).[83] I too must put in my two bits. I began by suggesting that Imperialism was cricket and Capitalism baseball. Psychoanalysis in its institutional practice, in its baseball mode, must incorporate the Marxian critique of capital and thus secure its own understanding of its game with more than just the sexual-difference application. (The mixing of the taxonomy (worse yet, the nosology) of psychoanalysis in an amateur way to the vaguest possible conception of the revolutionary agent seems to me to be an act of folly.) One might even add a word here about radical metropolitan multicultural psychotherapy. As follows:

MIGRANTS

In *The Wretched of the Earth*, Frantz Fanon speaks of the psychological effect of "brainwashing" on cricketers and future aspirants to baseball.[84] The first group – male Algerian "intellectuals" in the Franco-Maghreb mind set (epistemically enabled/violated by psych-ing out the culture of Imperialism) – fall into the see-saw (aporia) of enablement/violation: "The impossibility of explaining and defending any given position. Thought unfolds [se déroule] by antithetic couplings. Everything that is affirmed can, at the same instant, be denied with the same force." For the "non-intellectuals", the future aspirants to the baseball club, the hordes of migrants who will crowd the low-income housing projects of French towns in the decades following Independence, Fanon has this comment: "Here the disorders met with are not serious. It is the painful, suffering body that calls for rest and calm [apaisement]."

This is the origin of the gap between post-coloniality (via pre-Independence nationalisms) and (post-Independence) migrancy that many of us are busy foreclosing these days. In this gap, political mobilization for "fundamentalisms", the undoing of decolonization, festers and blooms.

What does this tough group (all male, of course) with non-serious disorders hold in reserve for the history of the present? Let us consider the nature of the brainwashing:

> (1) You must declare that you do not belong to the FLN. You must shout this out in groups. You must repeat it for hours on end. (2) After that, you must recognize that you were once in the FLN and that you have come to realize that it was a bad thing. Thus, down with the FLN. After this stage, we come to another: the future of Algeria is French; it can be nothing other than French. Without France, Algeria will go back to the Middle Ages. Finally, you are French. Long life France.

In the spirit, always, of French cricket, I offer a code phrase – "reaction-formation" – small r, small f. Here is a dictionary entry:

> Psychological attitude or habitus diametrically opposed to a repressed wish, and constituted as a reaction against it.... In economic terms, reaction-formation is the countercathexis of a conscious element; equal in strength to the unconscious cathexis, it works in the contrary direction.[85]

Eurocentric economic migration cannot live with the recognition that it offers proof of the enemy's brainwashing, that it agrees with the enemy. When in migrancy, the compromise of the exodus, the deep-seated want and need "to be French", to avoid the Middle Ages at home, cruelly denied by the Gaul (the racist self-description (*gaulois*) of the "real" French), formulates itself as a longing for the lost dynamic cultural base and an ambiguous and violent reaction to the metropolis, the gravity of the disorder is visible at last. Then the rules of baseball must be infiltrated, and the interventionist analyst must compute a multicultural psychoanalysis. Here that incorporated Marxist analysis – another universal baseball scenario – will come, one hopes, to her aid. Psychoanalysis must begin to work the left field, not only empathize "cultural difference". For the demand for cultural difference and the foreclosure of post-coloniality that is permitted to the typical well-placed migrant intellectual is a different hybridity, from above. What we need here is the "setting-to-work" of an ethico-political metapsychology, learning responsibility, but also savvy of global systems. The *ressentiment* of the typical post-colonial elite in the "mother-country" does not help much here either. I know whereof I speak, for I am a member of both groups. I search for the a-typical French cricketers, therefore, each with her own situational strategies – a Mahasweta Devi, an Assia Djebar, a Doris Lessing, a Melanie Klein. Cut then to Assia Djebar again.

The two groups Fanon discusses are male. (Since females are the exception in these cases, they are always conscientiously mentioned as such by Fanon.) Here are two moments from Djebar's novella "Women of Algiers in Their Apartments", which will figure the differences foreclosed by theories of hybridity.

If, in her essay "Forbidden gaze", Djebar longs for the impossible singular cathexis that will restore the cut-off lost history, in her novella she figures forth its necessary impossibility. The single spectator is a water-carrier in a women's public bath, daughter of a rural Algerian soldier of the Foreign Legion, devastated by the cruel usual marriage, flight, prostitution and the backbreaking work for women of a higher class. Attempting to describe her from the "inside" as she is carried off in the ambulance after an accident at the baths, Djebar produces a figured "example" of severed sound in her identity-delirium.[86] This sound is of course necessarily cut off when the water-carrier is "treated", by the only Algerian woman surgeon in the city. This is how the moment is staged: " '*I am – who am I? – I am the excluded one . . .* ' In front of Fatma's prostrate body the surgeon is concentrated in action [*se concerne en pleine action*]."[87] Here is Fanon's intellectual and non-intellectual in post-colonial womanspace. The one has no contact with the interiority of the other; it is only the body that longs for help. But the a-typical author attempts to cathect the singular mental theatre of that beaten body, the only possible hope against the ravages of mobilizing political cannon-fodder.

By contrast now, at the end of the story, let us look at the *pied-noir* white woman, with her own (sympathetically given) "psychological problems", deciding to forfeit her return ticket (after a projected short visit) to France, and to stay on in Algiers.[88]

> The plane Anne was supposed to take at dawn the next day was delayed for over an hour. . . . The two women waited among a group of migrant workers who had just spent their one month's paid vacation in their mountain village. Two or three of them, their faces tanned and more serene, were accompanied by their wives in long peasant dresses, a few with babies in their arms and their foreheads tattooed in minute detail. The loveliest one – Anne heard this from Sarah who exchanged a few basic words with her – had only that morning abandoned her veil. Young, her eyes blackened with kohl but her whole face sharp with hope, she maintained a stiff posture of expectation until the moment of boarding. "I'm not leaving!" Anne suddenly cried out. She stared intensely at the young woman traveler, smiled at her (that way this unknown woman would carry with her this sign of gratitude, as the others would take along their baskets and their pottery, all the way to the shantytown north of Paris that was waiting for them.)[89]

We will meet this woman next with her baby, in conversation with Daniel Sibony. And "the sharp hope" is the colonizer's brainwashing, long live

France! By pretending that the migrant has no history, by disavowing that in migrancy the nightmare of the civilizing mission of Imperialism becomes a dream only to become a nightmare again, we become part of the problem. And the question remains, what is the white woman's gratitude to the migrant? The French word is *reconnaissance*, gratitude to be sure, but also recognition, acknowledgement. What relay is passing on here, what exchange of places, woman to woman, colonizer to colonized? Is this what passes between Lynda/Martha using unorthodox healing procedures and the credulous clientele of Tantrism (see note 13)? A simple ethnocultural agenda will solve nothing.

Should we remember Freud's analysis of *"fausse reconnaissance"* and analogize with "group psychology"?[90]

Is this glance a sign of "you make visible what I have been"? I am back to my opening argument. Is that what we provide for you? but remember we belong to the team that cannot imagine a world without psychoanalysis. And the *reconnaissance* is *fausse*.[91]

NOTES

1 I refer to Jacques Derrida's discussion of iterability in "Signature event context", in *Limited Inc.*, ed. Gerald Graff, 2nd edition (Evanston: Northwestern University Press, 1988), pp. 17–19.

2 C. L. R. James, *Beyond A Boundary* (New York: Pantheon, 1984).

3 Ashis Nandy, *The Tao of Cricket: On Games of Destiny and the Destiny of Games* (New Delhi: Penguin, 1989).

4 I thank Thomas Keenan for listening to the first version of this essay at one sitting, and for correcting my baseball vocabulary. The understanding of the game is of course my own.

5 Neil Lazarus, "Cricket and national culture in the writings of C. L. R. James", in Paget Henry and Paul Buhle (eds), *C. L. R. James's Caribbean* (Durham: Duke University Press, 1992), p. 92.

6 Ashis Nandy, *The Intimate Enemy: Loss and Recovery of Self Under Colonialism* (New York: Oxford University Press, 1983).

7 Nandy, *Tao*, p. 3.

8 James Joyce, *Ulysses* (New York: Random House, 1961), p. 20.

9 See Maldwyn Allen Jones, *American Immigration*, 2nd edn (Chicago: University of Chicago Press, 1992), pp. 266, 267.

10 The work of the Graduate Center of the City University of New York with older immigrant groups in the New York metropolitan area bears comparison with the Birmingham School, for example.

11 Antonio Gramsci, "The intellectuals", in Quintin Hoare and Geoffrey Nowell-Smith (trs), *Selections from the Prison Notebooks* (New York: International Publishers, 1971), p. 21. The framing passage is from my Preface to Mahasweta Devi, *Imaginary Maps* (New York: Routledge, 1994). I apologize for a self-citation, but since the Gramscian passage alone may be read wrongly as a negative remark about Afro-America, I find it necessary to quote my comment together with the passage.

12 For "setting-into-work", see Jacques Derrida, "The principle of reason: the university in the eyes of its pupils", *Diacritics* (Fall 1983), p. 19. (*"Mise-en-oeuvre"* is translated "enactment" in the published version.) "The decision of

thought" – Derrida continues – "cannot be an intra-institutional event, an academic moment." The idea of the "setting-into-work of truth" in art is to be found in Heidegger's "The origin of the work of art" and elsewhere (Martin Heidegger, "The origin of the work of art", in *Poetry, Language, Thought*, tr. A. Hofstadter (New York: HarperCollins, 1975), pp. 15–87). Derrida's meticulously detailed critique of the itinerary of "the setting-into-work-of-truth" can be drawn from his *Of Spirit: Heidegger and the Question*, tr. Geoffrey Bennington and Rachel Bowlby (Chicago: University of Chicago Press, 1989). It should be contrasted to Gianni Vattimo's superficial and literalist account of this notion so that Derrida's elaboration of responsibility to the outside is not mistaken for a version of the particular Heideggerian enterprise (Gianni Vattimo, *The End of Modernity: Nihilism and Hermeneutics in Postmodern Culture*, tr. Jon R. Snyder (Baltimore: Johns Hopkins University Press, 1991), pp. 51–109).

13 Sadhna Mitra, "Adaptation of Kundu's neurotic personality inventory in Bengali", in *Indian Journal of Psychology*, vol. 45, no. 4 (1970) pp. 369–71.

14 Sudhir Kakar, *Shamans, Mystics and Doctors: A Psychological Inquiry into India and its Healing Traditions* (Delhi: Oxford University Press, 1982), pp. 151–90. This leads us into postmodern appropriations of the premodern. It is beyond the scope of this essay to ponder the problem that it is modernity that is not ceded without "modernization", entailing a(n economic) restructuring, part of the furniture of which can be the constitution of the appropriate analysand.

15 The feminist impulse is certainly present in Gananath Obeyesekere's work. Professor Obeyesekere, long domiciled in the United States and a professional anthropologist, is from the so-called Indian subcontinent, of Sri Lankan origin. Most interesting from this point of view is *Medusa's Hair: An Essay On Personal Symbols and Religious Experience* (Chicago: University of Chicago Press, 1981).

16 Sigmund Freud, *The Standard Edition of the Complete Psychological Works* (hereafter *SE*), tr. James Strachey, *et al.* (New York: Norton, 1961–), 14, pp. 76–7, and 22, p. 132.

17 Sigmund Freud, "Moses and monotheism", *SE* 23, pp. 83, 93.

18 Kumkum Sangari, "Figures for the 'Unconscious' ", *Journal of Arts and Ideas* 20–1 (1991), pp. 67–84. The two novels are R. C. Dutt, *Pratap Singh, the Last of the Rajputs: A Tale of Rajput Courage and Chivalry* (Allahabad: Kitabistan, 1943) and Arun Joshi, *The Strange Case of Billy Biswas* (New York: Asia Publishing House, 1971). I am grateful to Susie Tharu for bringing this piece to my attention.

19 "The growth of militant Islamic fundamentalism in areas adjacent to India underlines the possibility that New Delhi and Washington will share common security concerns" (*India and America after the Cold War: Report of the Carnegie Endowment Study Group on U.S.–Indian Relations in a Changing International Environment* (Washington, DC: Carnegie Endowment for International Peace, 1993), "Summary", n.p. My thanks to V. Siddharth for making this available to me.

20 Jacques Lacan, "Seminar on the purloined letter", in John P. Miller and William J. Richardson (eds), *The Purloined Poe: Lacan, Derrida, and Psychoanalytic Reading* (Baltimore: Johns Hopkins University Press, 1988), pp. 28–54, where the letter as clitoris hangs well hidden in the most obvious place between the columns of the gaping mantelpiece. Incidentally, when I speak of Father and Nephew, I am of course commenting on the Freud–Lacan relationship by referring to Marx's comments about the Napoleon–Louis Napoleon relationship in *The Eighteenth Brumaire*. At the Conference, Sarah Kofman referred to "*il n'y a que le premier pas qui coûte*" as being a citation of Freud. In another crowd, the Freud reference might have slipped by, but that Marx in *The*

Eighteenth Brumaire had used this time-worn phrase to speak about how the revolution became bourgeoisified would have been remembered.

21 Robert Coover, *The Universal Baseball Association, Inc., J. Henry Waugh, Prop.* (Random House, New York, 1968), p. 19.
22 Julia Kristeva, *Tales of Love*, tr. Leon S. Roudiez (New York: Columbia University Press, 1993), pp. 87, 263, 234. Consult also Kristeva, *Nations Without Nationalism*, tr. Leon S. Roudiez (New York: Columbia University Press, 1993).
23 Kristeva, *Tales of Love*, p. 251.
24 Michel Foucault, "On the genealogy of ethics: an overview of work in progress", in Hubert L. Dreyfus and Paul Rabinow (eds), *Michel Foucault: Beyond Structuralism and Hermeneutics*, 2nd edn (Chicago: University of Chicago Press, 1983), p. 231. Sentence order rearranged.
25 Jürgen Habermas, *The Philosophical Discourse of Modernity*, tr. Frederick Lawrence (Cambridge: MIT Press, 1987).
26 Eugene Converse Murdock, *Mighty Casey, All-American* (Westport: Greenwood Press, 1984). I thank Jerome Beatty for talking to me about Casey, especially for pointing out that these Irish names were often taken on by immigrant players with then "unacceptable" surnames. The Germans kept their names, and inevitably earned the sobriquet "Dutch". Who is playing Casey today?
27 Coover, *Universal*, pp. 240–1.
28 ibid., p. 242
29 Abdelkébir Khatibi, "Frontières", in "Entre psychanalyse et Islam", *Cahiers Intersignes*, 1 (Spring 1990), pp. 13–22.
30 Freud, "Moses", p. 92.
31 Ibid., p. 122.
32 Khatibi, "Frontières", p. 14.
33 Ibid., p. 17.
34 Ibid., p. 22.
35 Daniel Sibony, "Effets d'entre-deux-langues et exils d'origine", *Cahiers Intersignes*, 1 (Spring 1990), p. 82.
36 Ibid., p. 84.
37 Ibid., p. 83.
38 Martine Medejel, "L'exil d'un prénom étranger", *Cahiers Intersignes*, 1 (Spring 1990), p. 66.
39 Ernesto Cardenal, "Prayer for Marilyn Monroe", in *Marilyn Monroe and Other Poems*, tr. Robert Pring-Mill (London: Search Press, 1975), pp. 75–7. I am referring to the interpretation of the poem by the film of the same name produced by ICEAC.
40 Immanuel Kant, "Analytic of the sublime", in *Critique of Judgment*, tr. J. H. Bernard (New York: Hafner Press, 1951), pp. 89–106.
41 I use this idiomatic conjunctive expression from Marx's Eleventh Thesis on Feuerbach whenever I want to indicate the setting-to-work of interpretation (Karl Marx, "Theses on Feuerbach", in Karl Marx and Frederick Engels, *Selected Works* (Moscow: Foreign Languages Publishing House, 1949), vol. 2, p. 367).
42 Sigmund Freud, *Beyond the Pleasure Principle*, SE 18, pp. 7–64.
43 Jacques Derrida, "Différance", in *Margins of Philosophy* tr. Alan Bass (Chicago: University of Chicago Press, 1982), p. 12; translation modified.
44 Ibid., p. 15; emphases mine. Please forgive the running commentary. It reflects nothing more than the irascibility of a middle-aged academic, daily faced with tendentious misreadings dependent upon quick readings unable or unwilling to familiarize themselves with a dauntingly precise and admittedly somewhat cryptic language, but not therefore unable or unwilling to pose as sufficiently informed accusers.

45 For this earlier version, see Derrida, *Speech and Phenomena: And Other Essays on Husserl's Theory of Signs*, tr. David B. Allison (Evanston: Northwestern University Press, 1973), p. 146.

46 Sibony, "Effets", p. 82.

47 Freud, "An autobiographical study", *SE* 20, pp. 7–70.

48 Sibony, "Effets", p. 88.

49 These transgressions are bound to happen because we are in "history". They are not only marks of failure, but signposts for readers to go to work, to renarrativize, to rechannel. That is deconstruction if there is any. Incidentally, Jacqueline Rose's analysis of Freud's "failure" with Dora is precisely such a call to feminists to set Freud to work, thus to deconstruct him affirmatively (Rose, "Dora-fragment of an analysis", in *Sexuality in the Field of Vision* (London: Verso, 1986), pp. 34, 47 and *passim*).

50 Freud, "Moses", p. 88.

51 Ibid., p. 19.

52 Ibid., pp. 19, 22.

53 Ibid., p. 65.

54 Ibid., p. 60.

55 Ibid., p. 112. This is not an argument for a similarity between the British and the Jews. (The two are not, of course, mutually exclusive.) It is an analogy between the enduring spirit of Imperialism of the Eighteenth Dynasty of Egypt, carried forward by the Jews' contact to the culture of that imperialism through Moses's governorship and the spirit of the British Empire. As we will see in the case of Fanon, it is an argument for cricketers.

56 Nandy, *Tao*, p. 1.

57 Freud, "Moses", p. 57.

58 Would neighbourhood stickball – an improvisation on baseball – serve? Is that a serious question? Indeed it is. If the spirit of the US Constitution is being taught in the schools that the children attend, neighbourhood or street stickball is just an expediency. Yet, how about rural Black children? Inner city Black and Puerto Rican children in New York? Asian-American kids in San Francisco? You begin to get the point of how the "trace" works. It cannot suffice to bring about the necessary transgression. If you are sitting in the offices of the *Times Literary Supplement* – do they have offices? – wanting to make a nice ironic point – you dismiss all of this as "PC", and do not wait to ask what political point is precisely being made. Is it protection of "the discreet creative freedoms of the bourgeoisie"? I remain struck by the fact that the anti-PC voice is much more noticeably raised by liberals in Britain. PC offends the subdued camaraderie of cricket much more than it does the upfront politics of baseball. It is noticeable that in Britain the tactic is to trivialize criticism by identifying it with its most strident expression. Left-handed hitters, in truth playing baseball. In the US the opposition – right-handed hitters – embarrassingly seeks to protect "the American spirit". You get my point.

59 This section owes much to class discussion. I thank the members of my graduate and undergraduate seminars on "Feminist psychoanalysis" and "Literature and feminist psychoanalysis" respectively, at Columbia University in the Spring of 1993.

60 Assia Djebar, "Forbidden gaze, severed sound", in *Women of Algiers in their Apartments*, tr. Marjolijn de Jager (Charlottesville: University of Virginia Press, 1992), pp. 140–1; translation modified, emphasis mine.

61 Melanie Klein, "Love, guilt and reparation", in *Works* (New York: Free Press, 1984), vol. 1, p. 317 and *passim*.

62 Jacques Derrida, "Le Facteur de la vérité", in *The Post Card: From Socrates to*

Freud and Beyond, tr. Alan Bass (Chicago: University of Chicago Press, 1987), p. 465.

63 Freud, "Moses", pp. 101, 94. Sentence-order rearranged.

64 Notice, for example, the tacit weighing with signification of the word "tradition" in the following passage about the universally acclaimed first Algerian anti-imperialist hero:

Deriving prestige from belonging to a family with a religious position connected with the Qadiri order ['Abd al-Qadir (1808–83)], became the point around which local forces could gather . . . The symbols of his resistance to the French were *traditional* ones – his war was a *jihad*, he justified his authority by the choice of the *'ulama* and respect for the *shari'a* – but there were modern aspects of his organization of government.

(Albert Hourani, *A History of the Arab Peoples* (Cambridge: Harvard University Press, 1991) p. 270; emphasis mine)

For the restoration of the North African history of the region, see Mohammed Arkoun, *Actualité d'une culture mediterranéenne* (Tampere: TAPRI, 1990).

65 James McPherson, "Just Enough For the City", in *Elbow Room* (New York: Scribner's, 1987), p. 192. Mr McPherson supplied this answer to his use of French in a telephone conversation. With respect to the spirit of baseball, read the lovely "I Am An American" (pp. 113–32) in this collection.

66 Djebar, "Forbidden", p. 139; translation modified.

67 Ibid. p. 140.

68 Laura Mulvey, "Visual pleasure and narrative cinema", in *Visual and Other Pleasures*, (London: Macmillan, 1989), p. 14. I believe it is a sense of this precariousness that makes Mulvey date the piece in a footnote to the title, "trace" it within the fast-moving narrative of feminist intervention in the metropolis, in the anthology publication: "Written in 1973 and published in 1975 in *Screen*."

69 For the moment, it must suffice to quote her footnote in a footnote:

Veiled women are, in the first place, women who are free to circulate, therefore more advantaged than the women who are completely secluded, the latter usually being the wives of the most wealthy . . . In the town where I was born, in the thirties, the women used to go to the baths veiled, but they would go at night. The veiled woman who circulates during the day in the city streets is, therefore, a woman in the first stage of so-called progressive behavior. Since, furthermore, the veil signifies oppression of the body, I have known young women who, when they reached adolescence, refused the principle of having to be veiled when circulating. The result was that they had to remain cloistered behind windows and bars, and so see the exterior world only from afar . . . a half measure among the men of the new middle class: as much as possible, they let their women circulate in individual cars (which the women themselves drive), thus to shelter the body (steel playing the role of the ancestral fabric) and to circulate in a way that "exposes" them as little as possible.

(Djebar, "Forbidden", p. 153, n. 2)

For a detailed analysis of unveiling that resonates with feminist psychoanalysis, the text of the essay must be read carefully.

70 Freud, "The uncanny", *SE* 17, p. 243; translation modified.

71 Doris Lessing, *The Four-Gated City* (New York: Bantam Books, 1970), p. 504.

72 Ibid., p. 506. The passage begins with eyes drawn into the sky and then focuses on eyes as signs of being cut off from the present. Is anything to be gained by remembering Freud's recommendation that no "opponent of the psycho-analytic point of view [should] select this particular story of the Sandman with which

to support his argument that anxiety about the eyes has nothing to do with the castration complex" ("Uncanny", p. 230), when we are trying precisely to suggest that the narrative of castration may be the only explanatory narrative permitted by dominant gendering for the instantiation of being cut off?

73 Frued, "Uncanny", p. 238.

74 Lessing, *City*, p. 591.

75 Freud puts it by way of a more conservative theory of fiction: "it [*Fiktion*] contains the whole of the latter [experience – *Erlebnis*] and something more besides, something that cannot come forth under the conditions of experience [*unter den Bedingungen des Erlebnis nicht vorkommt*]" ("Uncanny", p. 249; translation modified). In other words, fiction makes visible the restrictions of "experience".

76 "As regards Jones, who no doubt wasn't so "hard"-headed about this as he said, why, in your opinion, does he compare, in 1926, the dangers of telepathy for psychoanalysis to the "wolves" who "would not be far from the sheepfold"? (Derrida, "Telepathy", *Oxford Literary Review* vol. 10, nos. 1–2 (1988))

77 Freud, "Uncanny", p. 245; translation modified.

78 Freud, "Fetishism", *SE* 21 pp. 152–3; translation modified.

79 The late essay "Femininity" is an example of such complications. It is instructive to read Freud's description of the "scientific" securing of analytic procedural exigencies in the development of the libido theory in *Beyond the Pleasure Principle*", pp. 50–1.

80 Derrida offers *différance* as a "translation" of this Hegelian description of "the limit or moment of the present [*der Gegen-wart*], the absolute 'this' of time, or the now" ("Différance", pp. 13–14).

81 For the connection between the intentional subject and responsibility, see Derrida, "Mochlos or the conflict of the faculties", in *Logomachia: The Conflict of the Faculties*, tr. Richard Rand and Amy Wygant (Lincoln: University of Nebraska Press, 1993) p.11.

82 Gramsci, "The intellectuals", p. 9.

83 Louis Althusser, "Freud and Lacan", in *Lenin and Philosophy*, tr. Ben Brewster (New York: Monthly Review Press, 1971); Fredric Jameson, *The Political Unconscious: Narrative as a Socially Symbolic Act* (Ithaca: Cornell University Press, 1981); Jean-François Lyotard, *Libidinal Economy*, tr. Iain Hamilton Grant (London: Athlone Press, 1993); Jean-Joseph Goux, *Symbolic Economies: After Marx and Freud*, tr. Jennifer Curtis Gage (Ithaca: Cornell University Press, 1990).

84 Frantz Fanon, *The Wretched of the Earth*, tr. Constance Farrington (New York: Grove Press, 1968), pp. 285–9. All the quoted passages are from this section.

85 J. Laplanche and J-B. Pontalis, *The Language of Psychoanalysis*, tr. Donald Nicholson-Smith (New York: Norton, 1973), p. 376.

86 Assia Djebar, "Women of Algiers in their Apartments", in *Women of Algiers*, pp. 37–43.

87 Ibid., p. 43.

88 Fanon has the account of a psychologically afflicted Frenchwoman as well (*Wretched*, pp. 275–77).

89 Ibid., p. 51.

90 Freud, "Fausse Reconnaissance (Déjà Raconté) in Psychoanalytic Treatment", *SE* 13, pp. 201–7.

91 *Conclusion*. Here, then, is my bid for "Speculation!" French cricket on the one side, and the field-work of the left field on the other. The institution as a necessary disadvantage, a clamp on responsibility that we cannot do without, rather than a claim to science. I had used the figure of polytheism at the Conference to describe the multitudinous situational strategies of what I call

French cricket in this version. Given the mobilization of Hinduism (as "ortho-doxized" in dystopic nationalism as Islam was "arabized" in its utopian national-ist moment) in India today – festering and blooming in the gap (between, for example, Freud's Jews returned to Sinai and the Mosaic few) that Fanon and other nationalist leaders did not work at "seriously" – I have deleted that figure.

5 The alibis of the subject

Lacan and Philosophy

Mikkel Borch-Jacobsen

Mikkel Borch-Jacobsen is Professor of Romance Languages at the University of Washington, Seattle. The following paper continues and extends his critical examination of the philosophical presuppositions of psychoanalysis, and his reopening of the philosophical significance of the hypnotic trance.

In *The Freudian Subject*, Mikkel Borch-Jacobsen undertook to examine the philosophical originality of psychoanalysis. Psychoanalysis supposedly began where hypnosis ended: both historically, and therapeutically, as regards that form of the trance known as transference. He showed that under the guise of a rejection of hypnosis, Freud repeated the Platonic relegation of mimesis. Freud linked desire with an object, rather than with mimesis, and installed a subject of desire as foundational, thus establishing a profound continuity between the Freudian subject and the metaphysics of subjectivity. Borch-Jacobsen argues that by rejecting the mimetic efficacity of the trance, Freud had thrown out what had made the "talking cure" possible in the first place. For Freud, the problematic of hypnosis later reappears, when he appeals to the riddle of hypnosis to account for the social bond. Borch-Jacobsen argues that through this internal overflowing of its limits, psychoanalysis becomes a mystery to itself.

The philosophical respectability accorded to Freud is largely due to the work of Jacques Lacan. Through Lacan's reading of Freud, the notion of a split, divided and decentred subject became one of the axioms of critical discourse. In the present paper, Borch-Jacobsen notes that whereas Freud never ceased to be haunted by the uncanniness of hypnosis, and kept returning to it, Lacan's gesture was that of peremptory refusal to have anything to do with it. He exposes Lacan's act as a shoring up of a Cartesian model of subjectivity through his representational model of the unconscious, far from the radical gesture that it proclaimed itself to be. This installation of a Subject obviates the trance: a pre-reflective immanence, or, in other terms – life itself.

SELECT BIBLIOGRAPHY

Borch-Jacobsen, M., *The Freudian Subject*, tr. Catherine Porter, Stanford: Stanford University Press, 1988.

—— *Lacan, The Absolute Master*, tr. Douglas Brick, Stanford: Stanford University Press, 1991.

—— *The Emotional Tie: Psychoanalysis, Mimesis, Affect*, tr. Douglas Brick *et al.*, Stanford: Stanford University Press, 1993.

* * *

Does psychoanalysis have anything to do with philosophy? As is well known, Freud answered this question with a serene "no". In the "Ego and the Id" he says that philosophers are simply incapable of understanding the idea of a psychical unconscious; and he continues:

> Here we have the first shibboleth of psycho-analysis. To most people who have been educated in philosophy the idea of anything psychical which is not also conscious is so inconceivable that it seems to them absurd and refutable simply by logic. I believe this is only because they have never studied the relevant phenomena of hypnosis and dreams, which ... necessitate this view. Their psychology of consciousness is incapable of solving the problems of dreams and hypnosis.[1]

It would be easy to demonstrate the naivety and even ignorance of this declaration of independence, and there has been no lack of professional philosophers to do so. If, however, the philosopher wants to consider the uncanny character of psychoanalysis, and not simply reduce it to the history of philosophy's "well-known facts", he must constantly keep Freud's declaration in mind. What, in fact, does Freud tell us? First of all, he says that the unconscious will always remain foreign and allergic to every philosophy that makes the psyche identical to being conscious. It may be said that this incriminates merely the philosophy of consciousness, which is not all of philosophy. But we would have to admit that, in fact, this is the dominant trait of modern philosophy, from Descartes to Husserl (and beyond): the total assimilation of being into being-represented, by and for a subject, by and for a *con-scientia*, which assures itself of itself by posing itself "before" itself, in the fashion of *Vor-stellung*. For such a philosophy, psychoanalysis represents a real scandal or, at best, a terrible embarrassment: in dreams, in symptoms, in the transference, something "happens", something comes to pass; that is, manifests itself, but without my representing it. "I" do not accompany all my representations, not because I cannot grasp myself in them (this is Lacan's interpretation, which we will examine in a minute), but because what happens to me does not happen in the mode of representation, does not take place in its space. What space, then? In an "other scene", one that has precisely nothing to do with representation, one whose uncanny characteristics Freud spells out for us: absence of delay and reflection, ignorance of negation and time, carelessness about contradiction and communication, lack of doubt, absolute "egoism" (that is, pre-egoism), and, finally, lack of knowledge of spatiality: "Psyche is extended; knows nothing about it."[2]

Here Freud produces two "witnesses" for the unlocalizable "place" of the unconscious, neither of which are acceptable in the high courts of consciousness and philosophy. The first witness is the dream, and the second, hypnosis. This second witness, however, is uncanny not only for philosophers, but for Freud's readers as well. For we can understand why Freud calls on hypnosis in this context: where could he find a better illustration or "proof" of what he calls the unconscious than in the hypnotic trance, that unquestionably psychical behaviour, which, nevertheless, is completely removed from the reflexivity proper to representative consciousness? (Just try to imagine, for example, a somnambulist's *Cogito* . . .) But we also know that Freud himself totally rejected the practice of hypnosis, preferring the method of free association and conscious recall of repressed-unconscious representations; just as we know that, in "Group psychology and the analysis of the Ego", Freud once again ran up against hypnosis and was forced to admit that it defied all "rational explanation", even psychoanalytic explanation.[3] In reality, by invoking hypnosis against the philosophy of consciousness, Freud calls up a phenomenon that escapes from his own theory of the unconscious. And it could be argued that the inability of psychoanalysis to establish a theory of hypnosis comes from its clandestine roots in the philosophical problematic of the subject, especially from its propensity for describing the unconscious in terms of "unconscious *thoughts*", "repressed *representations*", or "*Vorstellungsrepräsentanten des Triebes*". How then can it hope to account for so-called "unconscious" phenomena – those of hypnosis, in this case – if it retains the major concept of the philosophy of consciousness? The concept of "unconscious representation" is inconsistent not only from a philosophical point of view, but also from that of psychoanalysis, at least if psychoanalysis wants to understand why this so-called "representation" acts without being represented . . .

Perhaps these few remarks have managed to convey the uncanniness of Freud's statement, and by the same token the uncanniness of psychoanalysis for philosophy. For, it remains that Freud *does* oppose psychoanalysis to philosophy, and he found no better way to do so than by calling on a phenomenon that remains estranged not only from philosophy but from psychoanalysis itself. Could Freud have been trying to tell us that psychoanalysis is not really "itself" or "at home" except when estranged from itself? Such, then, would be its *Unheimlichkeit* for the philosopher, even for that (perhaps perennial) "philosopher", the psychoanalyst himself: that discourse on the unconscious speaks only in knowing that it can know nothing of what it speaks – and this, this *Unbewußte*, is what makes it speak.

If we now turn to that self-proclaimed Freudian heir Jacques Lacan, we are confronted by a totally different discursive stance. Obviously, Lacan does not have the same reservations about philosophy as did his predecessor, even though he regularly insists on the different status of psychoanalytic and philosophic discourse. Even the most cursory reading of the *Ecrits* suffices: it would be extremely difficult to avoid terms like "dialectic", "truth", "being", "intersubjectivity", "desire", or "subject" – all obviously philosophical. This immediately raises the question of the status of these "philosophemes" in Lacan's text. Are they simply "didactic" or "propaedeutic" references, as Lacan himself said in relation to Hegel and Heidegger (*ES*, p. 293; *SXI*, p. 18)? Or are they really reformulations of the "fundamental concepts" of psychoanalysis in terms of a particular philosophy – and, in that case, which philosophy? Hegel's? Heidegger's? or, as has been recently suggested, Kojève's or Sartre's?[4]

Lacan, however, generally refuses these filiations, preferring Descartes's patronage: "Freud's method is Cartesian – in the sense that he sets out from the basis of the subject of certainty" (*SXI*, p. 36). This statement is obviously a far cry from Freud's, in "The Ego and the Id", concerning the difference between philosophy and psychoanalysis. Indeed, doesn't this statement simply equate the Freudian unconscious and the subject of the *Cogito*, which Freud implicitly incriminated in speaking of "philosophy" and "psychology of consciousness"? Lacan, of course, would object that his "subject" is split, barred and divided by the signifier, and therefore not the subject of the *Cogito* – the subject that consciously assures itself of itself in its representations – but this same subject, separating itself from itself in the very act of self-representation, and dis-appearing into the gap between the *Cogito*'s enunciation and its statement: "I think where I am not, therefore I am where I do not think" (*ES*, p. 166); and in *Seminar XI*: "Of course, every representation requires a subject, but this subject is never a pure subject. . . . There is no subject without, somewhere, *aphanisis* of the subject" (*SXI*, p. 221).

This divided subject, nonetheless, divides itself only because it represents itself; therefore it is nothing but the Cartesian subject. In other words, the "subject of the unconscious" *is nothing but the subject of consciousness*, simply severed from the moment of self-presence. Indeed, Lacan constantly denounces every conception of the unconscious that tries to make it "other" than representative. As early as his "Remarks on psychical causality", he bluntly proposes replacing the word "unconscious" with "imaginary mode": "For I hope that people will soon stop using the word 'unconscious' for what takes place in consciousness" (*E*, p. 183). He then restates this theme most explicitly and dogmatically in "Position of the unconscious": "The unconscious *is not* a species that defines a circle in psychical reality of what does not have the attribute of consciousness" (*E*, p. 830).

In reality, the Lacanian unconscious is never anything but the unconscious of representative consciousness itself, and it obviously does not take long to discover this as a sort of radicalization of that old aporia, confronted differently by Leibniz, Kant, Fichte, Husserl and the Sartre of *The Transcendence of the Ego*: if transcendental consciousness is what it is, i.e., self-consciousness, only in being conscious of an object ("consciousness of . . ."), then that consciousness cannot be conscious of itself, since it can grasp itself only reflexively, by representing itself "before" itself as an object, a phenomenon, a transcendent *ego*, and so forth;[5] or, indeed, as a signifier, a *Vorstellungsrepräsentant*.

On this account, it could be said that the Lacanian unconscious is *the unconscious of philosophy*: the unconscious that the philosophy of consciousness presupposes while remaining ignorant of it – certainly; but it is also the unconscious *of* that same philosophy, *its* unconscious. For, once again, that "unconscious" cares very little about the affirmation made by psychoanalysis of a scene other than intentional, representative, cogitating consciousness. Another case, Freud would say, of the philosopher's eternal inability to admit that the psychical cannot be reduced to consciousness. Another sign (or symptom) of this could be seen in Lacan's obstinate refusal to have anything to do with hypnosis, either on the theoretical or the practical level. At this point, the difference between Freud's and Lacan's discursive stance becomes glaringly obvious: whereas Freud, despite all his ambivalence towards hypnosis, never stopped referring to it as the very enigma of the unconscious; Lacan simply did not want to hear about it, going so far as to make it the diametric opposite of psychoanalysis: a sort of shibboleth in reverse, which then signs Lacan's membership in the tribe of philosophers.

This is the suspicion, at least, that I would like to back up with the support of three passages from three different periods of Lacan's thought. Not that I want to prove that I know more about hypnosis than Lacan; I willingly confess that I do not know any more about it than Lacan, Freud or anybody else; and as far as that goes, I do not even have much to say about it. But the respect for its *Unheimlichkeit* strikes me as an excellent test of our capacity to respect the more general *Unheimlichkeit* of what Freud, for want of a better word, called "the unconscious". Either we will acknowledge its irrepresentability, the fact that our consciousness cannot be contemporary or commensurable with it; or, under the pretext of vigilance, we will lock ourselves up in the fortress of the representable and speakable – and then we will be on the side of those whom Freud called "philosophers", in their fundamental inability to do justice to the unknown.

I

The first text that I intend to examine, "Beyond the reality principle", is from 1936, a text from Lacan's youth, belonging to the period of theorization of "the mirror stage" and the imaginary-paranoiac constitution of the ego. There is, however, under the title "Phenomenological description of the psychoanalytic experience", a brief passage on the function of language in the cure, which, to a large extent, anticipates Lacan's future developments. "The given of that [psychoanalytic] experience", Lacan says, "is, first, language, that is, a sign" (*E*, p. 82); or, more precisely, a sign *addressed to someone* (i.e., what Lacan will later call "speech"). At first, removed from the demands of everyday communication, the patient's discourse signifies nothing; at least, it refers to no reality:

> But the psychoanalyst, in order not to detach the experience of language from the situation it implies, that of the interlocutor, touches on the simple fact that language, before signifying something, signifies for someone. By the sole fact that [the analyst] is present and listening, the man who speaks addresses himself to him; and because he imposes the condition of meaninglessness on his discourse, what that man *wants to say to him* remains. In fact, what he says may "make no sense," but what he says *to him* harbours a meaning.
>
> (*E*, p. 82–3).

In other words, the psychoanalyst knows that meaning is not to be found in *what* language says (in its statement), but in *the fact of saying it* (in its utterance). And this meaning, which is constituted in interlocutive speech and no place else; this "signified $= x$", is the subject (as Lacan already calls it), in so far as the subject "wants to say" (*veut dire*) and *ex*-presses itself to another. Note that this trait remains constant in Lacan, beyond all the ulterior changes: the essence of language is not to represent reality or communicate a pre-existing meaning, but solely to represent a subject, a subject reduced to the pure fact of speaking and communicating with another (of making itself common). Language, in its essence of speech (or, in Lacan's later terminology, of the signifier), *is* the subject, and, conversely, the subject *is* that speech (or signifier), which publicly manifests him and is his sole "place" or being-there. This explains why, for Lacan, analytic speech is not a matter of reality (of memory, for example, or of social adaptation), but solely of truth, in the sense of *certitude*. As he formulates in the overture to his *Seminar*: "What is at stake is the realization of the truth of the subject, like a dimension peculiar to it which must be detached in its distinctiveness in relation to the very notion of reality" (*SI*, p. 21).

Need I elaborate? This "dimension" is merely that of the *Cogito*, reformulated in terms of speech: the same *epoché* of any realistic reference, leaving only a pure subjective representation; the same certitude, inherent in the fact of thinking or speaking. Indeed, it is impossible for me to say something, no matter how meaningless, unless "I am", at the very moment of my saying it (even if I am nothing but that utterance or *pronuntiatum*): "This proposition [*hoc pronuntiatum*], *I am, I exist*, is necessarily true whenever it is put forward by me or conceived in my mind."[6] It might be said that Lacan makes much of the utterance of the *Cogito* – something that Descartes "forgets" (*SXI*, p. 36). It might also be said that the analysis described in "Beyond the reality principle" is a dialogue that takes time, not a solitary and instantaneous monologue. But this difference is merely the result of Lacan's then current formulation of the *Cogito* in Hegelian terms. If the subject must *speak* himself, and speak himself to another, it is because he can come to full self-consciousness only at the price of reflecting himself, of separating himself from himself in order to better (re)present himself "before" himself. The privilege accorded to speech and dialogue corresponds to the typically Hegelian demand for mediation: the subject manifests himself in his truth only by exteriorizing himself, alienating himself in a common language, and having himself recognized by someone else in the full light of a public space, an " 'I' that is 'We' and [a] 'We' that is 'I' ".[7] The *sum* presupposes an *existo*, an ek-sistence outside of oneself, which is the very condition of self-representation – in this case, of analytical auto-enunciation. In turn, that ek-sistence, in order to take place, presupposes the opening of a space (the same space-time that, according to Freud, the unconscious is ignorant of . . .).

This is confirmed in the rest of Lacan's text: the subject's auto-exteriorization in speech is made equivalent to the exteriorization of a specular *image*. At that time, as is well known, Lacan takes "image" to mean the principle of formation and identification of the "ego" (which he still does not clearly distinguish from the "subject"): the ego constitutes itself by identification with an image, whether its own or that of a specular *alter ego*. Because that image is seen spatially; the *ego*, from the very beginning, is an object for itself. This is the principle of its originary "alienation" (or "transcendence", as Sartre said at about the same time): the ego exists only as an image; it can represent itself (i.e., see itself) only at a distance from itself. It therefore misunderstands itself (*se méconnaît*) at the very moment it knows itself (*se connaît*). Self-representation, *precisely because it is a representation* (a *Vor-stellung*), is an absentation from self: an *alibi* of the subject. The subject is always elsewhere than where it is, because it can see and know itself only in an image of itself.

Lacan says that this alienating image is developed transferentially (but also like a photograph is developed), by projecting it onto that "pure mirror": the analyst (*ES*, p. 15). The patient speaks to the analyst, but he also speaks to him as an *alter ego*, as an ego-alibi. Speaking *of* his ego *to* his ego, he then progressively gains consciousness of the fact that the subject of the statement and the subject of the utterance (the allocutory and the locutor) are identical. Please allow me to quote at some length here, for Lacan's extremely ambiguous formulation is very instructive. He writes that in the patient's discourse

the analyst discovers the very *image* which, by means of his game, he has aroused from the subject, whose trace he recognized imprinted in his person [the analyst's person or the subject's? It is impossible to tell], that image . . . which, as he himself does for the patient, hid its features from his gaze [his or the subject's? Once again, a mystery]. . . . But the very image that the subject presents through his behaviour, and which continually reproduces itself therein, *is unknown to him.* . . . While the analyst finally recognizes that image, the subject, by the debate he is pursuing, finally imposes the role of that image upon him. It is from this position that the analyst takes his power to act on the subject. Henceforth, the analyst acts in such a way that the subject becomes conscious of the unity of the *image* that refracts through him into different effects, depending on whether he enacts, incarnates, or acknowledges them. At this point, I will not describe how the analyst proceeds in his intervention. . . . I will simply say that as the subject pursues the experience and lived process through which the image is reconstituted, his behavior ceases to mime its suggestion; his memories take back their real density, and the analyst sees the end of his power, now rendered useless by the end of the symptoms and the accomplishment of the personality.

(*E*, p. 84–5)

The notable expression "to mime the suggestion of the image" obviously brings us back to hypnosis. Analytic speech consists of a "de-suggestion", a "de-hypnotization"; or again, a "de-mimetization". As Lacan says, the patient "incarnates", "enacts" or "presents" the image with which he has identified himself, while remaining ignorant of it until the moment when, projecting it on that specular mirror, the analyst, he learns to recognize himself in it, to become conscious of himself in it by seeing himself at a distance from himself. The course of the analysis, which is conflated with that of dialogical speech, proceeds from a mimetic *Darstellung* to a specular *Vor-stellung*, from an unreflective identification to a reflective identification, from a miscognition (*méconnaissance*) of the other "in" oneself to a recognition of oneself in the other. This comes as somewhat of a surprise, since we thought we had understood that the *méconnaissance* inherent in the image came from its specular-alienating character. But now Lacan not only asks us to see the specularization of the image as the mainspring (the dialectical mainspring) of the subject's final de-alienation, but he seems to be imputing the initially "suggestive" or hypnotizing character of the image to a non-specular identification. This also allows us to clear up the ambiguity in the last citation: the "trace" of the image "hides its features from [*the subject's*] gaze" because it is "imprinted in *his* person", and thus he is condemned to repeat it in ignorance and "mime its suggestion". How could he possibly be conscious of it, since he could not see it in front of himself – since he "himself" *was* it, prior to any self-representation?

The stakes in this passage are considerable; what is in question is the very nature of the unconscious, the unconscious as it presents (rather than represents) itself in the repetition and affect of the transference. Also at stake is the way in which we understand the constitution of what Lacan calls the "subject" (or the "ego"): are we to understand it as constitution by image and self-representation, as Lacan usually affirms; or, as he suggests here, as an unrepresentational, hypnotic and prespecular constitution; and thus as a-subjective, profoundly blind and dispossessing, since anterior to every possession of a *self*? This last suspicion seems to be confirmed if we turn to the article "Family complexes" written two years later. Here again we find the theme of suggestion, this time explicitly linked to the imaginary formation of the ego, as part of what Lacan at that time calls the "intrusion complex" (instead of the "mirror stage"):

> As long as the image of the counterpart plays only its primary role, limited to the expressive function; it triggers similar emotions and postures in the subject. . . . But when he submits to that emotional or motive suggestion, the subject is not distinguished from the image itself . . . the image only adds the temporary intrusion of a foreign tendency. Call it narcissistic intrusion: nonetheless, the unity that it introduces into the tendencies contributes to the formation of the ego. But before the ego affirms its identity, it becomes one with the formative, yet primordially alienating, image.
>
> (*CF*, p. 45)

We understand why Lacan speaks here of "suggestion", qualifying it as "emotional": the image is truly irresistible, since the subject cannot distinguish himself from it by posing it before himself, and it is "affective" or affecting (as Freud also said of the identificatory *Gefühlsbindung*),[8] since it no longer pertains to representation. The image being an "intrusive" one (and, strictly speaking, this term is inadequate, since there is no ego before the intrusion); the image is not elsewhere, *alibi*, but here, *hic, da*; without the ego being able to separate itself from the image in order to be conscious of it. Therefore, it is no longer an *image*, but a "role", an obsession. One might object that Lacan does continue to speak of "image", "form" and "alienation", and this appears to retain us in the realm of visual representation; but Lacan alerted us to this problem earlier in the same article: the formative power of the image is itself pre-imaginary, in-formal. Behind the *imago* of the counterpart, which we have just been dealing with, lurks the maternal *imago*, whose character, as Lacan takes some pains to emphasize, is "affective", "proprioceptive" and non-imaginary: "At this point, I am not speaking, with Freud, of autoeroticism, since the ego is not yet constituted, nor of narcissism, since there is no ego-image" (*CF*, pp. 29–30). But it is from this irrepresentable (since non-objective) content of the maternal *imago*, that the later *imagos*, as Lacan emphasizes, take their "modelling" and "formative" power:

> That imago is given, in its content, by the sensations proper to first

infancy, but it *has no form* until they begin to mentally organize themselves. Since this stage is prior to the emergence of the form of the object, it appears that these contents cannot represent themselves in consciousness. But, as I already said, they reproduce themselves in the mental structures that *model* later psychical experiences. They are associatively re-evoked when these later experiences occur, but *they are inseparable from the objective contents that they in-form.*

(*CF*, p. 28; my emphasis)

There is not enough time to comment properly on this subtle blurring of the opposition between form and content (that is, of op-position, period). Suffice it to say that Lacan, from 1936 to 1939, is very close to founding the identificatory power of the image in a prespecular and affective identification or "suggestion", which, as he explicitly states, escapes from representation and consciousness, and to which he implicitly refers the phenomena of suggestion and transference. Later, however, he simply abandons this hypothesis, leaving no explanation of the *ego*'s constitution other than the imaginary-specular one. This abandonment, or so it seems to me, is in conformity with the dialectical model of the cure that we have seen sketched out in "Beyond the reality principle". If the objective of the cure is a *prise de conscience* of the subject's alienating image, it goes without saying that the cure cannot deal with anything but an *image*, precisely, one that can be ex-plicated by dialogical speech. By definition, everything that escapes from representative op-position, escapes from the *prise de conscience*. The result is that there is no reason to be concerned with it in the cure, and, in fact, there is every reason to avoid it. Better still, one must say nothing of it, not even of its possibility, since it goes against the proclaimed objective. Exit the "emotional suggestion" of the image, enter the specular, specularizable and dialecticable suggestion. The accent that the young Lacan puts on the *ego*'s originary alienation, far from contradicting the philosophical model of consciousness inherited from Descartes and Hegel, fully reinstates it and, in fact, has no other reason than its preservation.

II

Does this situation change after the "turning" of the 1950s, under the auspices of speech and language, and the beginning of the well-known "return to Freud"? It would seem so, since the dialectical speech that, in 1936, Lacan expected to relieve the symptoms and "complete the personality" is precisely the same speech that he then criticizes under the name of "empty speech", opposing it to "true" or "full speech". The "Rome discourse", the manifesto of the new theory of analysis, begins with precisely that observation. Implicitly contradicting his previous position, Lacan proclaims that in order to de-alienate the subject it is not sufficient to return his own image to him. On the contrary, that recognition in the mirror ends only in "his capture in an objectification – no less imaginary than before – of his static state or of his 'statue,' in a renewed status of his alienation" (*ES*, p. 43). This is the principle of " 'empty' speech, where the subject seems to be talking in vain about someone who, even if he were his spitting image, can never become one with the assumption of his desire" (*ES*, p. 45). In empty speech, the subject recognizes his ego (that is, his object), but not his desire (that is, himself, as non-object).

Hence, the *prise de conscience* (since that is what is at stake in recognition in the mirror) is no longer the objective of the cure. This is so true, that the theme of "full speech" is introduced through the example of the first cathartic cures under hypnosis, in which, as Lacan justly emphasizes, the *prise de conscience* was completely lacking. In fact, how is it possible to assimilate the "putting into words" of the traumatic experience with conscious recollection, as Breuer and Freud did, when "in the hypnotic state verbalization is dissociated from the *prise de conscience*" (*ES*, p. 46)? In reality, Lacan continues, the subject has remembered nothing, no real event, not even an image:

> He has simply recounted the event. But I would say ... that he has made it pass into the *verbe*, or, more precisely, into the *epos* by which he brings back into present time the origins of his own person. And he does this in a language that allows his discourse to be understood by his contemporaries, and which furthermore presupposes their present discourse. Thus it happens that the recitation of the *epos* may include a discourse of earlier days in its own archaic, even foreign language, or may even pursue its course in the present tense with all the animation of the actor; but it is like an indirect discourse, isolated in quotation marks within the thread of the narration, and, if the discourse is played out, it is on a stage implying the presence not only of the chorus, but also of spectators.
>
> Hypnotic recollection is, no doubt, a reproduction of the past, but it is above all a spoken representation – and as such implies all sorts of presences. It stands in the same relation to the waking recollection ... as the drama in which the original myths of the City State are produced before its assembled citizens stands in relation to history.
>
> (*ES*, p. 46–7)

Must we then conclude that "full speech", like the hypnotic "talking cure", is a presentative, mimetic speech; and that Lacan now believes in a sort of pure repetition of the unconscious, to the detriment of any *prise de conscience* of a self? Not in the least. In fact, two pages later, we come upon an unrepealable condemnation of hypnosis: "I ... repudiate any reliance on these states ['hypnosis or even narcosis'] ... whether to explain the symptom or to cure it" (*ES*, p. 49). Why is this? After all, Lacan had just used the example of hypnotized speech to demonstrate the effectiveness of "full speech". In reality, however, there was never any question in his mind of attributing the disappearance of the symptoms to hypnosis, but solely to the pure "speech addressed to the other" (*ES*, p. 48). Note the precautions, in this regard, with which Lacan envelopes himself at the moment he describes the hypnotic talking cure: the hysterical *epos*, he says, is admittedly a "drama", "played out" and rehearsed in "the present tense" with "all the animation of the actor", but it is suspended in the isolating quotation marks of an epic recitation, and, most importantly, is executed on a "stage", before [the] assembled citizens". In other words, what matters is not that the hysterics mimetically identify with their role, speaking "under the name of the other" (as Plato would have said); but only that they speak *to* the others, having their fiction recognized in a public place, and thus sealing their truth in the pact of speech. In other words, what matters is that they *put themselves in representation*, taking a pose before the other, and thus posing themselves before themselves, in a "distanciated" identification (Brecht). In short: *in not being hypnotized* ...

Here, once again, we find Lacan's original presuppositions, still just as disastrous for the hypnosis of "hypnotic" unconscious. The subject's truth resides entirely in the fact of being spoken, that is, in a performative auto-enunciation or representation (no matter how fictive and deceptive this utterance might be in relation to reality – that is, from a constative point of view); and this auto-representation presupposes an auto-exteriorization, a self-exhibition in the "place of the Other", where one has oneself recognized in speech. The problem, however, is that this recognition no longer has anything to do with a *prise de conscience*, if by that we mean self-recognition. Lacan now maintains that recognition of oneself in an other is the very principle of *méconnaissance* and imaginary resistance, whose hypnotic and suggestive traits he also emphasizes (*E*, pp. 377, 439). This assimilation of the specular *prise de conscience* with hypnosis is very significant; it testifies to a sort of retreat toward the front on the part of Lacan: the subject's truth is no longer his identification in (and even less *with*) the imaginary other in which he represents himself; his truth is now his non-identification in a symbolic "big Other", who represents the subject only by absenting him.

Why is this? Essentially because the subject who is to be recognized in speech is no longer the imaginary ego, but the subject of *desire*; and Lacan, under the influence of Alexandre Kojève's commentary on Hegel, conceives of this desire as the pure non-self-identity of a subject defined by his radical negativity. Which means that this "desire" has nothing to do with the Freudian *Wunsch*, or even with the Hegelian *Begierde*.[9] For, in Hegel, *Begierde* remains the desire of a *Selbst*, of a self-consciousness; whereas Kojève, in his anthropologizing and para-Heideggerian reading of Hegel, turns desire into the essence of a humanity dedicated to negating nature – that is, the "real", the self-identical "given being" – which this humanity *is not* and which it can never be: there is no identity between the real and the rational, because the real is impossible for man. Kojève says, in effect, that man can be what he is, i.e., a self-consciousness, only by transcending, and transcending himself in, every object, without ever being able to pose himself as a self, identical to himself. Therefore (as Sartre repeats), he is what he is not, and he is not what he is, because the condition of relationship with self is distance from self. It follows that his desire, in so far as it is conflated with that perpetual ek-static transcendence, is not the desire of any particular thing, but rather a "Desire of desire", or again, a "Desire of the desire of the other". This is Kojève's reformulation of Hegel's "desire of recognition": desire can be human only by negating itself as animal desire or need, and it must therefore be directed toward

> a non-natural object, toward something that goes beyond the given reality. Now, the only thing that goes beyond the given reality is Desire itself. For Desire taken as Desire – i.e., before its satisfaction – is but a revealed nothingness, an unreal emptiness. Desire, being the revelation of an emptiness, the presence of the absence of a reality, is something essentially different from the desired thing, something other than a thing, than a static and given real being that stays eternally identical to itself.[10]

All of these traits are to be found in Lacan. "Man's desire", he repeats, "is the desire of the other" (*SI, p. 146; SXI* p. 115); that is, the desire of no object, the desire of nothing (*SII*, p. 223), and, finally, the desire of death (*SII*, pp. 230–3). By the same token, we understand why no specular *alter ego* "can [ever] become one with the assumption of his desire": the subject-desire, who is to be recognized, is no longer a substantial "ego". Desiring the desire of the other, he admittedly desires "himself", but only as pure desire; that is, as never being "himself", as not "identical to himself", as always "beyond" himself. Therefore, if he "recognizes himself" in an other desire, it is only because the other "reveals" his own nothingness by "revealing" – *nothing*. Therefore, the analyst, who is the operator of this revelation, must be an "empty mirror" (*SII*, p. 246); that is, a pure desire.

On the other hand, the specular image does reveal *something* to the subject; namely, an ego-object, and as a result he cannot recognize himself (or have himself recognized) in the image as a subject, a transcendence toward nothing, and "being-toward-death" (*SVII*, p. 357). On the contrary, that image can be nothing but an alibi of the subject – not only because the image (re)presents him at a distance from himself, but because it causes him to appear there, where he is not: here, *da*, "before" himself; and not *illic, fort*, over there. The specular image or representation of self is an alibi of that radical alibi: the subject as a "creature of distance"[11] and absolute "Elsewhere" (*ES*, p. 193).

Nonetheless, the subject must manifest himself *somewhere* if, as Lacan says, he is to accede to his truth. In fact, Lacan strongly insists that desire is a desire of recognition (*ES*, p. 58; *E*, p. 343); this is the sign of his attachment to the idea of transcendent representation, understood as the only possible form of manifestation. Desire must have a *Da*, because it desires to have itself recognized, that is, exhibit itself outside, in the light of a public place. But where is this place, if desire is always "elsewhere"? On what scene (or stage) will it represent itself, if the place "in which the recognition of desire is bound up with the desire for recognition" is always "beyond" (*ES*, p. 172)? – Where else but that "Other scene" or "Other place", the place of speech and the signifier, since desire represents itself there, not in presence, but *in absence*.

In fact, this is precisely Kojève's lesson concerning Hegel: language, as the manifestation of a subject who poses himself by negating the real, performs the amazing feat of making be what is not.[12] By naming the rose, language abolishes it as a real rose, making it the *"absente de tous bouquets"*; and in that ideal rose, language manifests the negativity of a subject who is the rose's fading "being." In other words, language presents the absence of a subject who speaks himself in language by "nihilating" all reality, his own included. Thus, as Lacan translates, language is the *Da* of that *Fort*: "The symbol first manifests itself as murder of the thing, and this death constitutes the eternalization of the subject's desire" (*E*, p. 319).

This is why the subject, in "true" speech, does not have himself recognized as a meaning that would exist prior to the speech addressed to the Other. Truly "full" and "symbolic" speech occurs when the subject, quite literally, institutes himself in a speech pact that does not represent or constate some thing that would predate its enunciation. This speech presents – one could even say *performs* – the "nothing" that the subject is. "You are my wife", and thus I receive my own message in an inverted form: "I am your husband" – which I *was not* before uttering those words. Nothing changes, in that respect, when the theme of "full speech" gives way in Lacan to that of "autonomy" of the signifier. If Lacan finds it so important to emphasize, by way of Saussure and structural linguistics, that the signifier represents nothing – neither referent nor signified – it is because he wants to establish that it does represent (that is, manifest) the "nothing" that the subject is: "The signifier represents a subject . . . (not a signified); for another signifier (which means: not for another subject)" (R, p. 65).

As this last, famous, quotation clearly demonstrates, Lacan continues to define the subject in terms of representation. Admittedly there is no longer any question of intersubjective recognition, but only of a "discourse of the Other", in which the subject has himself represented by a signifier to another signifier, without ever being able to grasp himself as the elusive "signified" of that perpetual *"signifiance"*. The fact remains that the signifier represents nothing but the subject, who never stops speaking himself in the signifier while absenting himself in it, in some strange subjective *alētheia* – or better yet: that "signifier" is nothing but the subject "himself", incapable of relating to himself (that is, of being conscious of himself) except by separating from himself, absenting himself in the representation that manifests him outside, as the non-being transcendence that he "is": always elsewhere than where he is, always *alibi*. In short, that structure of referral of the signifier, identified by Lacan with the structure of the unconscious, truly is the structure of the *Cogito*, as Lacan himself clearly says; an empty *Cogito* – admittedly: the *Cogito* of a consciousness that appears to itself only in disappearing, but a *Cogito* all the same, always and forever defined in terms of auto-representation. And not the blind *Cogito* of a hypnotized person or of a dreamer, the unrepresentative *Cogito* of an unconscious "other scene".

III

Let us verify this one last time with the ultimate avatar of Lacanian theory: the *"objet petit a"*, as it functions in hypnosis and analysis.

By *"objet a"*, we know that Lacan means the object of phantasy, understood as the "object cause of desire". If it is necessary to say "object *cause* of desire" and not simply "object of desire", it is because, for the hyper-Kojèvian that Lacan continues to be, desire, strictly speaking, can have no object. Once again, desire is the pure transcendence of a subject who desires himself in negating/passing-beyond the object that he wants *not to be*; thus it goes without saying that he can desire himself only in (and as) a non-object: in the no less pure negativity of an other subject – that is, in his *desire*. Desire, Lacan repeats, after Kojève, is the "desire of desire" (*E*, p. 852), the desire to be desired by the Other; and not the desire to be the *object* of the Other's desire, a formula that defines instead what Lacan calls the "deceit of love" (*E*, p. 853), specifically that of transference love (*SXI*, p. 268). By identifying himself as "lovable", the subject of desire actually identifies himself as an object, whereas he is nothing – nothing but "lack-of-being" (*ES*, p. 164; as Sartre[13] also said), "want-to-be" (*ES*, p. 259), and ek-sistence without essence. More succinctly: he identifies himself, whereas he is perpetual non-self-identity and radical inquietude of the negative.

The problem, however, is that the subject of desire must simultaneously be "something", precisely in order to be it "in the mode of not being it" (Sartre). Here again, we find the request for transcendent manifestation, proper to the thought of representation: the *Fort* of ek-static transcendence must have a corresponding *Da* in which it can manifest itself *as it is not*, as the alibi and non-identity that it "is". As we have seen, the signifier has initially been given the role of presenting this absence, and we also know that this is especially true for the "signifier of signifiers" (*ES*, p. 265): the phallic signifier. Lacan tells us that this is the "signifier of a lack in the Other", with which the subject can identify only on the condition of the "Law" of castration, which commands him not to identify with it. But, starting in the 1960s, Lacan gives the *objet a* of phantasy the function of manifesting the subject of desire, as if he was not completely satisfied with that first "linguistic" solution. In the signifier, he admits, I simply cannot identify myself, because nothing responds to the question of what the Other "wants", and thus of what I am for him. *Ché vuoi?* How do you want me? Nothing but an immense silence from the Other, since he answers me only by referring me to a signifier that represents me to another signifier, and so on. In the phantasy, on the contrary, I really do get an answer, an answer as certain as it is enigmatic; and it is the undisclosable object that I myself am in the scenario that fascinates and "fixes" my desire. The *objet a* is that singular object that I put in the place of the lack in the Other (*ES*, pp. 320–1), and with which I identify to "prop" and "cause" my desire, which, in itself, is a desire of nothing.

For all that, is it simply a matter of a "stop-gap" object? An object destined to falsely fill the gaping wound of castration (i.e., of desire, i.e., of the subject)? No. As described by Lacan, that object has this original trait: it is not solely an imaginary object, the prop of a simply specular identification. If it was, it would not have the ambiguous function that Lacan gives it: that of "imaging" the unimaginable disappearance of the subject in the signifier. In fact, the subject identifies with that object only in so far as it is lacking in the Other, in so far as it is an "organ" (*SXI*, pp. 196ff.) or piece of the body from which the body separates itself in order to constitute itself in its corporeal unity: breast, faeces, phallus, voice or gaze. The result, according to Lacan, is that this "profoundly lost object" does not enter the specular image (*ES*, p. 316), unless as an incomplete part, a heterogeneous "stain", or a hole whose edge that object is: a disturbed, enigmatic image, in which the subject henceforth identifies himself, but without being able to recognize himself in it. The subject *sees* himself without seeing *himself* in it, and Lacan illustrates this structure by way of his own version of Sartre's famous analysis of the phenomenon of the gaze. In the gaze, I do not see myself in a mirror, as the other sees me (i.e., as he "loves me" or "wants me"). On the contrary, I see myself as the Other gazes at me, seeking my gaze (i.e., my desire) beyond the visible eye (the object) that I am for him. In short, I see myself in the gaze as I cannot see myself, as the lacking and "fundamentally lost" object of the desire of the Other: *as non-object* – that is, *as a subject of desire*. The scopic *objet a* (which Lacan significantly says is the phantasy object *par excellence*) thus has the remarkable property of making appear, in imaginary space, precisely what escapes in principle from every specular identification and objectification. There, in that non-specular image – i.e., the gaze (or painting, or stain) that "gazes at me" (or "concerns me")[14] before I see it – I am present in my absence; I identify myself in my non-identity, in my perpetual distance from myself: *ego sum alibi*.

Such is, according to Lacan, the objective of the analytic cure, and the principle of its radical difference from hypnosis: to bring the subject to that non-specular *Cogito*, through which his non-self-identity is finally revealed to him. Transference love, Lacan explains in the last lecture of his eleventh *Seminar*, consists of an identification "centred on the Ideal point, capital I, placed somewhere in the Other, from which the Other sees me, in the form I like to be seen" (*SXI*, p. 268): the subject sees himself in that point as "lovable" (*SXI*, p. 243), as the object capable of fulfilling the desire of the Other. On the other hand, the *objet a* is situated in that "other point where the subject sees himself caused as a lack . . . and where *a* fills the gap constituted by the inaugural division of the subject. . . . It is at this point of lack that the subject has to recognize himself" (*SXI*, p. 270). If, however, these two points are conflated, we obtain the phenomena characteristic of hypnosis. Put an "object in the place of the ego-ideal",[15] says Freud in *Group Psychology*, and you get the driving force behind the fascination of groups hypnotized by their *Führer*. Put the gaze of the analyst (or almost any shiny object) in the place of the subject's ego-ideal, Lacan adds, and you get the formula for that zenith of specular identification: hypnosis – "To define hypnosis as the confusion, at one point, of the ideal signifier in which the subject is mapped with the *a*, is the most assured structural definition that has been advanced" (*SXI*, p. 273). This is also the definition of bad (fascist) analysis, characterized by "identification with the analyst" (*SXI*, p. 271).

"Now", Lacan continues, "as everyone knows, it was by distinguishing itself from hypnosis that analysis became established."

> For the fundamental mainspring of the analytic operation is the maintenance of the distance between the I – identification – and the *a*. . . . [The analyst] isolates the *a*, places it at the greatest possible distance from the I that he, the analyst, is called upon by the subject to embody. It is from this idealization that the analyst has to fall in order to be the support of the separating *a*, in so far as his desire allows him, in an upside-down hypnosis, to embody the hypnotized patient. This crossing of the plane of identification is possible.
>
> (*SXI*, p. 273).

Therefore, the true analysis, in conformity with its name, is one that dissolves and separates. It separates itself from hypnosis by separating the point in which the subject sees himself as the object that *fulfils* the desire of the Other from the point in which he sees himself as the object that the Other *lacks* (as that "fallen" object which hypnotizes the analyst . . .). In sum, the analyst "breaks" the identification by separating the subject from his specular object, i.e., "himself". In that ungraspable separation, which confuses the imaginary fascination, the subject can finally see himself dis-appear, appear before himself as the non-object or "nothing" that he is. There, the analyst says, you are there, in those bleeding eyes that fall from me "like scales" (*SXII*, 18 March 1970), and which, as blind as they may be, "*gaze at you*": in them you may see the truth of your desire to see (*voir*) and to know (*savoir*), which is also mine.

"Upside-down hypnosis", Lacan says, meaning that the subject, after the "crossing of the phantasy", can no longer see *himself* – that is, identify himself – in the gaze of the Other. An upside-down *Cogito*? So it seems, since, earlier, Lacan characterized the scopic *objet a* as the "underside of consciousness" (*SXI*, p. 83), explicitly opposing it to the "I see myself seeing myself" of the *Cogito* (*SXI*, p. 80). In fact, the "crossing of the phantasy" is equivalent to an upside-down *Cogito*, since the subject identifies himself in it as non-self-identity, becoming conscious of the "underside of consciousness" that he himself is. And yet, however reversed that *Cogito* is, it is, nonetheless, a *Cogito*, if only because it requires a gaze, an "object" that it itself is at a distance from itself – that is, a self-representation. That gaze is perhaps blind, but at the very least the subject *sees* himself in it as incapable of seeing. In that opaque mirror, the subject reflects his reflection, and he specularizes his unspecularizable negativity. Let us say that he becomes conscious of the impossibility of his consciousness becoming conscious of itself, except by becoming conscious of an object that it *is not*. But never does this subject lose consciousness. However much he faints (or fades) into the object that represents him in his absence, he never faints without knowing it – without fainting, therefore.

This is a far cry from the blind *Cogito* presented by the young Lacan in the "suggestion" of the image, and equally far from the enigma of the unconscious that Freud called "hypnosis". For, as I hope you have seen, the hypnosis that Lacan claimed as the diametric opposite of analysis is really nothing but an alibi-hypnosis: a specular, specularizable, representable hypnosis – a hypnosis kept at a distance, precisely, so that one can become conscious of it. It is the hypnosis of consciousness, placed on the scene to exhibit one's own night and nightmares – not that completely other hypnosis, which seizes us "before" any consciousness, where there is nothing to see (*voir*) and nothing to know (*savoir*). Where is that, you ask? Right here, not *elsewhere*: in that "other scene" of the unconscious, which haunts the scene of consciousness before consciousness is even aware of it. "Psyche is extended; knows nothing about it."

Translated by Douglas Brick

ABBREVIATIONS

CF Lacan, *Les Complexes familiaux dans la formation de l'individu*
E   Lacan, *Ecrits*
ES Lacan, *Ecrits: A Selection*
R   Lacan, "Radiophonie"
SE Freud, *The Standard Edition of the Complete Psychological Works of Sigmund Freud*
SI Lacan, *The Seminar of Jacques Lacan, Book I*
SII Lacan, *The Seminar of Jacques Lacan, Book II*
SVII Lacan, *Le Séminaire, Livre VII*

SXI   Lacan, *The Four Fundamental Concepts of Psycho-analysis*
SXII Lacan, *Le Séminaire, Livre XII*

NOTES

1 "The Ego and the Id", in *The Standard Edition of the Complete Psychological Works of Sigmund Freud*, (hereafter *SE*), ed. J. Strachey, (London: Hogarth Press, 1953–74), 19 p. 13.

2 "Findings, ideas, problems", *SE* 13, p. 300.

3 "Group psychology and the analysis of the Ego", *SE* 18, p. 115:

> Hypnosis would solve the riddle of the libidinal constitution of groups for us straight away, if it were not that it itself exhibits some features which are not met by the rational explanation we have hitherto given of it as a state of being in love with the directly sexual trends excluded. There is still a great deal in it which we must recognize as unexplained and mysterious.

4 On the relationship between Kojève and Lacan, see Elisabeth Roudinesco, *La Bataille de cent ans: Histoire de la psychanalyse en France* (Paris: Seuil, 1986), pp. 149ff.; and Philippe van Haute,"Lacan en Kojève: het imaginaire en de dialectiek van de meester en de slaaf", *Tijdschrift voor Philosophie*, 48 (1986), 391–415. On the relationship between Sartre and Lacan, see van Haute, "Psychoanalysis and existentialism: on Lacan's theory of subjectivity", *Stanford Literature Review*, 8(1–2) (Spring-Fall 1991), 19–37.

5 On this question, see the important developments made by Michel Henry in *The Essence of Manifestation*, tr. Gerard Etzkorn (The Hague: Martinus Nijhoff, 1973), Book I, sec. I; and *Généalogie de la psychanalyse* (Paris: Presses Universitaires, 1985), 352–3. See also Manfred Frank, *Die Unhintergehbarkeit von Individualität* (Frankfurt: Suhrkamp Verlag, 1986), the chapter entitled "Subjectivity as self-consciousness or as consciousness of consciousness".

6 René Descartes, *Philosophical Writings of Descartes*, tr. John Cottingham, Robert Stoothoff and Dugald Murdoch (Cambridge: Cambridge University Press, 1984), vol. 2, p. 17.

7 G. W. F. Hegel, *Phenomenology of Spirit*, tr. A. V. Miller (Oxford: Clarendon Press, 1977), p. 11.

8 Sigmund Freud, "Group psychology", *SE* 18 p. 107: "Identification is the original form of emotional tie [*Gefühlsbindung*] with an object."

9 Translator's note: both of these terms are currently translated in French as *désir*.

10 Alexandre Kojève, *Introduction to the Reading of Hegel*, tr. James H. Nichols, Jr (Ithaca: Cornell University Press, 1969), p. 13.

11 Martin Heidegger, *The Metaphysical Foundations of Logic*, tr. Michael Heim (Bloomington: Indiana University Press, 1984), p. 221.

12 Kojève, *Hegel*, p. 141.

13 Jean-Paul Sartre, *Being and Nothingness*, tr. Hazel E. Barnes (New York: Philosophical Library, 1956), p. 88: "Desire is a lack of being. It is haunted in its inmost being by the being of which it is desire. Thus it bears witness to the existence of lack in the being of human reality."

14 Translator's note: "qui me regarde" means either "which gazes at me" or "which concerns me".

15 Freud, "Group psychology", pp. 113–16.

BIBLIOGRAPHY

Descartes, René, *Philosophical Writings of Descartes*, tr. John Cottingham, Robert Stoothoff and Dugald Murdoch, Cambridge: Cambridge University Press, 1984.

Frank, Manfred, *Die Unhintergehbarkeit von Individualität*, Frankfurt: Suhrkamp Verlag, 1986.

Freud, Sigmund, *The Standard Edition of the Complete Psychological Works of Sigmund Freud*, ed. James Strachey, London: Hogarth Press, 1953–74.

Hegel, G. W. F., *Phenomenology of Spirit*, tr. A. V. Miller, Oxford: Clarendon Press, 1977.

Heidegger, Martin, *The Metaphysical Foundations of Logic*, tr. Michael Heim, Bloomington: Indiana University Press, 1984.

Henry, Michel, *The Essence of Manifestation*, tr. Gerard Etzkorn, The Hague: Martinus Nijhoff, 1973.

—— *Généalogie de la psychanalyse*, Paris: Presses Universitaires, 1985.

Kojéve, Alexandre, *Introduction to the Reading of Hegel*, tr. James H. Nichols, Jr, Ithaca: Cornell University Press, 1969.

Lacan, Jacques, *Ecrits*, Paris: Seuil, 1966.

—— *Le séminaire, livre XII: L'envers de la psychanalyse*, unpublished manuscript copy (1969–1970).

—— "Radiophonie," *Scilicet* 2/3 (1970).

—— *Ecrits: A Selection*, tr. Alan Sheridan, New York: W. W. Norton, 1977.

—— *The Four Fundamental Concepts of Psycho-analysis*, tr. Alan Sheridan, New York: W. W. Norton, 1977.

—— *Les complexes familiaux dans la formation de l'individu*, Paris: Navarin Editeur, 1984.

—— *Le Séminaire, livre VII: L'éthique de la psychanalyse*, Paris: Seuil, 1986.

—— *The Seminar of Jacques Lacan, Book I: Freud's Papers on Technique*, tr. John Forrester, New York: W. W. Norton, 1988.

—— *The Seminar of Jacques Lacan, Book II: The Ego in Freud's Theory and in the Technique of Psychoanalysis*, tr. Sylvana Tomaselli, New York: W. W. Norton, 1988.

Roudinesco, Elisabeth, *La bataille de cent ans: Histoire de la psychanalyse en France*, Paris: Seuil, 1986.

Sartre, Jean-Paul, *Being and Nothingness*, tr. Hazel E. Barnes, New York: Philosophical Library, 1956.

Van Haute, Philippe, "Lacan en Kojève: het imaginaire en de dialectiek van de meester en de slaaf", *Tijdschrift voor Philosophie* 48 (1986), 391–415.

—— "Psychoanalysis and existentialism: on Lacan's theory of subjectivity", *Stanford Literature Review* 8 (1–2) (Spring-Fall 1991), 19–37.

6 "It's only the first step that costs"

Sarah Kofman

Sarah Kofman is Professor of Philosophy at the University of Paris I, Panthéon-Sorbonne. Her work has involved a lengthy engagement with psychoanalysis, in its rapport with philosophy, femininity, art and literature. In particular, she has been concerned with tracing the proximity between the separation from the philosophical tradition inaugurated by psychoanalysis and the formal deconstruction of western metaphysics, as inaugurated by Nietzsche and carried forward by Derrida. She distinguishes herself, in the interior of this deconstructive field, by the very precise research of the instinctual bases of the great philosophical and literary texts.

In *Freud and Fiction* she figuratively places herself in Freud's chair, analysing Freud's treatment of various fictional works that came to function as privileged exemplars or speculative mirrors for psychoanalysis.

In the present paper, she is in particular concerned with the unique status of psychoanalysis, as limit-discipline between science and philosophy. She analyses the twists and turns of Freud's troubled relation to what he termed "speculation". She examines his avowed positivism, which she traces back to the influence of Auguste Comte (a figure she has dealt with at length in her *Aberrations: the Becoming-woman of Auguste Comte*), which draws out the philosophical roots of Freud's "denial" of philosophy. Comte, the father of positivism, had designated metaphysical speculation as a prescientific stage to be surmounted by the stage of scientific knowledge. In "Freud and Empedocles" (1970) (reprinted in *Freud and Fiction*) she showed how Freud's recourse to speculation had renewed the link with the pre-socratic tradition which had been ostracized by science and metaphysics. Taking up again this problematic, Kofman argues that despite Freud's insistence to the contrary, he is himself a 'speculator', nevertheless. She concludes that his unwitting denial of speculation hinders his step at the very approach to sexual difference.

SELECT BIBLIOGRAPHY

Kofman, S., *The Enigma of Woman: Woman in Freud's Writings*, tr. Catherine Porter, Ithaca: Cornell University Press, 1985.

—— *The Childhood of Art: An Interpretation of Freud's Aesthetics*, tr. Winifred Woodhull, New York: Columbia University Press, 1988.
—— *Freud and Fiction*, tr. Sarah Wykes, Cambridge: Polity Press, 1990.

* * *

THE FATE OF PSYCHOANALYSIS

In an old film of Christian Jacques, *La Loi c'est la Loi* [*The Law is the Law*][1] Fernandel the gendarme, on the lookout for smugglers in a village on the French-Italian border, suddenly discovers that he is Italian, not French as he had always thought. He thus finds himself obliged to set off for Italy to be naturalized as French, so he can be recognized as a full citizen in France. But the bureaucratic wrangles are such that neither country, France nor Italy, wants anything more to do with him and he is turned back by customs on both sides of the border. As if paralysed, he is unable to take a step in either direction without risking a beating.

The fate of psychoanalysis seems to resemble Fernandel's: Freud himself says so. More precisely, he compares its fate to that of individuals placed between two enemy nations, belonging to one by birth and to the other by choice and residence: always at war, first with one, then the other: "It was their fate [*Schicksal*] to be treated as enemies first by one side and then, if they were lucky enough to escape, by the other. Such might equally be the fate [*Schicksal*] of Psychoanalysis.[2]

The above appears in a text written in 1921, not long after the end of the 1914–18 war. It was during this war, Freud says, that he first heard talk of these people who are doubly at risk by virtue of their position on, we might say, the "*borderlines*".[3] And while his eldest son is fighting at the front, causing him nightmares,[4] he is also thinking incessantly of his other child, psychoanalysis, whose fate preoccupies him at least as much as that of his own flesh and blood. If the 1914–18 war is sure to come to an end one day, the war which threatens his spiritual child looks likely to continue indefinitely. Indeed, despite the arguments over priority and above and beyond his acknowledged indebtedness to poets, collectors of myths and philosophers,[5] Freud continually repeats his claim: psycho-analysis is his creation.[6] If his "discovery" is fragile (in a dream he compares it to a glass hat that he has on his knee while making a train journey),[7] it is this discovery alone that makes its creator a great man, fulfilling that destiny prophesied for the child Freud by a fortune teller. A prophesy about her beloved son which his mother believed.[8] A belief in destiny held by all those who (in their desire to anticipate, to speculate on, the future), consult card readers, mediums or graphologists, despite the refutations of reality.

In this same text of 1921, Freud speculates on three cases of this kind of prediction and makes a veritable inflation of the word "destiny" around which the whole text revolves. In what is an extremely *unheimlich* manner, he returns to the word eight times, mimicking by his very repetition the ineluctable nature of every Fatum. Thus among other "destinies" (as if he smuggles this term belonging to the occult "sciences" into his own domain to assimilate it by surreptitiously appropriating it), Freud lingers over the destiny of psychoanalysis, also apparently stemming from an ineluctability. Translated into analytic language, it stems from its creator's compulsion to repeat. A compulsion which keeps him/it (Freud or psychoanalysis, but can we still make a distinction between them?) in a state of perpetual conflict, caught in an interminable war between two combative enemies, persecuted first by one, then by the other. Constantly on his guard, never at peace: as soon as he has finished with one enemy, the other starts up again. Such is the diabolical fate of psychoanalysis, and of Freud, its father, who has fully identified himself with this child whom he has made "his" thing. Freud is therefore never at peace (*ruhig*). But what can he do in order to be able to work at constructing his "science" without being constantly preoccupied by this state of war which keeps him on the defensive, always caught between two enemies, as if suspended on a frontier that he cannot cross for fear of finding himself maltreated and of losing his whole system of security?

He would like to be able to work in peace, move forward step by step, at his own pace, without having to worry about prohibitions that are external to science. But his destiny, rooted in his instincts, which are symptomatic of his fundamental and deep-rooted dualism[9] and of his ambivalence, keeps him in a state of conflict and his creation, psycho-analysis, in the uncomfortable position of a border-discipline.

A BORDER-DISCIPLINE

Psychoanalysis, on the point of articulation between the natural sciences where its origins lie ("analysts cannot repudiate their descent from exact science")[10] and philosophy, where its prediliction would lie, if it did not refuse to abandon itself to philosophy on the pretext of a lack of "talent", is never really on one side or another. It claims to belong to both, according to the needs of its cause.

Above all it is in its beginnings, when the destiny of the house of analysis has not yet been determined, when it has not yet set up shop on its own, when it enjoys no notoriety, no prestige, and displays no noble titles, that Freud seizes upon the mask of science and of its authority: the only guarantee of infallible success. Even more so because he is only a poor Jew whose speculations no one would give any credit to unless they were covered with the illustrious name of science.

> When I assured my patients that I knew how to relieve them perma-
> nently of their sufferings they looked around my humble abode,

reflected on my lack of fame and title, and regarded me like the possessor of an infallible system at a gambling resort, of whom people say that if he could do what he professes he would look very different himself.[11]

But, although he needs the authority of an exact science and uses it as a cover, he in fact finds it difficult to tolerate because of the pressure exerted by its rigid rationalism on anything which strays from what is solidly established and recognized. Freud has always refused to bow down to this authority and has never conformed to it. He has continually denounced the false precisions (*Wissendünkel*) of the educated representatives (*Gebildeten*) of Official Science and placed greater importance on the spontaneous wisdom of common experience.

The wisdom of poets who predict, intuit and anticipate in an indestructible, if obscure, manner the truths of psychoanalysis.[12] How could he have any sympathy for that science which has always treated his creation in a disdainful and haughty manner, suspecting it of mysticism and charlatanism and classing the unconscious among "one of the things between heaven and earth which philosophy [*Schulweisheit*] refuses to dream of"?[13] Because psychoanalysis concerns itself with things that are "uncanny", it has itself been considered particularly *unheimlich*[14] and because it uses dreams as the royal road to the knowledge of its object it has been judged the province of dreamers and visionaries.

Which is why, when the aforementioned science wants nothing to do with occultism, which affirms the real existence of "more things in heaven and earth than are dreamt of in our philosophy",[15] Freud (who ten years or so later in *Dreams and Occultism* (1933) once again uses this expression taken from the mouth of Hamlet, the madman who knew more about it than any sage) is quite ready, confident in the support of the great Shakespeare, to ally himself with this new victim of persecution. Or at least he is firmly resolved not to confine himself to the views of the academy and thoroughly determined to believe anything that is made plausible to him. In the war between occultism and science, the first gesture of Freud's rejecting any limiting authority, is his siding with the occultists.

However, things are not so simple because such an alliance could prove dangerous for psychoanalysis. The motivations of the occultists in rejecting scientific authority are not, in fact, those of Freud. What motivates him is a thirst for knowledge (*Wissbegierde*) that nothing can check, the shame of seeing science neglect certain undeniable problems and the need to bring it to bear on new fields of phenomena. The occultists are not moved by a desire for knowledge: they are true believers looking for justifications. They would like psychoanalysis's support in order to further impose their beliefs on people. Occultism is "either the old religious faith which has been pushed into the background [*zurückgedrängt wurde*] by science in the course of human development, or another one, even closer to the superseded convictions of primitive peoples"[16] (the belief in the omnipotence of thoughts) and which is making its return in a completely *unheimlich* manner.

In this respect, psychoanalysts belong to the representatives of the exact sciences – suspicious of all those whose research is motivated by the force of their beliefs, of their desires, whose omnipotence psychoanalysis has been the first to reveal. Freud does not give in to [*sacrifier*] scientific authority, nor does he to desire and the pleasure principle.

On the contrary, he is ready to "sacrifice" them all in exchange for even the smallest fragment of objective certainty: "Moved by an extreme distrust of the power of human wishes and of the temptations of the pleasure principle, they (the psychoanalysts) are ready, for the sake of obtaining some fragment of objective certainty, to sacrifice everything".[17] Everything? That is to say the pleasure of the blinding brilliance of a flawless theory (*der blendende Glanz einer lückenlosen Theorie*), the exultant consciousness of possessing a conception of the world that is nicely whole and rounded, the peace of spirit that derives from generously motivated ideas of a useful and ethical action. This is the kind of pleasure that philosophical speculation offers, the speculation by which Freud was seduced in his youth. It was to such speculation that he felt himself destined,[18] before being put on his guard by the philosopher Brentano who, above all, recommended that he read the English empiricists and August Comte, inducing him not to set off on the slippery paths of reason because, as Freud says:

> on this score, the same goes as for the doctor specialising in mental illness who, admittedly, remarks at first that things are not right among the madmen but who soon becomes accustomed to it and often turns into a slight crackpot himself. Among the moderns, he recommended A. Comte to us, touching upon his life.[19]

Brentano, who in his youth when he began to read the philosophers, was himself disappointed to the point of beginning to doubt his aptitude for philosophy,[20] succeeded in convincing Freud that he too was not very intellectually "gifted",[21] at least not for the study of metaphysics, for whose aberrations, like Comte,[22] he displays a very positive contempt.[23] Unless such a parade of his lack of "talent" is well and truly a negation which allows him to renounce his deep desire to philosophize. By philosophizing, by allowing too free a rein to the imagination[24] and the personality,[25] one runs the risk of speculative madness, in the strict sense in which Comte uses the term,[26] of becoming, as he says, a bit of a crackpot, of losing one's head, one's reason, one's equilibrium. In the same way, he prefers to deny his originality (he has always had precursors, he has absorbed the principle ideas of psychoanalysis by means of cryptoamnesia), for fear of being taken for, and of being, "an original" in the pejorative sense of the word – a crank.[27] Thus what he fears about philosophical speculation is that by being too seduced, attracted, bewitched by it, it will end up "leading him astray", "disorientating" him, giving him delusions, forcing him off the straight and narrow path of Science, of "the correct steps".[28] This means advancing step by step,[29] without rushing to arrive at a conclusion, without being in a hurry to construct a unifying system,[30] a vast synthesis at the expense of certainty[31] by abusing the power of thought,[32] which makes one regress to a superseded age, a period which should, in adulthood, have been surmounted.

This is exactly why Comte criticizes metaphysics. A normal mode of thought at a specific period in the development of the mind (in adolescence), it becomes abnormal, pathological, when it persists into the positive virile age, thus endangering the proper order, the just hierarchies, the mental health of both the individual and society. Metaphysics is a "fantastical" philosophy that rambles, wanders, oscillates between two ages: it is fundamentally ambiguous. It is a strange (*unheimlich*) manner of philosophizing because it reproduces on the level of the species the return of something familiar to all individuals but which, at a given moment in the course of their evolution, has been repressed or surmounted, or at least should have been by the age of virile maturity. Metaphysics is *unheimlich*, a retrograde, archaic vestige, an eternal persistence of what should have been left behind.

Thus for fear of falling into the worst aberrations and of "regressing" to the magical stage of animism, Freud renounces what all his "disciples" will increasingly abandon themselves to, be it Jung, Adler, Groddeck, Rank, Ferenczi: to the pleasure of the blinding light, the systematic unity of a conception of the world that is flawless and definitive. In order to make do with the "fragmentary crumbs" (*fragmentarischen Brocken*) of a knowledge and propositions whose foundations are imprecise and perpetually open to revision. At the banquet of science Freud is forced, like a beggar, to satisfy his hunger with crumbs, without ever really feeling the contentment of someone with a nicely rounded belly, someone for whom everything is easy and moves along of its own accord [*pour qui ça va toujours tout seul*]. That is, someone for whom things always roll along smoothly of their own accord like the originary human beings of the Aristophanes myth in the *Symposium*, who move by rolling themselves forwards like balls and who are narcissistically flawless, conceived by Plato/Aristophanes on the lines of the Empedoclean Sphere.

Thus in accordance with the object of his science and the material at his disposal, which is always lacunal and obscure, Freud claims his theory's right to the fragmentary, the lacunal, in opposition to a narcissistically reassuring unity and totality.

In opposition to the blinding, the all too-blinding light of speculation, he claims his right to obscurity and likens his vision to a mole's[33] rather to than to a lynx's – the ideal of philosophical vision for Aristotle, the first great Speculator.

Finally, against the definitive, the absolute and the invariable, symptoms of the speculative-metaphysical, indeed magical, nature of those theories which emerge complete in a single blinding flash, Freud (once again like Comte) demands his right to the relative, to the continual, slow and gradual revision of a theory which is never complete, which calls on experience and observation alone. For example in *My Views on the Part Played by Sexuality in the Aetiology of Neuroses* (1905) he writes:

> My theory of the aetiological importance of the sexual factor in the neuroses can best be appreciated, in my opinion, by following the history of its development. For I have no desire whatever to deny that it has gone through a process of evolution and been modified in the course of it. My professional colleagues may find a guarantee in this admission that the theory is nothing other than the product of continuous and ever deeper-going experience. What is born of speculation, on the contrary, may easily spring into existence complete and thereafter remain unchangeable.[34]

The flip side of such facility being a lack of substance, proof and fruitfulness.[35] In *Instincts and their Vicissitudes*, he shows how no science, even the most (so-called) exact science starts from fundamental, transparent and clearly defined concepts and that the advance of knowledge does not tolerate any rigidity of definitions: "Physics furnishes an excellent illustration of the way in which even basic concepts that have been established in the form of definitions are constantly being altered in their content."[36] In *An Introduction to Narcissism*, Freud the heir of Comte, with regard to the necessary distinction between sexual libido and ego libido – the aim of the entire text being to counter the monist speculations of Jung and Adler (it is always his rivals who speculate, and each time Freud polemically opposes observation and speculation it is to emphasize that he is in perfect mental health while his rivals are deluded, like paranoics who build "speculative systems" resembling "philosophical systems"[37] – opposes observation to the sterility of theoretical debates and a science founded on the interpretation of phenomena to a logically flawless speculation that leads nowhere:

> It is true that notions such as that of an ego libido, an energy of the ego instincts, and so on, are neither particularly easy to grasp nor sufficiently rich in content: a speculative theory of the relations in question would begin by seeking a sharply defined concept as its basis. But I am of the opinion that this is just the difference between a speculative theory and a science erected on empirical interpretation. The latter will not envy speculation its privilege of having a smooth, logically unassailable foundation, but will gladly content itself with nebulous, scarcely imaginable basic concepts, which it hopes to apprehend more clearly in the course of its development, or which it is prepared to replace by others. For these ideas are not the foundation of science, upon which everything rests, that foundation is observation alone; they

are not the bottom but the top of the whole structure and they can be replaced and discarded without damaging it. The same thing is happening in our day in the science of physics, the basic notions of which as regards matter, centres of force, attractions etc, are scarcely less debatable than the corresponding notions in Psychoanalysis.... In the total absence of any theory of the instincts which would help us to find bearings, we may be permitted, or rather, it is incumbent upon us, to start off by working out some hypothesis to its logical conclusion, until it either breaks down or is confirmed ... let us face the possibility of error but do not let us be deterred from pursuing the logical implications of the hypothesis we first adopted or an antithesis between ego instincts and sexual instincts (a hypothesis to which we were forcibly led by an analysis of the transference neuroses), and from seeing whether it turns out to be without contradictions and fruitful and whether it can be applied to other disorders as well, such as schizophrenia.[38]

The remainder of the text takes issue with Jung, who has claimed hastily (at least without sufficient evidence) that libido theory is incapable of explaining schizophrenia, at least without being expanded and in the process being deprived of all sexual content. Freud blames Jung for decreeing instead of arguing, for anticipating his decision and for economizing on discussion: in short, for speculating in a vain and sterile fashion. This is not the only text in which he heaps reproaches on him as if he had committed the worst kind of offence.[39]

But it is his correspondence with Lou Salomé that is of greatest interest in this respect: in fact it is to her alone that Freud seems able to reveal his relation to philosophical speculation with a certain amount of serenity, without a background of rivalry or polemic. In Lou alone he recognizes the qualities, the talents he says he himself does not possess – but Lou is not duped – those of synthesis,[40] of unity, visionary talents[41] which enable her always to steal the march on Freud – the mole who reveals only fragmentary writings,[42] *disjecta membra* that Lou is able to complete, transforming them into a construction, a living organism. He remains incorrigibly, interminably an analyst,[43] focusing all his light on one point and renouncing the coherence of the whole:

I cannot always follow you, for my eyes, adapted as they are to the dark probably can't stand strong light or an extensive range of vision. But I haven't become so much of a mole as to be incapable of enjoying the idea of a brighter light and a more spacious horizon, or even to deny their existence.[44]

Every time I read one of your letters of appraisal I am amazed at your talent for going beyond what has been said, for completing it and making it converge at some distant point. Naturally I do not always agree with you. I so rarely feel the need for synthesis ... what interests me is the separation and breaking up into its component parts of what would otherwise revert to an inchoate mass.[45]

I strike up a mostly very simple melody; you supply the higher octaves for it; I separate the one from the other, and you blend what has been separated into a higher unity.... I tend to exclude all opinions except one, whereas you tend to include all opinions together.[46]

In her replies to Freud or in her Journal, Lou refutes his modesty. Of *Of Metapsychology* she says that there can be no question of "the fragmentary", that "every argument is related ever more cogently and inevitably to every other.... It must be admitted that Psychoanalysis has made vast strides".[47]

At the same time she recognizes that he is the perfect researcher, "advancing quietly and working tirelessly", his theory never definitively complete but continually being modified as he goes along, in accordance with his experience, and that this "tireless advance" is punctuated at intervals by limits only in order to help those who are following him in his investigations.[48]

She acknowledges that psychoanalysis, which has its own particular methods and means, has the right to impose its own obscurity, instead of disappearing into a pseudo-clarity which is foreign to it. Because if the psychical and the physical can represent one another, they do not condition one another, any more than they are expressions of one another and they cannot therefore intervene for each other.[49] And she is grateful to Freud for being the only person, thanks to his scientific rigour, to make her feel secure ("I continued to feel so wonderfully safe and secure only with you"[50]), for being the only person who could have invented psychoanalysis, since "other researchers would have mixed it up in an overly mechanical way with a whole host of things which they would have been drawn to by the fantasies of their secret desires"[51], and which would have seduced her too. This is because, Freud's creation running counter to his personal tastes, which did not in any way direct him to the "dredging up of discoveries from such profound depths", he has been able to "subject them to a doubly exacting and sober scrutiny, so that their value might in no way be overestimated".[52]

However at the same time, Lou knows how to defend those who, like Adler or Groddeck, indulge (in Freud's view) in a little too much speculation, who go a little too far or too high, which is perhaps highly seductive but removes the certainty for which Freud has sacrificed everything: unity, wholeness, the feeling of intellectual satisfaction. Regarding one of Groddeck's books which Freud has sent her emphasizing Groddeck's tendency to exaggeration, to unification and to a certain mysticism, and declaring that he goes further than him (Freud), that his "Id" is more than Freud's unconscious and is badly defined, despite his feeling that there is something authentic in it,[53] Lou retorts by insisting on the fruitful results of the speculations of such a bold thinker, whom she astutely likens to Freud himself:

> If he now manages on his own territory to conquer a small area, that is excellent for the future of Psychoanalysis. . . . He is clearly one of those who make use of our theories, in order to be unimpeded in the range and boldness of their researches, and in the light of these researches to be able to abandon or modify their theories as the case may be. And that after all is your stand point too: for me at least the way you made use of any particular theory as well as your dislike of philosophising was an expression of this determination and resignation.[54]

Later, in *Analysis Terminable and Interminable*,[55] Freud, who seems to have understood Lou's lesson, writes that "without metapsychological speculation and theorising, I had almost said 'phantasying' we shall not go another step forward".[56] And yet if he has given into this fantastical self (this demon of creative speculation which, like a compulsion, forces one to take one's investigations ever further) more readily in the last twenty years of his life, he has kept it in check, during the long years of his scientific work. In his *On the History of the Psycho-analytic Movement* (1914), reflecting on his beginnings, he declares that, despite his "splendid isolation" this was a noble and heroic period because, as he says: "I learnt" (thanks to a long and hard self-imposed discipline which included giving up the pleasure of reading philosophy, notably Nietzsche, and book learning in order to study things themselves), "to restrain speculative tendencies".[57]

There is therefore a certain Freudian "resignation", a certain evasion. And Lou is not deceived by it: the theoretical renunciation of a perfect unity goes hand in hand with a vital renunciation. It is symptomatic of a certain lack of euphoria which hides behind rationalizations. The rational need for a definitive unity between things springs from an anthropomorphic source and customs, and would involve a regression to infantile questioning, thus disturbing individual positive scientific research:

> Freud acknowledged that this striving for unity has its ultimate source in narcissism. But according to his own view that is also the source of our love for life. Where joyousness prevails, there also does the longing for unity and vice versa. But to admit that much is also to confess that our life in its depths is at one accord with it, and we could not struggle against it without choking the source of all our individual activities as well. Our thirst for life and our thirst for thought are stilled in the depths of the same stream. . . . In fact, scientific activities, the orientating as well as the practical, also are undertaken on behalf of man's euphoria – only by a detour from the "pleasure principle" by way of the "reality principle" and back to pleasure. . . . Thus it is for him at most a displacement which is involved in this; lack of euphoria would be the only

reason for our lack of interest in philosophy (or art). If someone objects (as Freud did) that this simply amounts to aggression, to the infantile way of putting questions, that may once again be a case of confusing "primitive" with "primary". The fact that something pursues us in some form or other from our very earliest childhood might lead only to the conclusion that there is a decline in the fullness of life. But further I have often found that such a renunciation following the philosophical or artistic enthusiasm of youth, betokens not only weariness but actually a kind of self stupefaction that results from devotion to absorbing activities of a scientific or practical kind. A sort of repression of one's self with the aid of resignation.[58]

Thus Freud denies himself a certain euphoria, the joy of limitless speculation. He denies devoting himself to the study of occultism which, if he were again at the start of his scientific career, he would make the entire object of his research, as he says in a letter.[59] Occultism could be called a pathology of speculation, speculation taken to its extreme, to its highest and furthest. It shows, written large, what occurs in normal speculation, in the strictest sense of the term.

THE DEMONIC WINGS OF SPECULATION

Which is the reason why, in the war between official science and the occultists, Freud will not take one side or the other. While the occultists seek to escape recognized physical and chemical laws, Freud hopes to discover broader natural laws that he is prepared to accept. He remains an unredeemed mechanist and materialist. If he devotes himself to the study of occult material, it is solely because he hopes to be able to definitively exclude from material reality the productions of human desire. Far from allying himself with the occultists, the analyst must exclude them from any possible common task and – this is a veritable duty, a prohibition that must not be ignored – he must not abandon (*es nicht verlassen soll*) his own field of research: the unconscious. The analyst must remain in his *Arbeitsgebiet* and not cross its limits. He must not fix his eyes [*guetter*] (*lauern*) elsewhere, look higher or further. To be on the lookout [*guetter*] is, if you remember the first sense of the word, *speculation*. If one refers to the Latin verb *speculor*, from which speculation is derived, one finds in the *Gaffiot*: *Speculor*: first meaning (paradoxically): to observe, to be on the lookout for [*guetter*], to watch closely, to spy.

Speculation, before being contemplation, is an act of espionage; the speculator's relation to the spy comes first. Before being an observer of phenomena, he is an observer in the sense of a spy, a scout, a messenger. The danger for psychoanalysis would be that, on the lookout to denounce possibly suspect occult phenomena, it no longer sees what is closer to it, neglecting what is near in favour of what is far away (*was ihm näher liegt zu übersehen*). Like Thales it risks falling into a well while contemplating the sky, for the greater joy of a Thracian servant. Since a certain dream – to which I will return – Freud has known that he has been ordered to keep his eyes shut, not to spy too much . . . not to open his eyes too wide, too far. That, among other temptations[60] he must resist that of speculation, and not try to derive greater pleasure from seeing too far, on pain of no longer being able to see what is near. On pain of being punished in the very place he has sinned: blinded to reality for having tried too hard to get pleasure by looking elsewhere, towards forbidden, blinding heights. In wanting to look too far, too high, Freud could well lose the analytical armour and equipment which are his protection against the omnipotence of his desires and the pleasure principle. He risks losing his lack of bias, his impartiality, his lack of expectations.

Thus he will no longer keep his eyes open for occult phenomena but will wait for them to impress themselves upon him. If they do, he will not avoid them (*aus dem Weg gehen*), any more than he would other phenomena but, for fear of being drawn to this fascinating research at the expense of his proper object, he will protect himself by means of a strict self-discipline. The real danger of an alliance with occultism lies elsewhere: if the factuality of a single occult phenomenon were confirmed the occultists would quickly claim victory, extending the belief accorded to a single observation to all other occult phenomena. Science would have been only a pretext for them to rise above it, a mere ladder to ascend to the heavens and fly away (*zu erheben*). The real danger is the risk of this limitless ascension. Worse than this, it would be a real calamity, because nothing would hold them back any longer (*sich aufhalten*); "heaven help us if they ever climbed to such a height!":[61] no more limits, nothing further to prevent their advance. Everything that has been repressed (religious belief) and surmounted (the belief in magic which goes back to the animist stage) would return at one fell swoop. Like a horde of demons. And what is more serious, they would appear as the liberators of the repressed, whom everyone is ready to welcome since they would allow the rediscovery of a source of lost pleasure and the possibility of economizing on the expenditure which the laborious work of psychoanalysis demands:

> There will be no scepticism from the surrounding spectators to make them hesitate, there will be no popular outcry to bring them to a halt. They will be hailed as liberators from the burden of intellectual bondage [*Denkzwang*], they will be joyfully acclaimed by all the credulity lying ready to hand since the infancy of the human race and the childhood of the individual.[62]

The danger is the collapse of critical thought and the need for determinism. The analytical project would not escape such a collapse of values (*Wertsturz*). Its laborious (*mühevoll*) work would be of absolutely no interest when faced by those who claim to possess the ultimate truths thanks to familiar spirits. Who would want to carry on working if they could enrich themselves by a single wave of a magic wand, by a successful piece of speculation?

> The methods of analytic technique will be abandoned if there is a hope of getting into direct touch with the operative spirits by means of occult procedures, just as habits of patient humdrum work are abandoned if there is a hope of growing rich at a single blow by means of a successful speculation.[63]

Freud does not take the path of speculative or occultist desire, he does not give into it because he knows only too well – he has a final example in his Uncle Joseph – that wanting to get out of working, to get rich quickly by just about honest means leads to prison – or at least to punishment of one kind or another.

He must therefore always work, always pay the cost [*que cela lui coûte*] so as to avoid it costing him even more, to avoid having to pay at some time or another. Because he has never wanted to resemble his uncle, the "simpleton" [*cette tête faible*], the "criminal" who made his father Jakob's hair turn grey overnight and for whom Freud feels a strange repulsion, as the dream in which he aspires to be a professor extraordinarius shows. In this dream he plays the role of a minister who is maltreating a Jewish colleague in the form of Uncle Joseph, simply because he is a Jew.[64] Perhaps it is also simply because he is a Jew that Freud has a strong (repressed) inclination for speculation and because of the double sense of the word which he plays upon (again like Comte who admires the spontaneous wisdom of a language whose polysemy is never accidental and knows instinctively that there can be no theoretical speculation that does not bring its author some fruitless interest or profit)[65] Speculation, when he allows himself to indulge in it, could not fail to remind him in one way or another (and not always very pleasantly) of his Uncle Joseph and his Jewish origins.

His relation to these origins is not without ambivalence. It is therefore easier to understand why, in reply to a letter from Jones which reproaches him for not having been able to keep quiet about his newfound belief in occultism, thus damaging the reputation of psychoanalysis, almost as if he had professed a belief in Bolshevism, Freud is able to write:

> when anyone adduces my fall into sin, just answer him calmly that conversion to telepathy is my private affair, like my Jewishness, my passion for smoking and many other things, and that the theme of telepathy is in essence alien to psychoanalysis.[66]

And Jones, quoting the letter in his *Life of Freud*, Volume 3, comments "there was nothing more to be said".

Perhaps he could have added that his taste for occultism, for speculation, the fact of his Jewishness, and his passion for smoking are three "facts" which are not wholly independent and which are all connected with origins which are just about accepted. Both accepted and rejected, since it is not coincidental either that, in the dream which follows the death of his father (at least as he relates it in the *Traumdeutung*) the poster on which he sees written "You are requested to close the eyes" or "You are requested to close an eye"[67] reminds him of the "Smoking is prohibited" notices that are found in station waiting rooms. Nor is it coincidental that at the moment when he can no longer smoke as he pleases – the moment it would have cost him dearly to do so – he says that he no longer has any desire to write.[68]

Thus to avoid the fate of the poor Jew, the simpleton, to prevent misfortune falling upon his head because he has tried to climb higher, and see further than he is allowed to, Freud accepts his fate – because destinies must be borne whatever they may be.

Thus he does not turn aside from psychoanalysis as a rigorous science, and he renounces, to a greater or lesser extent, that magical speculation which makes and unmakes fortunes in the twinkling of an eye. He remains forever trapped between his desire for a positive science and his desire to speculate, perpetually caught in the cross-fire, between two enemies. He accepts his fate, that is, tries to find compromise solutions between two opposing instincts, under threat of remaining paralysed at the frontier, unable to take a single step forward.

For example, as regards occultism, the compromise entails assimilating the enemy, the foreign body, by transforming those mysterious phenomena which are its object into psychoanalytic "facts", by showing they are only facts when interpreted in the light of psychoanalysis. By reducing, therefore the two instances of occult phenomena which he examines in the text of 1921 to cases of thought-transference,[69] selecting, paradoxically, those instances of predictions which are not fulfilled, he shows how, despite their failure, they have had a remarkable effect on the people concerned, who consider them extraordinary. In this they behave towards the prophets or clairvoyants concerned like the flock of the chief rabbi of Cracow. The latter, "zyeuting" as far as Lemberg "saw" the town's rabbi lying dead. It is later revealed that he is not dead, but despite the fact that the prophecy is belied by reality, the faithful continue to demonstrate an unconditional admiration for the rabbi and, concealing his deficiencies and his death wishes behind an appearance of logic, stress his long-sightedness: "the Kuck from Cracow to Lemberg was a magnificent one".[70] The words of the believer who actualizes the sublime look (*Kuck*) preserve intact the father's phallus despite reality and logic.

In *Jokes*, where Freud relates his Jewish tale, it is not insignificant that he tries to remove its specific Jewishness[71] from the story, despite its characteristic Yiddish jargon, by reducing it to a cynical critique of religion which attacks both miracle workers and miracles. He universalizes its significance by relating it to a verse of the Latin poet Propertius "*In magnus rebus voluisse sat est"* ("In all things important it is enough to have wished"). In the text of 1921 he alludes to the "rabbi's look" (*coup d'œil*) endowed with such powerful vision, in connection with the admiration professed by one of his patients for a famous fortune-teller, a great professor – despite the obvious errors he has made. What this story and other similar cases that are related prove is that, as regards prophecies, the essential thing is not the relation to future events but on the contrary, the relation to former, extremely powerful desires which only psychoanalysis can reveal. Thus only psychoanalysis can transform the ravings of the occultists into psychic facts. The "clairvoyant's" work consists of an activity designed to divert his or her own psychic forces by means of some anodyne occupation, so that receptive and permeable to the thoughts of the other person working upon him or her, he or she can truly become a medium. What psychoanalysis shows is that what is communicated is never an indifferent piece of knowledge but always an extremely strong desire; the content of the prediction always coincides with the realization of a suppressed desire.

Of all the other miracles occultism claims, Freud declares he has nothing to say. And, indeed, to have brought into the realm of analysis the single instance of thought – induction might seem insignificant in comparison with the great magical world (*Zauberwelt*) of the occult. And yet Freud has scarcely taken this first step in the direction of a world that is completely other when, as if gripped by an obsessional fear, he steps back and attempts to erase all traces of his advance. In effect, he weighs the serious consequences of this step into the beyond from the present perspective of psychoanalysis, were it to accept even the single idea of thought-transference.[72]

What lies behind this fear? Listen to the story of St Denis and you will be transfixed. After his head has been cut off St Denis is said to have lifted it up (*aufgehoben*) and walked on quite a distance carrying it under his arm as Jacques de Voragine's *The Golden Legend* [*Legenda aurea*] recounts.[73] Freud adds that what the custodian of St Denis used to remark remains true, that is that *"Dans des cas pareils, ce n'est que le premier pas qui coûte"*[74] ["in such cases, it's only the first step that is difficult/that costs"]. He quotes this in French, no doubt taking it from Mme du Deffand's letter to Horace Walpole (6 June 1797) in which she claims to have made this witticism in response to the Cardinal de Polignac, "a great talker, a great storyteller and exceedingly credulous" who recounted not only "what everyone knows" (that St Denis carried his head under his arm) but also that "having been martyrised on the Hill of Montmartre he carried his head all the way to Saint Denis, which is a distance of two full leagues".[75] It was at this point that she cried out: "Ah, I said to him, Monseigneur, I would have thought that in such a situation it is only the first step that is difficult" [*il n'y a que le premier pas qui coûte*] – a witty remark made apparently to ridicule such credulity but also to overcome the feeling of horror this tale of the martyr's death inspires. "It's a horror story", she says, and as if perfectly naturally, moves on to discuss the breaking-off of Walpole's cousin's marriage – no doubt her suitor was himself seized by a holy terror.... As for Freud, he adds after the story, and this time in German: "The rest is easy" [the rest follows of its own accord]: *Das Weitere findet sich*. A saying that can be linked to the following: "Once the devil is unleashed, he cannot be stopped." He writes this in a letter to Ferenczi (6 Sept 1924), in which he complains of the ravings of Rank, who also seems to him to have lost his head: "Once he has recovered his wits, then it will be the time to forgive his ravings and restore him to his place.... I dare not however believe it: experience proves that once the devil is unleashed, he cannot be stopped."[76]

The demon of speculation cannot be stopped. He is present in the very first step which is always already one step too many. He does not release you and can easily make you lose your head, and the rest.... A severed head, legs which seem to move by themselves, the devil, here we are right in the middle of a horror story and of the uncanny:

> Dismembered limbs, a severed head, a hand cut off at the wrist... feet which dance by themselves ... all these have something peculiarly uncanny about them especially when as in the last instance they prove capable of independent activity in addition.[77]

And Freud adds that this peculiar impression stems from its relation to the castration complex. It is hardly surprising that the text which immediately follows that of 1921 in the *GW* is *Medusa's Head* (1924). Thus if Freud draws back, having advanced a step in the direction of occultism, it is because, with this first step, he has already gone too far and the demon of speculation would not release him, were it not for the good double he also has within him, a guardian demon who, like that of Socrates, criticizes him and holds him back when he seems to be going forward. So that he never entirely sells his soul to the devil, even if sometimes, as in *Beyond the Pleasure Principle*, he advocates it: for fear of suffering the same fate as St Denis, because one is always punished in the place where one has sinned.[78] In fact a closer reading of the *Legenda aurea*[79] reveals that St Denis, who at the end of Freud's text makes his shattering appearance in an apotropaic guise, is not simply a saint destined like many others to be the object of numerous miracles. This martyr, and it is as such that he is exemplary for us, was a speculator *par excellence*. He is in fact Denys Areopagites. His forename means: he who flees with force. What? The world: by abnegation, to raise himself up to the contemplation of spiritual things. One of his surnames is the Theosophist: one who is educated in the divine sciences. The sages of Ancient Greece call him "The wing of heaven" because he is said to have taken his flight towards the heavens on the wing of spiritual intelligence. From Plato to Nietzsche, the metaphor of speculative knowledge taken to its extreme, furthest from the sensible world and from practice, from all that is earthly, too earthly, is that of a winged knowledge directed towards celestial, divine heights which the eye of the soul tries to contemplate. It is not coincidental that certain birds which are called *spectabilis* have a patch on their wing like a mirror which is referred to as a speculum. Thus in *Philosophy During the Tragic Age of the Greeks*, Nietzsche declares that Thales is more than a sage, he is the first philosopher worthy of the name because he was able, with a single beat of the wings of intuition, to hit upon the unity of Being, proceeding directly with his subtle and sound judgement to what is essential, in contrast to the scholar who advances heavily and carefully, step by step, without anticipating the results of his research:

> With Thales especially one can learn how philosophy has behaved at all times when she wanted to get beyond the hedges of experience to her magically attracting goal. On light supports she leaps in advance; hope and divination wing her feet. Calculating reason too clumsily pants after her and seeks better supports in its attempts to reach that alluring goal at which its divine companion has already arrived. One sees in imagination two wanderers by a wild forest stream which carries with it rolling stones; the one, light-footed, leaps over it using the stones and swinging himself upon them ever further and further, though they precipitously sink into the depths behind him. The other stands helpless there most of the time; he has first to build a pathway which will bear his heavy, weary step. Sometimes that cannot be done and then no god will help him across the stream. What therefore carries philosophical thinking so quickly to its goal? Does it distinguish itself from calculating and measuring thought only by its more rapid flight through large spaces? No, for a strange illogical power wings the foot of philosophical thinking and this power is fancy. Lifted by the latter, philosophical thinking leaps from possibility to possibility, and these for the time being are taken as certainties; and now and then even whilst on the wing it gets hold of certainties. An ingenious presentiment shows them to the flyer, demonstrable certainties are divined at a distance to be at this point. Especially powerful is the strength of fancy in the lightening-light seizing and illuminating of similarities.[80]

Freud denied himself the pleasure of reading Nietzsche, he says. The fact remains that at the end of *Beyond the Pleasure Principle*,[81] to console himself for having scarcely, after a thousand detours, advanced in his attempts to justify his speculative theory of the instincts, he also reintroduces the same metaphor of winged thought. He quotes a poet, Ruckert Makemem Des Hariri in his version of one of the Maqamat of al-Harir: "What we cannot reach by flying we must reach by limping. The Book tells us it is no sin to limp."[82]

To limp along, this is the *Ersatz* with which those who cannot, or will not, fly – for fear of being led too far or too high, to too much pleasure

[*Jouissance*] and the punishment which is its price – make do. Freud recalls in the *Traumdeutung*[83] that flying dreams are common but that, according to him, he has no personal experience of them. He has never allowed himself, even in dreams, to rise up into the skies with a real feeling of pleasure. He adds that, in general, these dreams can be interpreted as erection dreams, with the absence of the sensation of heaviness. He corroborates his interpretation by a reference to the winged phallus of the Ancients. Denys does not seem to have been afraid of losing either his phallus or his head (can we still distinguish between them?) – his particularly speculative head.

In the *Littré* under the entry for "Speculative" the only quotation given is: "He has a head for speculation."[84] A cool head concerned only with reasoning, without attachment to fact or practice; someone who invests everything in their head. Hardly surprising then that it ends up getting cut off, since it was always already lost in some form of celestial contemplation. Because, like Thales, Denys was a *speculator*. The first sense of this term is someone who observes the stars (the second being a sentry, the third someone who devotes himself to theoretical speculation). It was through his devotion to studying the heavenly bodies that Denys first acquired his knowledge of God. The *Golden Legend* recounts that he was an eminent philosopher called the Ionian and that he was renowned for his perfect knowledge of divine names.

The day of Christ's Passion, when an eclipse throws the whole world into darkness, Denys cries out: "This night which we wonder at like a novelty, reveals the coming of the true light which will illuminate the whole world." He is attributed with the miracle of having restored a blind man's sight and with the gift of prophecy. How true that only the first step is difficult.[85] From astral speculation he moves to philosophical speculation then to a belief in heaven; he becomes a miracle worker and is himself the object of several miracles.

In fact Domitianus, who treated the Christians with great cruelty, seizes him, has him thrown to the wild beasts, roasted alive and thrown into a furnace. He resists it all as if his attention was focused entirely on the divine light. (He says that Christ appears to him in an immense light.) He does not feel or see anything else. He is completely blinded by it. After this, he and his companions are subjected to new tortures. The heads of the three confessors of the Trinity are chopped off with axes in front of Mercury's idol. You know the rest of the story, except that Jacques de Voragine specifies that it is led by an angel and preceded by a heavenly light that Denys rises up, puts his head under his arm and carries on walking.[86] The rest does not follow of its own accord . . . without the aid of some divine or diabolical power it would not follow at all.

The story could have ended here, but the author, whom the devil will no longer release, sees fit to add one final anecdote. He relates that in 644 (Denys died in 96 under Domitianus) King Dagobert, who since childhood had held the saint in great veneration, used to take refuge in his church when he had occasion to fear his father Clotaire's anger. After his death, when evil angels wanted to drag him off to Hell, St Denis intervened on his behalf. The sudden apparition of King Dagobert's father threatening his son with castration (after such a story who could seriously suggest otherwise) and the son finding shelter at the side of a decapitated saint leaves us with a strange impression to say the least. Decapitated and still moving by himself, guided by the divine light, blinded by it. Castrated by it.

LOSING ONE'S HEAD

Medusa's Head, written a year after the text in which Freud tells the story of St Denis begins thus: "We have not often attempted to interpret individual mythological themes, but an interpretation suggests itself easily in the case of the horrifying decapitated head of Medusa."[87] Decapitate = castrate. The terror induced by Medusa's head is thus the fear of castration connected to the sight of something. "This situation is familiar to us from numerous cases. It occurs when the boy who previously did not believe in the threat sees an adult organ surrounded by hair, fundamentally his mother's." Such an interpretation suggests itself easily, it follows without saying, of its own accord. . . . Freud is so well aware of this that he does not publish the text, just as he does not publish the text mentioning Denys.[88] He considers them to be too "speculative". And doubtless he only allowed himself to write them as a form of amusement. The constraints of thought being what they are, it is both good for one, and enables one to bear such constraints better, if one lets oneself go from time to time and indulges in speculation, if one "plays at speculation". As if unwinding thread from a reel, since even if the speculative instinct is reined in, stopped, repressed, it continues to exist and to seek an occasion on which to return.[89] Just as in Plato's *Phaedrus* it is a good idea to take up writing, preferably in old age, as a means of amusement. *Medusa's Head* ends in effect with a disavowal of its seriousness: "In order *seriously* [my emphasis] to substantiate this interpretation it would be necessary to investigate the origin of this isolated symbol of horror in Greek mythology as well as parallels to it in other mythologies."[90]

A note in *The Infantile Genital Organisation*[91] stresses that it was Ferenczi who first considered such an interpretation and that Freud's contribution has merely been to add that the Medusa's head is in fact the mother's genital organ. Once again it is others, not Freud, who are speculating – in this case Ferenczi. Freud plays at speculation but does not risk publication, releasing as the results of psychoanalytical science what stems, more or less, from his personal fancy. It is for the same reason that he does not publish the text of 1921: for fear of being likened to the occultists. He warns against the latter while at the same time appropriating, swallowing, the foreign body of the phenomena they study, in order to turn it into the matter of psychoanalysis, its thing.

It is only in 1933, when the risks seem to him to have diminished for his child, when he has more confidence in its strength, that Freud allows himself in *Dreams and Occultism* to publish a text in which he is not afraid to display his "secret inclination towards the miraculous".[92] It is this inclination which urges him to consider favourably the production of occult phenomena and to doubt his own scepticism:

> When they first came into my range of vision more than ten years ago, I too felt a dread of a threat against our scientific *Weltanschauung*, which I feared was bound to give place to spiritualism or mysticism if portions of occultism were true. Today I think otherwise. In my opinion it shows no great confidence in science if one does not think it capable of assimilating and working over whatever may perhaps turn out to be true in the assertions of occultists.[93]

By publishing this text he also repays his debt to those who came to see him in the Harz (Abraham, Eitingon, Ferenczi, Rank, Sachs, Jones) and whom on that occasion, by means of a fine parapraxis, he did out of a promised third case of occulticism.

But in 1921 his hat is still too fragile for him to be able to risk seeing it shatter by coming to the aid of the occultists and abandoning himself to the pleasure of speculation. At this date, it remains an almost solitary pleasure. He does not publish this text and he does not even give it a title (which is why until now, I have only referred to it as the text of 1921). On its publication in 1941, it was the *GW* which felt obliged, or at least took it upon itself, to give the text the title *Psychoanalysis and Telepathy*. This text, which ends with the horrifying vision of the decapitation of St Denis is itself decapitated – "unheaded" as the *Standard Edition* says. With neither head nor tail,[94] since at the end the promised third case of occultism is missing, in place of which, in the form of a supplementary prosthesis, there is a story about graphology. *Psychoanalysis and Telepathy*: a text with neither head nor tail, the opposite of a good discourse according to Plato. And thus particularly *unheimlich*.

With neither head nor tail, unpublished by Freud precisely because of his fear of losing his own head and/or tail,[95] a symbolic equivalance Freud puts forward in texts he considers to be "more serious" than *Medusa's Head*. For example the *Taboo of Virginity* in which Judith's decapitation of Holofernes is interpreted as castration[96] and above all in *The Interpretation of Dreams*. In this text – in which Freud claims to found his observations solely on clinical experience, on his patients' or his own dreams – he gives two examples of castration dreams. One of a small child aged 3 years 5 months who is visibly put out by the return of his father and who wakes up one day disturbed, excited, asking "Why was daddy carrying his head on a plate last night?".[97] The other of a student who dreams he goes to the hairdresser to get his hair cut. A woman with a severe face – his mother – comes up to him and cuts off his head.[98]

Elsewhere in dream symbolism the head, the male genital organ and the hat are all equivalent. A text of 1916, *A Connection Between a Symbol and a Symptom*[99] corroborates this with evidence from the cases of certain obsessional neurotics. The latter are said to exhibit a greater degree of horror and indignation at the punishment of decapitation (*Strafe des Köpfens*) than they do for any other kind of death. This can be explained because they treat the fact of decapitation (*Geköpftwerden*) as a substitute for castration. The symbolic meaning of hat derives from that of head, since the hat can be considered a prolongation of the head but a head that is suitable for removal.

> When they [obsessional neurotics] are in the street they are constantly on the look out to see whether some acquaintance will greet them first by taking off his hat, or whether he seems to be waiting for their salutation: and they give up a number of their acquaintances after discovering that they no longer greet them or do not return their own salutation properly. It makes no difference to their behaviour when we tell them . . . that a salutation by taking off the hat has the meaning of an abasement before the person saluted.[100]

Given the parallels that Freud establishes it is curious that he did not interpret the dream in which his creation, psychoanalysis, is identified as a glass top hat he keeps on his knee as a castration dream. Read in this light, how can one fail to see that the correlation to the pleasure of inventing psychoanalysis, which erects him into a great man, is the threat of castration? As if he could not quite completely let himself be the hero his father Jakob was unable to be the day he, too, was involved in a story concerning a hat. The day when a Christian threw his fur hat into the mud and ordered him to get off the pavement and he did as he was told and got down into the gutter to pick it up. He bowed down, humiliated himself, castrated himself before the Christian and in the presence of his son Sigmund who, identifying himself with Hannibal, swore to revenge both himself and his father.[101]

To avoid being castrated in his turn, Freud in his dream castrates himself and makes sure that analytical speculation is an orginal speculation that never crosses a certain threshold, certain limits. A speculation that will never be "pure", allowing him the pure pleasure of thought without constraints, the pleasure of giving himself up to the omnipotence of this thought: except from time to time to "have fun" and to play as in *Beyond the Pleasure Principle* or again in his old age. At the end of *Constructions in Analysis* (1932), for example, Freud is in effect seduced by a series of analogies[102] which allow him to establish connections between apparently heterogeneous objects. These analogies, which are a means of invention and expansion for the mind and the imagination, are no less dangerous because this time they came from within the limits of experience. At the end of this text Freud lets himself go along this dangerous and fascinating path and, advancing effortlessly from analogy to analogy, indulges in a vast speculative construction. First, he makes an analogy between the constructions of patients suffering from delusions and constructions elaborated in the course of an analysis, an analogy between psychosis and neurosis, the latter itself then being made analogous to hallucination which is in turn analogous to *überdeutlich* memories. He moves from analogy to analogy, until, finally, he allows himself to summarize the aetiology of all illness in one simple and striking formula previously applied only to hysteria: the patients are "suffering from their own reminiscences".[103] Then, continuing his vast analogical journey, he links individual psychoses to the collective psychoses of humanity which have given rise to veritable delusions – delusions impervious to all logical criticism and contradictory to reality. The aim of this great speculative sweep is to guarantee the truth of the analytical construction which would be proved by the force of conviction it carries.

Thus in *Constructions in Analysis* the now aged Sigmund, having forgotten Brentano's warning, has let himself go down the slippery slope of analogy. He has given in to his need to establish reassuring connections, his need for unification. He who would always denounce this need in his rivals, putting forward his dualism as the sign of the scientific seriousness of his investigations and of his mental health. It all seems as if, at the end of his life, faced with the fragmentation which threatens him, with the death instincts, he feels the need to build a reassuring construction in which everything is unified and holds together perfectly. As if at the moment when everything is collapsing within him, he needs to feel that psychoanalysis is not a fragile glass hat and that the analytical abode at least, is still standing on a common ground.[104]

A pardonable weakness in an old man – a weakness which reveals even more clearly the discipline Freud has subjected himself to so as not to allow himself the perpetual pleasure of delusion. The singular function of psychoanalysis, its fate as a borderline-discipline, is therefore inseparable from Sigmund's fate, for the fact of having had, apart from an uncle who was excessively speculative, a Jewish father who was not made of the stuff of heroes.

The dream Sigmund has the night after his father's burial "You are requested to close the eyes"[105] further corroborates this "point of view". The way in which the dream is inserted into a letter written to Fließ (2 November 1896) is particularly interesting. Announcing the death of his father, Freud writes that he has been profoundly affected by it and feels completely distraught. In the next line he adds as if moving on to something completely different: "Apart from this I am working on cerebral palsies (*Die infantile Cerebrallähmung*): Pegasus put to the yoke!"[106] Finally he relates his dream, attributing a universal significance to it: the feeling of guilt that regularly surfaces in the living after a death.

Curiously, writing about cerebral palsies as if the circumstances were not there to explain why, Freud finds himself seemingly paralysed – things really are no longer moving along of their own accord. The death of his father seems to have cut off his arms and legs and he will continue, it seems, from this day on, to fear for his legs, to fear they will be broken by going forward over ground which is too slippery and yet so comfortable to walk on. In the famous Brucke dream,[107] wandering aimlessly towards an unknown destination where he has never set foot before, his legs feel so tired that he is afraid that they will not carry him to the end, and that he will never, therefore, conquer the coveted immortality that he abandons to his children. Freud is so afraid for his legs that we may well ask whether, as in the Jewish story recounted in *Jokes*,[108] he would actually have preferred to be always already crippled, never able to take a single step, because in this case "it is at least a fait accompli".[109] He would no longer have to fear feeling paralysed, a feeling, if we are to believe the *Traumdeutung*, that is so close to anxiety, when it occurs in a dream in which one wants to walk and yet is unable to move from one's place, thus betraying a conflictual state, a contradiction within the ego.

He emerges from this state of conflict in which his father's death leaves him by means of a compromise. He does not become paralysed (as in the Goethe dream) but clips his wings and henceforth will advance by limping. He will no longer be Pegasus (the winged horse that sprang from Medusa's blood when Perseus had cut off her head). His father's death cuts short all flight, all inspiration and aspiration towards ethereal heights. It brings him back to earth, transforms him into a beast of burden put to the yoke. It forces him to renounce the winged and effortless flight of speculation so as to dedicate himself to the hard labour of psychoanalysis, groping his way blindly forward among the deep shadows of the psyche like a mole.

HE MUST "SWALLOW IT" OR: TO SAVOUR OR SUFFER

So as to avoid losing his head and the rest, his father's death forces him always to have to pay. A poor Jew who has the audacity to aspire to become a great man, or at least to go further than his father, must not expect to see his way clear after making the first step. All his steps must be difficult, must be costly. And yet he would so much have liked not to pay!

The dream which serves as the main thread of Freud's argument in *On Dreams (Über den Traum)* is revealing in this respect: Freud is dominated by the thought that he will never enjoy, as others do, a free gift (the gift of speculation which his rivals or the poets possess). This thought is replaced in the dream by the thought "Will I never enjoy anything for which I don't have to pay the cost?" The dream-work plays upon the double sense of the German word *kosten* – to cost and to taste. A plate of spinach is served up at a *table d'hôte* to which Freud is invited: a dish which, as a child, he did not enjoy at all but nevertheless had to "swallow" [*déguster*] because his mother, by deeming there were other children who would be only too happy to eat spinach, persuaded him to taste it (*kosten*). Whatever the cost he already had to swallow it. "There are children who are only too pleased to have spinach"[110] as his mother used to say. In other words: if you don't eat your spinach I could easily replace you with another child, give my love to someone else. Because, don't delude yourself, you are not irreplaceable. "You are not loved just for the sake of your beautiful eyes", as you would like to be. The dream analysis reveals the bitterness Freud must have felt over the unconditional love that is refused him, and the wish he forms for a distinterested love which would not cost him anything. This is the idea that is concealed behind the allusion to the spinach and a phrase from the dream in which someone says he has always had such beautiful eyes; that "people have always done everything for you for love: you have always had everything without paying for it".[111] Freud comments "The truth is, of course, the contrary. I have always paid dearly for whatever advantage I have had from other people."[112] In contrast to what usually happened, on the eve of the dream one of his friends had offered him a free car ride. Normally he has hardly got into a taxi, taken his place, when, eyes fixed on the meter, he is already in debt. Like at the *table d'hôte* where he feels himself growing greedy and egotistical by thinking of the debt which is growing too quickly and where he is afraid of not getting his money's worth. He has hardly taken his place in the world before he finds himself indebted to his parents who put him back in his place and threaten him with losing it if he doesn't pay back his debts, if he thinks he can live without any effort, that he is welcomed into the bosom of the family simply because of his beautiful eyes.

He associates this dream with the following lines from Goethe which he takes up once more in *Civilisation and its Discontents*: "Ihr führt uns ins Leben hinein – Ihr lasst den Armen schuldig werden" ("You lead us into life – you make the poor man fall into debt").[113] It is in the context of this dream that he recounts the dream about the glass hat which he interprets as the discovery of psychoanalysis which could make him rich and independent, enabling him to "succeed in everything in this world" and, perhaps, finally, to pay off his debts towards his parents. The chain of associations in the dream (in which the free car ride of the previous evening reminds him of other, more expensive rides with a member of his family on whom, shortly before the dream, he has spent a large sum of money) forces Freud to admit that he regrets this expense. What he would like, therefore, is a love which does not entail any expenditure. A disinterested love: he wants to be loved for his beautiful eyes alone. Which seems, in fact, to have been Goethe's lot rather than his own. Goethe, the happy child favoured by fortune: fate keeps him alive when he is taken for dead on entering the world and at the same time supplants his brother, leaving him with his mother's undivided love.

Freud concludes from this in his text about Goethe's *Dichtung und Wahrheit* that "if a man has been his mother's undisputed darling he retains throughout life the triumphant feeling, the confidence in success, which not seldom brings actual success along with it".[114]

We know that at the end of his secondary school studies (when he craved knowledge but was afraid of being dominated by the abstract speculations to which he felt so strongly inclined),[115] it was his reading of Goethe which influenced him to "bravely step back" from such speculations and enrol in the faculty of medicine. More precisely, he switched to science after having heard Dr Carl Bruel read "Goethe's beautiful essay on Nature"[116] at a public lecture at the end of his secondary school studies.

In this essay, Goethe portrays nature as a generous mother granting her favourite children the privilege of exploring her secrets. Very soon, however, Freud's curiosity turns to the secrets of human nature, a compromise between his taste for philosophical speculation and the constraints of the strict scientific discipline he imposes upon himself. As if he thought he could compete more successfully with Goethe in the psychic sphere. In the *Goethe* dream, Goethe treats Freud and his friend as if they are mad but the dream thoughts say "naturally, it's he (my friend Fließ) who is the crazy fool and it's you (the critics) who are the men of genius and know better, surely it can't by any chance be the reverse?". As if he feared that the mother, that nature did not love him enough to reveal her secrets to him without it costing him anything. Because precisely what his mother reveals to him in the *Dreams of the Three Fates*, what she displays before him *ad oculos*, as she kneads the meat balls, the *Knödel*, in her hands, is his necessary mortality. A lesson which, in *The Theme of the Three Caskets*, Freud translates into the necessity for all men to repay their debt to Nature by returning to her the life she has lent them. The mother could only agree to reveal her secrets, without it resulting in the threat of death for her and her son, to someone who had surmounted the fear of incest. Because knowing the secrets of Mother Nature implies, by discovering, by uncovering her, committing incest with her, Freud renounces the natural sciences and, as the father has ordered, prefers to "shut his eyes" on the Mother. And when, at a late stage in his work, he attempts to resolve the enigma of women, he repeatedly indulges in pure speculation and at the very same time, more polemically and dogmatically than ever, he opposes speculation and observation.[117] While, always elsewhere, he recognizes that in accordance with the strictest positivism, there can be no observation without a minimum of speculation.[118]

Which is why, when he claims to divulge the secret of the feminine enigma, the much-vaunted "penis envy" that he proposes as its solution serves only to cover up women's sex and sexuality[119] with a thick veil. Like children who invent "false theories" about sex which cover up an earlier knowledge closer to the truth, Freud seems to have assigned his thought to the single task of warding off a terrible threat to the masculine sex and, guided by an *idée fixe*, to have imposed penis envy as a cheering solution for men.[120]

Freud, we know, fancied himself to be the gynaecologist of the psyche. He wanted to be the saviour of women on the single condition that they, unlike Turkish women, do not only let him feel their pulse through a hole in a partition, but let him look into their depths, through his *Speculum*.[121]

But this *Speculum*, has it not been too blurred by a certain number of fantastical, masculine, aberrations? Aberrations that are too masculine to allow the gynaecologist to really make his observations without any bias? Can this *Speculum* have allowed Freud, despite his denials, to indulge in anything other than pure speculation? Is it enough for women to give them credit in order to be saved? Putting their money on such speculations could perhaps cost women rather more than the first step.

Translated by Sarah Wykes

NOTES

All notes are the author's except when indicated otherwise by TN (translator's note).

1 TN. My parentheses.
2 TN. *Psychoanalysis and Telepathy* (1921) in *The Standard Edition of the Complete Psychological Works of Sigmund Freud* (hereafter *SE*), ed. J. Strachey (Hogarth Press, 1953–74), 18, p. 180
3 TN. In English in the original text.
4 He relates one of these nightmares in *Dreams and Telepathy* (1922) [*SE* 18, pp. 195–220] as an example of a "telepathic" dream later contradicted by reality.

> For example I once dreamt during the war that one of my sons then serving at the front had been killed. This was not directly stated in the dream, but was expressed in an unmistakeable manner, by means of . . . well-known death symbolism. . . . My son however, whom the dream pronounced to be dead, came home from the war unscathed.
>
> [*SE* 18, pp. 197–8]

5 Cf. on this subject my *L'Enfance de l'Art*, (Payot, 1970 and Galilée, 1986, tr. as *The Childhood of Art*, Columbia Press, 1988) and *Pourquoi rit-on? Freud et le Mot de l'Esprit* (Galilée, 1987).
6 Cf. Freud: *On the History of the Psycho-analytic Movement* [*SE* 14, pp. 1–66]: "No one need be surprised at the subjective character of the contribution I propose to make here to the history of the psychoanalytical movement, nor need anyone wonder at the part I play in it. For psycho-analysis is my creation."
7 Cf. *Über den Traum*, *On Dreams* (1901) [*SE* 5, pp. 629–86]. Freud's associations are as follows: "If you go hat in hand, you can cross the whole land" [p. 652 – a German proverb]. Then he thinks of an "incandescent gas Mantle" [a bec Auer] and of his compatriot Dr Auer de Welsbach:

> I soon saw that I should like to make a discovery which would make me as rich and independent as my fellow countryman Dr Auer von Welsbach was made by his and that I should like to travel instead of stopping in Vienna. In the dream I was travelling with my discovery, the hat in the shape of a glass cylinder – a discovery which, it is true, was not as yet of any great practical use.
>
> [p. 652]

8 Regarding this dream in which his ambition is to be a *professor extraordinarius*, Freud writes:

What, then, could have been the origin of the ambitiousness which produced the dream in me? At that point I recalled an anecdote I had often repeated in my childhood. At the time of my birth an old peasant woman had prophesied to my proud mother that with her first born child she had brought a great man into the world. Prophecies of this kind must be very common: there are so many mothers filled with happy expectations and so many old peasant women and others of the kind who make up for the loss of their power to control things in the present world by concentrating it on the future.

[*SE* 4, p. 192]

9 Cf. especially *On Narcissism: An Introduction* (1914) [*SE* 14] and *The Freud Journal of Lou Andreas Salomé*, entry for 11/12/1912 [tr. S. A. Leavy, Hogarth, 1965].

10 TN. *Psychoanalysis and Telepathy* [*SE* 18, p. 178].

11 "The future prospects of psycho-analytical therapy" (1910) [*SE* 11, p. 146].

12 On this Aristotelian gesture of Freud see my *Quatre romans analytiques* (Galilée, 1974, tr. as *Freud and Fiction*, Polity Press, 1990).

13 TN. *Psychoanalysis and Telepathy* [SE 18, p. 178].

14 Cf. *The Uncanny* [*SE* 17].

15 TN. *Dreams and Occultism* (1933) [*SE* 22, p. 31].

16 TN. *Psychoanalysis and Telepathy* [*SE*, 18 p. 178].

17 TN. ibid., p. 179.

18 Cf. Freud's *Letter to Silberstein*, 8/11/1874. He writes that, a doctor and an atheist empiricist, he has signed up for two philosophy courses and is reading Feuerbach. In his letter of 11/4/1875 he states that he is undecided whether to opt for natural sciences or philosophy and for the moment has postponed his decision. Around 9 September 1875, he seems to undergo a change of mind. He writes that the works of English scientists have favourably disposed him towards them and adds "I am more suspicious than ever of philosophy" [TN. My translation from Walter Boelich (ed.), *Sigmund Freud, Jugendbriefe an Eduard Silberstein, 1871–1881* (S. Fischer Verlag, 1989). Freud's letters to Silberstein are unavailable in English]. Cf. also Freud's *Letter to Flieβ*, 2/4/1896: "As a young man my only longing was for philosophical knowledge, and now that I am changing over from medicine to psychology I am in the process of fulfilling this wish. I became a therapist against my will" (Sigmund Freud, *Letters of Sigmund Freud 1873–1939*, ed. E. L. Freud, tr. T. and J. Stern (Hogarth, 1961), p. 241).

19 Cf. *Letter to Silberstein*, 15/3/1876 [TN. My translation].

20 Ibid.

21 Cf. *Letter to Putnam*, 8/7/1915. After telling him he could well bear a grudge against God for not having endowed him with a greater intellect he adds: "I think I ought to tell you that I have always been dissatisfied with my intellectual endowment" [Freud, *Letters*, p. 451].

22 Cf. my *Aberrations, de devenir-femme d'Auguste Comte* (Flammarion-Aubier, 1978).

23 Cf. *Letter to Werner Achelis*, 30/1/1927:

Other defects in my nature have certainly distressed me and made me feel humble; with metaphysics it is different – I not only have no talent for it but no respect for it either. In secret – one cannot say such things aloud – I believe that one day metaphysics will be condemned as a *nuisance* [in English in the letter], as an abuse of thinking, as a survival from the period of the religious

Weltanschauung. I know well to what extent this way of thinking estranges me from German cultural life [he would be separated from it by an unbridgeable gulf].... However this may be, it is certainly simpler to orientate oneself in "this world" of facts than in the "other world" of philosophy.

[Freud, *Letters*, pp. 375–6]

24 Cf. *Letter to Marie Bonaparte*, 12/11/1938: "A certain aversion to my subjective tendency of granting everything too free a rein has always held me back [from acquainting people with his latest ideas]". [Freud, *Letters*, p. 451].

25 "Philosophical theories and systems have been the work of a small number of men of strong individuality. In no other science does the personality of the scientific worker play anything like so large a part as in philosophy", *The Claims of Psycho-analysis to Scientific Interest*, (1913) [*SE* 13, pp. 163–90, p. 179].

26 For Comte the speculative process of the brain functions like a mirror. The ultimate aim of speculation is to achieve a faithful representation of the outside world, to "transform the human brain into an exact mirror of the external order" (*Système de Philosophie Positive II*, pp. 381–3 [TN. My translation]. The aim of positive science is to see the true state of things without impediments and to reproduce this vision in theory. Aberrations are the result of a poor, fantastical vision, a vision that is more or less a hallucination, a consequence of the poor quality of the mirror. The speculative aberration is the result of an incorrect, inexact vision of the world, a vision refracted through a deforming mirror, and clouded by man's illusions, projections and phantasms which obstruct the direct observation of natural phenomena. Instead of seeing things as they are, man therefore sees only what he is inclined to see. The brain is not an exact mirror from the onset. The whole history of human thought is a long process of progressive transformation towards the elimination of such illusions and projections in order, finally, to produce a faithful representation of the real.

Normality can only be achieved by the subordination of the internal to the external, the interior to the exterior, the subject to the object. Madness is always the excessive and illegitimate predominance of the subjective and of ideality. If the mental mirror is unrepresentative, it is because a whole collection of subjective phenomena come between it and the world. Only the predominance of external spectacle over internal contemplation can, by its regulatory effect on the subject, put an end to pathological wanderings and ravings: "Successful speculation always depends on a noble submission of subjective inspiration to objective impressions.... If ideality is no longer subordinated to reality, it pushes us directly into madness by developing an excess ... of subjectivity" (Comte, *Système III*, pp. 225–6) [TN. My translation].

27 Cf. Freud's *Letter to Groddeck*, 5/6/1917. Freud reproaches him for having failed to master the ambition which makes him aspire to originality and priority and adds:

a man with unbridled ambition is bound at some time to break away and, to the loss of science and of his own development, to become a crank.... Why do you plunge from your excellent vantage point into mysticism?... and commit yourself to philosophical theories that are not called for?

[Freud, *Letters*, p. 324]

In *On the History of the Psycho-analytic Movement*, he says that he decided to forego the pleasure reading philosophy, notably Nietzsche, gave him in order to remain free of all influences external to the elaboration of the psychoanalytical project itself: "I had therefore to be prepared ... to forego all claims to priority in the many instances in which laborious psycho-analytic investigation can merely confirm the truths which the philosopher recognised by intuition" [*SE* 14, p. 16].

28 Cf. *Letter to Lou Andreas Salomé*, 13/7/1917.

29 Cf. ibid. In this slow and progressive "advance" Freud is again drawing on the positivist tradition but also, among others, on the Idéologue Destutt de Tracy (whose "positivist advance" Comte recognizes even if he did stop short on such a promising path). In his Introduction to *Elemens* [*sic*] *d'Idéologie* he writes that

The human mind always moves forward step by step, its progress is gradual, so that no truth is more difficult to grasp than any other when one understands what comes before it.... Thus there is no science in itself that is more obscure than any other, everything depends on advancing in an orderly fashion to avoid taking strides that are too great.

[TN. My translation]

Comte uses the same metaphors when he speaks of a "fundamental gradual advance", of an indispensable "march" towards universal education [TN. My translation]. But this is not merely a metaphor. The smooth running [*la bonne marche*] of the mind or, conversely, its wandering, depends essentially on the body. The whole of Comte's political stance in favour of housing for the proletariat is aimed at tying them down to a dwelling place, a shack, a land, a patria – so as to remove them from their state of "camping", of nomadism, of vagrancy. Because the absence of a fixed home prevents both body and mind from settling down, from forming attachments, and without attachments there can be no development of the desire for a durable order. When the body wanders and roves around, the mind strays, in thrall to the worst aberrations. As for Comte himself, he tried to guard against the dangers inherent in any unstable and shifting position for fear of losing his equilibrium.

30 Cf. *Letter to Groddeck*, 5/6/1917: "I am afraid that you too are a philosopher and have the monistic tendency to disparage all beautiful differences of nature in favour of tempting unity. But does this help to eliminate the differences?" [Freud, *Letters*, p. 324].

31 Cf. *Letter to Putnam*, 8/7/1915:

For the time being psycho-analysis is incompatible with various *Weltanschauungen*. But has it yet spoken its last word? For my part I have never been concerned with any comprehensive analysis, but invariably with certainty alone. And it is worth sacrificing everything for the latter.

[Freud, *Letters*, p. 315]

32 Cf. *Letter to Werner Achelis*, 30/1/1927.

33 Nietzsche also compares himself to a mole in *Daybreak* (preface, paragraph 1), because his work is that of a "subterranean" being who bores, excavates and mines in the depths, deprived of light and air.

34 TN. *SE* 7, p. 271.

35 Cf. *Remarks on the Theory and Practice of Dream Interpretation* [*SE* 19].

36 TN. *SE* 14, p. 117.

37 Cf. *On Narcissism: An Introduction*:

the activity of the mind which has taken over the function of conscience has also placed itself at the service of internal research, which furnishes philosophy with the material for its intellectual operations. This may have some bearing on the characteristic tendency of paranoics to construct speculative systems.

[*SE* 14, p. 96]

Freud specifies that if he neglected the part auto-observation – in the sense of delusions of paranoid observation – plays in dream formation, a variable contribution, it is probably because: "it does not play any great part in my own dreams; in persons who are gifted philosophically and accustomed to introspection it may become very evident." [ibid.].

In *Totem and Taboo*, Freud says that paranoid delusion is a deformed philosophical system.

Cf. the Preface to Reik's *Ritual: Psycho-Analytic Studies* [*SE* 17, p. 261]: "the delusions of paranoics [*sic*] have an unpalatable external similarity and internal kinship to the systems of our philosophers".

38 TN. *On Narcissism, SE* 14, pp. 77–9.

39 Cf. for example, *On the History of the Psycho-analytic Movement* [*SE* 14] where he shows the discovery of the importance of infantile sexuality has only been made possible by the "method of analysis" [p. 18] of tracing neurotic symptoms back to their ultimate sources. As for Jung, he arrived at different results but this is because he begins by elaborating

a theoretical conception of the nature of the sexual instinct and then seeks to explain the life of children on that basis. A conception of this kind is bound to be selected arbitrarily or in accordance with irrelevant considerations. . . . It is true that the analytic method, too, leads to certain ultimate difficulties and obscurities in regard to sexuality. . . . But these problems cannot be got rid of by speculation, they must await solution through other observations or through observations in other fields.

[p. 19]

In the same text he notes what Jung has in common with Adler – a man of "unusual ability, combined with a particularly speculative disposition": both advance certain considerations of a high order and try to look at things *sub specie aeternitatis*. Both – and nothing could be more dangerous – want to introduce personal choice into scientific matters. Adler proclaims the right of the individual personality to creatively shape the material science provides and Jung insists on youth's right to liberate itself from the chains that tyrannical Old Age, locked in its rigid concepts, wishes to impose upon it. Such discretion can only disqualify psycho-analysis's claims to be a science. Adler, whose theory has, from the onset, been a system, has only been able to maintain this system by completely disregarding psychoanalytic observation and technique. Observation has for him merely been a spring-board to climb to new heights. By seriously deviating from reality as revealed by observation, he has rendered himself guilty of the greatest possible mental confusion, confusing in his theory of masculine protest the biological, social and psychological senses of the words "masculine" and "feminine". Freud ends his piece by wishing "an agreeable upward journey" to those who have been unable to bear their sojourn in the "underworld of psycho-analysis" [p. 66].

Cf. also Freud's *Letters to Romain Rolland* of 20/7/1929 and 19/1/1930, in which, having recalled in the first letter that for him "mysticism is just as closed a book as music" [Freud, *Letters*, p. 389], he adds in the second that until now Hindu mysticism has been quite foreign to him due to "an uncertain blending of Hellenic love of proportion, [σωφροσύνη] Jewish sobriety and philistine timidity" and that "it isn't easy to pass beyond the limits of one's nature". Conversely, he says that "C. G. Jung is a bit of a mystic himself and hasn't belonged to us for years" [Freud, *Letters*, p. 392].

40 Cf. *Letter to Lou Salomé*, 22/11/1917 and 22/5/1931 [in *Sigmund Freud and Lou Andreas Salomé – Letters*, ed. E. Pfeiffer (London, 1963)].

41 Cf. *Letter to Lou Salomé*, 13/7/1917.

42 *Letter to Lou Salomé* 13/7/1917, 22/11/1917 and 2/4/1919.

43 *Letter to Lou Salomé* 30/7/1915.
44 *Letter to Lou Salomé* 25/5/1916.
45 *Letter to Lou Salomé* 30/7/1915, [*Freud and Salomé – Letters*, p. 45].
46 *Letter to Lou Salomé* 23/3/1930.
47 *Letter from Lou Salomé to Freud*, 20/6/1918.
48 Cf. Salomé, *The Freud Journal*, entry for 30/10/1912 where she makes this remark after Freud, with reference to neuroses, had used the expressions "my latest formulation" [p. 37].

   Cf. also Freud's *Letter to Lou Salomé* 13/5/1926 "We have not yet earned the right to dogmatic rigidity and . . . must be ready to till the vineyard again and again", *Freud and Salomé – Letters*, p. 163].
49 Cf. Lou Salomé's *Journal* of 5/3/1913: this is said in protest against Adler's "organ-feeling" [Salomé, *The Freud Journal*, p. 111].
50 TN. Freud, *Letters*, p. 180.
51 TN. ibid.
52 *Letter from Lou Salomé to Freud*, 14/7/1929. This is said in disapproval of Thomas Mann's portrait of Freud in which Mann describes him as a thinker who is secretly and naturally inclined to mysticism and all things that are obscure and profound. Above all, Mann admires Freud's resolute and open opposition, despite his own inclination, to everything which is outdated and his devotion to progress:

   He does not realise that, as you yourself have described it, you originally not only had quite different plans than to pursue the "obscurities", but also that your preoccupation with such things was often enough thoroughly distasteful to you, and that nothing was more truly abhorrent to you than the thought that your investigations might be grist to the mill of those who are mystically inclined.

   [*Freud and Salomé – Letters*, p. 180]

53 *Letter to Lou Salomé*, 7/10/1917.
54 *Letter from Lou Salomé to Freud*, 15/10/1919 [*Freud and Salomé – Letters*, p. 64].
55 Sigmund Freud, *Gesammelte Werke* (*GW*), 18 vols (vols 1–17: London, 1940–52: vol. 18: Frankfurt am Main, 1968), 16, p. 69.
56 TN. *SE* 23, p. 225.
57 TN. *SE* 14, p. 22.
58 Lou Salomé's *Journal*, 23/2/1913; *Visit to Freud, Freud and Philosophy*.
59 Cf. *Letter to Carrington*, 24/7/1921.
60 In a *Letter to Eitingon*, 4/2/1921, who had sent him some books on occultism, Freud writes "the thought of this bitter apple make me wince, but there is no way of avoiding *biting* it" [TN. My translation].
61 TN. *Psychoanalysis and Telepathy*, *SE* 18, p. 180.
62 TN. ibid.
63 TN. ibid.
64 *The Interpretation of Dreams* [*SE* 4, p. 138]:

   There was an unhappy story attached to him. Once – more than thirty years ago – in his eagerness to make money, he allowed himself to be involved in a transaction of a kind that is severely punished by the law, and he was in fact punished for it. My father, whose hair turned grey from grief in a few days, used always to say that Uncle Josef was not a bad man but only a simpleton: those were his words.

   Cf. Also his *Letter to Martha*, 10/2/1886 [Freud, *Letters*, pp. 222–3]:

I have never told you about my uncle in Breslav because I never think of him. I have seen him three times in my life, on each occasion for a quarter of an hour. He is a younger brother of my father, a rather ordinary man, a merchant, and the story of his family is very sad. Of the four children only one is normal and married in Poland. One son is a hydrocephalic and feeble-minded; another, who as a young man showed some promise, went insane at the age of 19, and a daughter went the same way when she was 20-odd. I had so completely forgotten this uncle that I have always thought of my family as free of any hereditary taint. . . . Fortunately, of us seven brothers and sisters there are very symptoms of this kind to report except that we, Rosa and I, (I don't count Emanuel), have a nicely developed tendency towards neurasthenia.

65 Cf. for example, Comte's *Letter to Valat* in which he points out his different motives for writing. After he has commented on the first three he says "I was forgetting a fourth which is as yet a speculation because I am terribly self-interested. I feel that the scientific reputation I could acquire would lend more weight, more value, more useful influence to my political sermons" [TN. My translation]. More generally, Comte shows that there are always practical and affective motives behind speculative research. It is only at the end of a long process of evolution, in the positive age, that disinterested speculative research becomes possible. But in my *Aberrations, le devenir-femme d'Auguste Comte*, I have shown how Comte's positive system – which is presented as the culmi-nation of the entire development of human thought, human reason finally having reached maturity – is in fact motivated by the most regressive fetishistic and narcissistic impulses; motives that are the source of his entire speculation. For Comte, however, this would not invalidate the truth of his system in the least, since even if the speculative faculties need to be stimulated by the affective and practical faculties in order to be shaken from their torpor, they possess a force and energy of their own. Theory begins with practice or feelings but it is not derived from them. Similarly, in *On the Interest of Psycho-Analysis* [*SE* 13], Freud recognizes that

psycho-analysis can indicate the subjective and individual motives behind philo-sophical theories which have ostensibly sprung from impartial logical work, and can draw a critic's attention to the weak spots in the system . . . however . . . the fact that a theory is psychologically determined does not in the least invalidate its scientific truth.

[p. 179]

66 TN. *Letter to Jones*, 7/3/1926, quoted in E. Jones, *Sigmund Freud – Life and Work*, Vol 3 (Basic Books, 1957), pp. 423–4.

67 TN. *SE* 4, p. 317.

68 Cf. *Letter to Arnold Zweig*, 2/5/1935: "Since I can no longer smoke freely, I no longer want to write – or perhaps I am just using this pretext to veil the unproductiveness of old age" [Freud, *Letters*, p. 421].

69 The third case will have formed the subject of a lapse which reveals Freud's resistance to occultism: he forgets to take the material with him and uses another example instead.

70 TN. *Jokes*, *SE* 8, p 63.

71 Cf. on this subject my *Pourquoi rit-on?*

72 Cf. *The Future of an illusion* (*SE* 22), "If by this means [i.e., looking around for evidence] we could succeed in clearing even a single portion of the religious system from doubt, the whole of it would gain enormously in credibility" [p. 27].

Cf. also *Dreams and Occultism* in *New Introductory Lectures on Psycho-*

analysis XXX, [SE 22]:

all the signs, miracles, prophecies and apparitions... which we thought had long since been disposed of as the offspring of unbridled imagination.... If we accept the truth of what, according to the occultist's information, still occurs today, we must also believe in the authenticity of the reports which have come down to us from ancient times. And we must then reflect that the tradition and sacred books of all peoples are brimful of similar marvellous tales and that the religious base their claim to credibility on precisely such miraculous events and find proof in them of the superhuman powers. That being so, it will be hard for us to avoid a suspicion that the interest in occultism is in fact a religious one and that one of the secret motives of the occultist movement is to come to the help of religion, threatened as it is by the advance of scientific thought. And with the discovery of this motive our distrust must increase and our disinclination to embark on the examination of these supposedly occult phenomena.

[p. 34]

73 TN. Jacques de Voragine, *La Légende dorée* (Garnier Flammarion, 1967), vols 1–2. Cf. *Psychoanalysis and Telepathy, SE* 18, p. 193.
74 TN. ibid.
75 TN. My translation.
76 TN. My translation.
77 TN. Cf *The Uncanny* [*SE* 17, p. 244].
78 "Because you sought to misuse your organ of sight for evil sensual pleasures it is fitting that you should not see anything at all anymore", *The Psycho-analytic View of Psychogenic Disturbance of Vision* [*SE* 11, pp. 209–18, p. 217].
79 Cf. Voragine, *La Légende dorée*, vol. 2, p. 278
80 TN. Cf. Nietzsche, *Philosophy During the Tragic Age of the Greeks* (1873), tr. M. Mugge, ed. O'Leavy (T. N. Foulis, 1911), pp. 87–88.
81 On Freudian speculation in *Beyond the Pleasure Principle* [*SE* 18], I refer the reader of course to Jacques Derrida's "To speculate – on 'Freud' ", in *The Post Card – From Socrates to Freud and Beyond*, tr. Alan Bass (University of Chicago Press, 1987) and also my *Freud and Empedocles* in *Quatre Romans analytiques* (Galilée, 1974) and to Rodolphe Gashe's *La Sorcière métapsychologique* in *Diagraphe 3*, Galilée.
82 TN. *Beyond the Pleasure Principle, SE* 18, p. 64 note.
83 TN. *The Interpretation of Dreams, SE* 4, p. 271.
84 TN. "C'est une tête Spéculative."
85 Voragine, *La Légende dorée*, vol. 2, p. 275. Freud says to Jones, who had asked him where such beliefs in occult phenomena would end (if one were to believe in mental processes floating in the air, why not believe in angels?), thus putting an end to their discussion: "Quite so (one could believe in) even *der liebe Gott*" (quoted by Jones in *Sigmund Freud – Life and Work*, vol. 3, p. 408).
86 Voragine, *La Légende dorée*, vol. 2, p. 277.
87 TN. *Medusa's Head, SE* 18, p. 273.
88 The first was published in 1940 in the *GW*, the second in 1941.
89 From the very beginning, when life takes us under its strict discipline, a resistance starts within us against the relentlessness and monotony of the laws of thought and against the demands of reality-testing. Reason becomes the enemy which withholds from us so many possibilities of pleasure. We discover how much pleasure it gives us to withdraw from it, temporarily at least, and to surrender to the allurements of nonsense. Schoolboys delight in the twisting of words, make fun of their own activities, even earnest-minded men enjoy a joke. More serious hostility to "Reason and Science, the highest strength possessed

by man" (Goethe, *Faust*, part I, scene 4) awaits its opportunity; it hastens to prefer the miracle-doctor or the practitioner of nature-cures to the "qualified" physician, it is favourable to the assertions of occultism so long as those alleged facts can be taken as breaches of laws and rules; it lulls criticism to sleep, falsifies perceptions and enforces confirmations and agreements which cannot be justified. If this human tendency is taken into account, there is every reason to discount much of the information put forward in occultist literature.

[Freud, *Dreams and Occultism* in *New Introductory Lectures*, pp. 33–4]

90 TN. *Medusa's Head*, SE 18, p. 273.
91 *SE* 19, p. 144.
92 TN. *SE* 22, p. 53.
93 TN. ibid., p. 55.
94 TN. "Sans tête ni queue."
95 Lou Salomé in her *Journal* from 21 August to 5 September 1913 (pp. 166–7) uses the same equivalence with references to Tausk:

Tausk, endowed by nature with a philosophical head, has so to speak, cut it off instead of using it, at least on holidays. When he engages in synthetic thought he promptly "thinks it over" with a bad conscience, since basically he always thinks of his *own* practical analysis alone – *never* synthetically; hence his position with regard to psycho-analysis is at once too uncritical and (through resistance) excessively critical. . . . As if by a thought transference he will always be busy with the same thing as Freud, never taking one step aside to make room for himself. . . . A certain gap in creativity is filled by identification with the other (sonship) which constantly begets the illusion of having attained the anticipated position.

96 Cf. my *Judith* in *Quatre Romans analytiques*.
97 TN. *The Interpretation of Dreams*, SE 4, p. 366.
98 TN. ibid., p. 367.
99 *GW* 10 [*SE* 14].
100 TN. *SE* 14, p. 340.
101 *The Interpretation of Dreams*, SE 4, p. 197.
102 On analogy and its seductions, cf. one of Freud's favourite texts, *Analysis Terminable and Interminable* [*SE* 23] in which he allows himself to be seduced by an analogy between Eros and Love, the death instinct and hate as they are poetically represented by Empedocles: "This made me all the more pleased when not long ago I came upon this theory of mine in the writings of one of the great thinkers of ancient Greece" [pp. 244–5].
103 TN. *SE* 23, p. 268.
104 Cf. S. Kofman, *Un Métier impossible: Lecture de "Constructions en analyse"*, final chapter (Galilée, 1983).
105 TN. *SE* 4, p. 317.
106 TN. Freud, *Letters*.
107 TN. *The Interpretation of Dreams*, SE 4.
108 The story concerns the fiancée who has one leg shorter than the other and limps. The match-maker tries to marry her off by using a specious reasoning designed to convince prospective husbands that it is better to take a wife who is already lame because at least it's a *fait accompli*. I have commented on this story and Freud's reading of it in *Pourquoi rit-on?*
109 TN. *Jokes*, SE 8, p. 107.
110 TN. *SE* 5, p. 639.
111 TN. ibid., p. 638.
112 TN. ibid.
113 TN. *Civilisation and its Discontents*, SE 21, pp. 637–8.

114 TN. *A Childhood Recollection from Dichtung und Wahrheit*, SE 17, p. 156.
115 Cf. *An Autobiographical Study*, SE 20, p. 8.
116 Ibid. Cf. also *The Interpretation of Dreams* [SE 5] on the *Goethe* dream, which is the story of an 18-year-old patient and the different interpretations of his cry *"Nature"*. In this dream Goethe treats his friend (Fließ), that is, Freud himself, as a madman. Thus alluding in this way to the fact that he is in conflict with the majority of his profession because of his theory of the sexual aetiology of psycho-neuroses, Freud confirms that beneath his friend's traits the dream is really referring to himself, because the study of Goethe is mentioned. He adds: "When at the end of my schooldays I was hesitating in my choice of a career, it was hearing that essay read aloud at a public lecture that decided me to take up the study of natural sicence" [p. 441].
117 Cf. my *L'Enigme de la femme*, 1980 [tr. as *The Enigma of Woman*, Cornell University Press, 1985], in which I showed that behind a pseudo-scientific discourse that he claims to be based purely on observation, Freud was pursuing phallogocentric aims.
118 This is what Comte referred to as the "circle of method". In order to make observations, one needs a hypothesis; in order for the hypothesis to be positive it must rest on observation. For Comte, normality does not consist in eliminating subjectivity; only an excess of subjectivity leads to madness. Excessive objectivity is also, in its turn, idiocy. The accuracy of the mirror does not imply the passivity of the subject. A normal rationality is at once submissive and active, and positivism is not a realism nor a "fatalism". The rational and positive mind selectively divides up its field of observation by using as its criterion what is useful to mankind. An observation merely subject to facts is chimerical. The exactness, the precision of the mirror is measured by the requisites of human needs, which act as an indispensible discipline to prevent thought straying into the vague opinions of ancient philosophy. The "real", as opposed to the illusory, is reduced to what is accessible to the field of intelligence and becomes relative to human needs. It excludes impenetrable mysteries, an infantile area of investigation which the mature mind rejects as useless and unnecessary. Thus the "real" implies the intimate combination of the subjective and the objective. Moreover, for Comte, in order for the positive age to have come into being at all, a continual speculative advance has been necessary, an advance which the constitution of a purely intellectual class has helped to sustain. A class cut off from practice and whose research has not been at the service of, or limited by, any practical end. Only *limitless* speculation has brought about the development of the positive mind. Indeed, the first step of the positive mind. Indeed, the first step must have been costly so as to be able to stop further on.
119 TN. "Le sexe de la femme."
120 I have developed this idea at length in my *L'Enigme de la femme*, and in "Ça Cloche" in *Lectures de Derrida* (Galilée, 1984), ed. Hugh Silverman in *Derrida and Deconstruction*, (Routledge, 1989).
121 Cf. "The future prospects of psycho-analytic therapy", SE 11, pp. 139ff.

7 Lust

Alphonso Lingis

Alphonso Lingis is Professor of Philosophy at Pennsylvania State University. He is one of the foremost commentators and translators of contemporary continental philosophy.

In *Libido* he traces the disruptive effect of the perturbations and convulsions of eroticism: voluptousness, langour, torpor, bondage and obsession, upon traditional philosophical categories of desiring subjectivity. The recognition that the body laid out as a spectacle for theoretical observation does not comport itself as the orgasmic, lustful body, leads Lingis to abandon the sobriety of traditional philosophical language, and pursue an ecstatic, carnal phenomenology.

His *Excesses* is articulated around the possibility of encounter in non-western societies, of a contact with the other otherwise than through the cultural exchange systems of productive labour, commerce and the transactions of interpersonal "communication". The encounters form limit situations, that challenge the categorical norms by which "western" identity erects itself – instinctual renunciation, Oedipal prohibition, castration, lack, etc.

The following paper evokes the lustful interrogation addressed to the westerner by the Bangkok transvestite theatre. Lingis's depiction performatively restages and enacts the unease occasioned by the traversal of the constraints that would bind and tie the movements of lust as attributes of subjective identity conceived of as auto-representation. In the process, the psychoanalytic props that are used to confine the multiple and vagrant stirrings of the erotic as signs and symptoms of disorder are discarded.

SELECT BIBLIOGRAPHY

Lingis, A. *Excesses: Eros and Culture*, New York: State University of New York Press, 1983.
—— *Phenomenological Explanations*, Dordrecht: Martinus Nijhoff, 1986.
—— *Deathbound Subjectivity*, Bloomington: Indiana University Press, 1989.

—— *The Community of Those Who Have Nothing in Common*, Bloomington: Indiana University Press, 1992.

* * *

The Calypso. It's the biggest theatre on Thanon Sukumvit, Bangkok's Fifth Avenue. It has seats for three thousand; expensive seats so there will be businessmen and yuppies, German and Japanese and American and French and Hong Kong and Singapore and Saudi and Kuwaiti, in them. There is a cast of a hundred, a different show each night. Palaces, skyscrapers, desert oases drop upon the huge stage in outbursts of electric lightning. There is the Empress of China seated on the uplifted hands of naked body-builders metallized in gold. There is Mae West with a chorus line of nuns. There is Madonna competing with Grace Jones. Now the stage fills with ballerinas spinning out adagios and minuets from Swan Lake. Now gongs and the shakuashi propel the advance of a traditional transvestite dancer of Japanese Kabuki theatre. The Michael Jackson is – really – better still than the real one; Marilyn Monroe resurrects with puckered lips to coo for diamonds, your incredulous fingers want to feel for the wound to be sure. Vamps, divas, *grandes dames*, pop superstars, they are all, of course, men in their early twenties. You know that. Now there is the stripper. With rose-blushed complexion, under an auburn river of Farrah Fawcett hair, she uncoils in the cone of a spotlight, silver-sequinned gown cut to the navel revealing the contours of creamy breasts, slinking on spike heels. Her sultry eyes fix you as she approaches, her lips tremble and part, her silvered fingernails clutch at her sides, grip her breasts, slide down between her thighs. She unbuckles her waist-sheath with convulsive movements, flings off her skirt. You slide into the movement: artifice and style and props being shed to reveal flesh and nature. But now you find your mind getting twisted behind your eyes: at each stage of the strip the more is exposed of her body the more female she gets! Soft belly, ample thighs, full breasts are revealed. At each stage a more and more violent contradiction splits your head between what your prurient eyes see and what your mind knows. Finally she snaps off the *cache-sexe*: you see pubic hair, mons veneris. Her eyes are pulling at you with torrid magnetism. How the hell could she gyrate like that with her cock somehow pulled between her thighs? Then abruptly, for just a second, the cock flips out and the spotlight goes off and she is gone.

This now must be the last number. A big iron cage is wheeled out by a stout matron in safari clothing and wielding a whip. Inside the cage a dozen extravagantly beautiful women. There is a Thai in royal courtesan costume, an Indian in a sari, an Indonesian in a sarong, a Filipina in a *barong*, a Vietnamese in an *ao dai*, a Cambodian in court dress. They are clinging to the bars of the cage, shivering with fear and weeping. On the right side of the stage there is a gathering of men, German and Japanese and American and French and Hong Kong and Singapore and Saudi and Kuwaiti. The matron in the safari suit unlocks the cage and brings out the women one by one for their inspection. One by one the men make each his selection and leave until the stage is empty.

After some moments the audience applauds briefly. Then they file out, looking at the floor, past the performers who are lined up in the lobby their hands folded in the traditional *wai* greeting.

One could with Freud understand transvestism as transsexualism and explain it by our biological bisexuality. The Oedipus triangulation fixes each sex in a specific gender identity upon which the reproductive family will be built, as well as a good deal of the division of tasks in our society. But since the reduction of bisexuality was done by repression, there is a return of the repressed in the form of a compulsion to cross-dress.

One hardly ever notices transvestism in the streets in Bangkok; the cabaret is its space, and there, in the cheaper places, the Thai crowds obviously love it more than the foreigners, who don't get a lot of what is going on, especially when the numbers are Indochinese female imperson-ations with Indochinese songs.

There is the specific pleasure of theatre. The cabarets of Bangkok com-pete in sumptuous costuming, dazzling stage effects, an array of more glorious and hilarious female types than one had realized recent culture had created. The performers, superlative dancers and *poseurs*, virtuosos in an enormous range of moods and expression, queens in the succession of populations across the planet, radiate an infectious vitality. When I left Bangkok two years ago for Paris I went to see the shows in the Alcazar and the Madame Arthur and found them really uninventive by comparison. And there is the specific pleasure of transvestite theatre. There is not a script for which a director seeks actors who are naturals for the part. They don't do plays, stories, they just do the *femme fatale*, the Czarina, the college cheerleader, the Brooklyn Jewish mother.... Each the matrix of an indefinite number of plots, intrigues. They have no director, no one is a natural for a role, each one inverts and transposes his nature entirely into a representation. Each one a parthenogenesis in his own laser-beam planet.

You envy, are excited by the audacity, the cheeky freedom of these 20-year-olds. What an enormous quantity of psychic energy each of us has invested since childhood and to this day in fixing a specific male or female identity in ourselves! Now, tourist in another country, you watch these young guys creating to perfection the most extreme female identities for themselves, one after another, through two dozen acts a night, changing the show nightly. This theatre is a saturnalia of freedom, human bodies emanating, delighting in, flaunting, one-night-stand sexual identities which we in the audience have known as destinies and obligations.

Anti-feminist theatre: glorification of all the feminine types. Transvestites are more sensual, more charming, more tantalizing, more seductive than one has ever seen debutantes, fashion models, starlets or British princesses. They are the ones who have cut through all the inhibitions to achieve that feminine look, "that", Baudelaire said, "blasé look, that bored look, that vaporous look, that impudent look, that cold look, that look of looking inward, that dominating look, that voluptuous look, that wicked look, that sick look, that catlike look, infantilism, nonchalance and malice compounded".[1]

They always let you know. Something shows through – the body underneath not female and not masculine, virile, either, the stubble on the shaved legs, the pelvis too thin for maternity, the unmuscled but squarish shoulders – the indeterminate carnality. They lip-synch to perfection songs of a dozen languages they do not know, but you do see that it is not these Adam-appled throats that are trilling and warbling these soprano songs. If the performer has finally had so much plastic surgery done and is so artfully costumed that you no longer see the squarish male shoulders or the unfecundatable pelvis, then the magic is gone and there is just an ordinary female singer imitating an act another woman created. These performers are not males pathetically trying to look and act like women; if to become a woman is an artwork, they try harder than women, dare more, outdo women.

The apparatus of femininity, the artifice, the seductive appearance, the vaporous look, sick look, feline look, etc., is not a plumage that evolves out of biologically female bodies; it is, Baudrillard says,[2] a harness men buckle upon women in order to appropriate them to their uses. An apparatus given to women as their own in order to take back the women. The transvestites take back the apparatus too. They make it look so easy, to be a white superstar, these 20-year-old farm boys from the rocky Himalayan foothills of the Isaan who just got to Bangkok last year.

And you who paid the bucks and are sitting here feel somehow you are once again being taken for a ride. You feel something aggressive against you in all this glamour and gaiety, with it brash edge, reminding you that it is a guy like you that created this allure that you, after showering and shaving, would never dare try to concoct. You only wanted the woman in the harness. They are making a mockery of all the identities we have invested such a disproportionate amount of our psychic energy to fixing ourselves into and which we have hallowed with morality and religion. It's not spectator but participationist theatre; you are part of the show.

One can say, with Baudrillard, that men who take the harness contrived for women, the blasé look, impudent look, infantilism, nonchalance and wickedness compounded, etc., and who appropriate it for themselves doubly appropriate women; one can say that of transvestites in the street. But when transvestism occurs in theatre, it is not simply a ploy in the arena of the Hegelian or Freudian dialectic of the sexes. For the theatre is the space of the confrontation of real society – a configuration of political and economic forces – and its representation. The confrontation has its uses; the real society contemplates its image disengaged and illuminated with glamour and glory. But theatre is an appropriation of all the shapes into which human bodies are bent by the armour of political castes and the harnesses of economic power, for its own uses. In theatre transvestism is put to the uses of theatre.

Transvestism is theatre, the extreme degree of theatre, pure theatre, cut loose entirely from narrative, what is left of theatre when you take away everything that could be done in cinema. And theatre is transvestite. It is only bourgeois theatre, which Artaud and the Balinese and everybody else says is not theatre but recited novels and pop psychogogy, that is not transvestite. Primal theatre that recommences today in rock concerts and Harlem discos rediscovers transvestism. In Elizabethan theatre all the actors were men; female roles were played by boys. In this theatre of the greatest and most single-minded age of English imperialism, these boys are parodies of imperial males. The Queen found much of Shakespeare to her distaste. In Japanese theatre Nô theatre, the high theatre of the ruling samurai caste which glorifies their Zen ideals, all the roles are played by mature men. Kabuki, the low theatre of the merchant class, originated in the red-light district of Kyoto and its plots parody the plots of Nô theatre. Female prostitutes played all the roles; Kabuki was performed as an entertainment for male merchants. But it happened that Kabuki was so rich in theatrical innovations that it attracted clandestine visits from the samurai, who soon upgraded it, composed music and text for it, appropriated it, and it too came to be performed entirely by male actors. The T'ai people are profoundly matriarchal, and rural Thailand, Laos and parts of Myanmar are to this day. Patriarchal culture entered Siam late, through the royal family, which, though to this day Buddhist, in the late Sukhothai period – as Angkor long before it – imported Brahminical priests, and with them, Vedic patriarchal culture. Under King Chulalongkorn's programme of modernization, large numbers of Chinese coolies were imported, to build the land transportation system across this river kingdom; these were to stay on and settle into the traditional commercial activities of Chinese everywhere in the cities of South Asia; today a third of Bangkok is Chinese. They are the second entry of patriarchal culture into Siam. Since the Sukhothai period, in the now patriarchal court of the king, all the roles in the high court theatre of Siam were performed by women; it was conceived as an entertainment for the king. But throughout Siam village culture centred in the *wats*, which are regularly the scene of religious feasts and fairs. There low theatre was developed, popular theatre. Entertainment, featuring rogues and outlaws, burlesquing, as low theatre everywhere, the manners and heroic legends of the court. And working in under cover of comedy ridicule of state policy and even of the monks. Low theatre inverts and parodies high theatre. The popular theatre of matriarchal plebeian Siam put males in and out of all the roles.

In the cabarets of Bangkok today this Siamese popular theatre has been thoroughly internationalized. Although every show contains some acts from Siamese popular theatre, in the sound systems, the disco music, the female superstars being impersonated, the cabaret is very western and Hong Kong–Singapore–Tokyo. This occurred recently, when the military junta put in by the Americans during the Vietnam war realized that the planeloads of dollars that came into the country with the tens of thousand of GIs on R'n'R in Bangkok and Pattaya could be kept coming by maintaining Thailand as the R'n'R place for businessmen and yuppies; today 82 per cent of the tourists are unaccompanied males. It is not the Buddhism allegedly free of Judaeo-Christian sexual hangups that explains why Bangkok is the wide-open place it is. And traditional popular Siamese low theatre reoriented itself to an international audience. Even in the cheap cabarets full of Thais, the *farang* tourist has the impression that it is being performed for him. Here are the real women, the Onassis and Donald Trump kind of gal, sashaying for the credit-card troops, who frankly can't relate too well to these little Siamese dolls swarming around the barstools. You there, from Cincinnati, you from Frankfurt, you haven't seen half these, your women, back home; here in Bangkok you can see them all in a single night. Here there are more women for you, and more than the women. Oh come on, we're all bisexual; you really would dig a blow job from a Thai boy wouldn't you, only 500 baht? What's that? You say, frankly you would from a Greek sailor, but Thai men, well, are just not your type? Okay, just give me a half-hour – Now how do I look to you? Madonna!

You are sitting there, digging the show they are putting on for you, a little abashed at how far they are willing to go to be sex objects for you, to the point of changing their sex, to the point of themselves glorying in being the latest kind of corporate-produced media siren. But the cheaper places full of Thais who have paid to get in have the same kind of shows. They all seemed to be honoured to stand in the dark and watch the high theatre created for the entertainment of the white kings. Yet they have inverted it: all the voluptuous super-females are played by men. Might it not be for the Thais around you low theatre, travesty of the manners and intrigues and even of the state policy of the white court? In old Siam the kings used to go in disguise to the fairs in the village *wats*; the players had to learn to cover well their ridicule with entertainment. In Bangkok the white kings are welcomed, they pay; the ambiguity of low theatre has to be yet more elusive.

Yet you do feel uneasy in those places. There is something derisive in the ease with which they outdo it, the Marilyn Monroe and Ella Fitzgerald number. Even more sophisticated that number where a Thai boy suggests having a very female, pansy, body, to do a Thai girl doing impersonations of western matinée idols, Rock Hudson, Tom Cruise or John Travolta. The spotlights swing, intersect, blaze, the numbers follow one another very fast, you watch the conflagration of all our identities, all that we export, our music, our sybarite luxuries, our idols, our horny bodies.

They do try to put you at your ease, these charmers chatting with you so ingratiatingly at intermission, greeting you by name like your friends already in the lobby after the show. Yet you leave without one of them. They have made you feel inferior, sexually inferior, not as daring, not as attractive. You don't go back; the next night you go to the massage parlours, where there are a hundred straightforward, country girls, seated in banked rows behind a one-way plate glass window, with numbers on their bosoms, where you can pick one and she will massage, blow and spread for you. But they have spoiled it for you, on the stage at the Calypso, with their last number with the cage and the matron with the safari suit. The one you picked spreading the baby oil now on your thighs is after all just a farm girl from the Isaan in Bangkok to put her kid brothers and sisters through school. You think of the glamorous ones, of the Calypso stage, you toy with the idea of going back and taking one of them to your room, taking up the challenge. Taking one of these guys that dares everything back to your room, and taking off the clothes, and seeing what would happen, between two more or less bisexual guys without the apparatus. The theatre, *le symbolique* killed the lust. You have a visceral urge to kill all this *symbolique* with your lust.

It's the show in the world's biggest sex resort, but you are not sitting there with a newspaper over your lap. The libido in this libertine theatre is not a matter of nerves going soft, postures caving in, lungs heaving, sweat pouring, vaginal and penile discharges. The theatre of sex is a theatre of representation. A woman in Las Vegas with her voice, her movements, her own concupiscence had the spunk to create an erotic presence, a number, a representation of herself; it is transported whole to the other side of the planet, she factors out, her very physical nature of being female factors out. It is the representation of the self that carries the erotic charge. But the performer – this male Thai – is there, and shows through, and is now blended into the act to heighten its brazen glamour. What makes the number the more wanton and suggestive is that he is there as a representative male (his own specific maleness all covered over, factors out), and also as a Thai doing an American woman – a representative of the ethnic, economic and geopolitical layout that is Thailand. You went for the charge, but then to those who hold themselves to be serious cultural travellers and not gross tourists and who go to the performances of Siamese classical dance the Ministry of Tourism puts on at the National Theatre you say: if you really want to know about Thailand go to the cabarets! It is not just the physiognomy, the swagger, the *enfant terrible* of the Vietnam-War-torn 1960s Janis Joplin that is being represented; it is a Thai representing her that is being represented, representing inevitably with himself the position of low theatre with respect to the ruling icons and effigies, representing economic and cultural subordination, representing a certain moment of geopolitical history – smelted into an erotic trope. And you are there as a representative; those who go to the performances of Siamese classical dance don't want to be stock tourists, more ugly Americans in post-Vietnam-War Southeast Asia.

It is the specifically erotic figure, and not the classical dancers, that has this representational power, because it implicates you. Not only because the cabaret show is also the presentation of the charms of the escorts, all of whom are available to you to take back to your hotel, but because even while you are sitting there just watching the show you feel yourself being challenged to an intercontinental sexual duel. The erotic theatre is participationist, the decent theatre is spectator theatre; those who go watch the performances of Siamese classical dance at the National Theatre or in the restaurant of the Oriental Hotel are watching a representation of a moment of Siamese cultural, political-economic history from which the passage of time has separated them, as well as the ushers, the *maitre d'*, the waitresses, the restaurant owner and the performers themselves, from involvement.

It is because one is horny that one is a representative. The farm boys from the Isaan whose libido can be contained within the confines of village possibilities and constraints are in Bangkok for a few years working on construction gangs or in the sweatshops; it is those with an unrestrained libido who are working out in gyms, in dance classes, grooming themselves, cultivating suggestive gestures, learning English, learning the rhetoric of seduction. When you take out your more rakish shirt from the suitcase, splash cologne over the greasy pores of your carnivorous body, go and pay for the ticket, speaking English to the teller, your national prestige, your money, your profession, your boutique-bought shirt and your suave and unflappable manners are so many props in the theatre of libido. All your words are phallic symbols; if you mention the plane to Hong Kong you have to catch tomorrow, if you mention the comfort of the Oriental Hotel, if you mention your company, your high place in a research institute or a university, all this is so many tropes in the rhetoric of seduction. What you want, here in Bangkok, is of course not some meat to get off on; you want Miss Thailand. To tell the truth, the lay will not be very good, the bodies are too mismatched, in the end you will do a kind of pathetic reciprocal masturbation in the dark. That is why, in the sex resorts, they do not just line the street with naked young women and men; they put on the theatre. The whole theatre of the international beauty contest, in which Miss Thailand wins one year. And the cabarets featuring Mae West, Tina Turner, Margaux Hemmingway or Margaret Thatcher. Where it could be that you are challenged by his provocations, his twitting at your western manhood, feel a lascivious urge to take him up on it: after the show, in my hotel room Mr Cincinnati and Miss Bangcock! On stage or in the hotel room, the libidinal encounter is a rhetoric of signs, a transaction not with body parts but with representatives of self, themselves representatives of Oedipal personages, castes, classes, cultures, nations, economies, continents. The difference between him and you is that he is a representative of a backward Isaan economy whose only productive resources are bodies, the unreproductive bodies of the Bangkok sex theatre, whereas you are a representative of a productive economy that produces bodies such as yours, professionally qualified bodies, assets with which you acquire productive wealth.

And back in the company lounge, when you are asked about your trip to the notorious Bangkok, what you will tell is not about the clumsy peasant girls lined up by the hundreds waiting for somebody to fuck them for a few bucks; you will tell about having Miss Thailand in your room for a night, you will tell about the Calypso. We all know the classicalized genre of the narrative: there she was, at the bar, the most gorgeous thing you ever saw, huge boobs, et cetera . . . and then when we got back to the room at the Oriental and I got her dress off, I couldn't believe my eyes, imagine my disgust! . . .

The libido makes the self a representative. Libido is not nostalgia for, and pleasure in, carnal contact. One was a part of another body, one got born, weaned, castrated. Libidinal impulses are not wants and hungers but insatiable compulsions, sallies of desire which is desire for infinity, for *l'objet a*. The libido does not adhere to the present but bounds toward the absent, the future; it extends an indefinite dimension of time. What makes this craving insatiable is the way back blocked, the way back to symbiotic immediate gratification. Every present object that excites it represents the absent; the love it knows is the gift from the other of what the other does not have. It is libidinous desire that stations the self in the Oedipal theatre, in the polis, on the field of objectives which is the objective universe and which is the universe of objectives of desire, in the world market, in *le symbolique*. If our libido is a part of ourselves, the libidinous gesture or move represents the whole self. The pansexualist psychoanalysis turns into a science of the subject.[3] And the self is a representative of *le nom-du-père*, the Oedipal theatre, the reason and the law, the corporate state, the cybernetic digital communication chains, the West. The libidinous gesture or move does not transact with another for discharge into a set of carnal orifices but for another libidinous gesture which is a representative of another self, a representative of another reason and law, transnational corporation, corporate state, continent.

One would have to read the libido, see it in its context, interpret it. Our phenomenology of sex is an interpretation of intentionalities, representatives, a decoding of barred objectives of desire, a transcription of dyadic oppositions, an inscription of *différance*. Tracking it down we end up, like Plato, finding the whole of culture. Including its technology and its relationship with the material, the electromagnetic universe. Lately we have also been doing a machinics of libidinal bodies, a mechanic's analysis of what the parts are, the couplings, how they work, what they produce.[4] We find with Ballard in *Crash*[5] our landscape of automobiles, high-rises, multiballistic missiles and computer banks very sexy, representative of our own libidinal machinery. We have also been doing, with Lyotard,[6] a micro-engineer's account of freely mobile excitations, inductions and irradiations, and bound excitations. We represent our erotogenic surface as an electromagnetic field. The I or the *Ca* that is aroused in the Calypso is a representative of *le nom-du-père*, of the phallus, of the text of culture, the technological industry, the electromagnetic universe. Intelligent talk about sexual transactions among us is talk about transactions with representatives of the self.

But on stage at the Calypso you caught sight of something else – the body underneath not female and not masculine, virile, either, the lean thighs, the pelvis too narrow for maternity, the still adolescent shoulders – the indeterminate carnality. Something troubling. You remember passing by this young guy in jeans and sneakers heading for the backstage entrance. That body, now slippery with greasepaint and sweat, belly marked with the tight plastic belt, feet with red marks from the spike heels. You see the impudent glamour of the performance, something in you wonders how it would feel. He came from a rice-paddy in the Isaan, you came from a farm in Illinois, a working-class apartment in Cincinnati. If one could somehow join, immerse oneself in the physical substance of that body, one would have a feel for the weight and the buoyancy, the swish and the streaming, the smell and the incandescence of the costumes, masks, castes, classes, cultures, nations, economies, continents that would be very different from understanding the signs, emblems, allusions, references, implications. You watch the effigy being paraded, but there is an undercurrent of feeling in you that is asking a question words cannot answer. What is this flesh he pushed into that mummified skin of Marilyn Monroe? How does it feel? Something in you would like to know how it feels to be that bare mass of indeterminate carnality being stuck in spike heels, sheathed in metallized dress, strapped to a filmy fibreglass wig, become phosphorescent in a pool of blazing light. Something in you that would like to make contact with that body from within. Something which is the stirrings of lust.

Lust does not know what it is. The mouth loosens the chain of its sentences, babbles, giggles, the tongue spreads its wet over the lips. The hands that caress move aimlessly over flesh, no longer exploring or discovering, in random unendingly repetitious movements that have no idea of what they are looking for or what they are doing. The body tenses up, hardens, gropes and grapples, pistons and rods of a machine that has no idea of what it is trying to achieve. Then it collapses, melts, gelatinizes, runs. There is left the coursing of the trapped blood, the flush of heat, the spirit vapourizing in exhalations.

There is the horrible in lust. The story, by Flannery O'Connor, of the petrified, or petrifying, woman, A huge mass of carnal flesh, which – like Flannery O'Connor herself, who was to die of a degenerative bone disease – has lost the diagrams of its skeletal force, its muscular elasticity, and which is turning to stone. Such bodies to be sure fail to arouse first the movements of tenderness and sensuality in us, to the contrary chill us with cold horror. The landscape of horror is strewn with Hieronymus Bosch and Salvador Dali bodies with faces softening and oozing out of their shapes, limbs going limp and shrivelling like detumescent penises, their extremities melting and evaporating, flesh draining off the bones, bones crumbling in the sands. Yet this horror troubles us not in our minds, which compulsively fix substances in their boundaries and in their material states, but in our loins. There is lust in the fascination with the domain of horror. Lust is the dissolute ecstasy by which the body's ligneous, ferric, coral state casts itself into a gelatinous, curdling, dissolving, liquefying, vapourizing, radioactive, solar and nocturnal state. *Exstase matérielle*, transubstantiation.

Lust is flesh becoming bread and wine and bread and wine becoming flesh. It is the posture become dissolute, the bones turning into gum. It is the sinews and muscles becoming gland – lips blotting out their muscular enervations and becoming loose and wet as labia, torso becoming belly, thighs lying there like more penises, stroked like penises, knees fingered like montes Veneris. It is glands stiffening and hardening, becoming bones and rods and then turning into ooze and vapours and heat. Eyes clouding and becoming wet and spongy, hair turning into webs and gleam, fingers becoming tongues, wet glands in orifices. Moslems say they have to veil their women in public, because when lust stirs it takes over the whole of a woman's body; but Arnold Schwarzenegger, to those who objected that most women really don't find these Conan the Barbarian bodies sexy and anyhow how can anyone get it up spending as much time in the gym hoisting barbells as you do, Arnold answered: it *is* sex, getting horny is gorging the penis with blood but that is exactly what pumping the barbells is and what the feeling is! Pumping iron is better than humping a woman; I am coming in my whole body! The orgasm continues in the jacuzzi where the hard wires of the motor nerves dissolve into sweat and the pumped muscles float like masses of jelly.

The supreme pleasure we can know, Freud said, and the model for all pleasure, orgasmic pleasure, comes when an excess tension built up, confined, compacted, is abruptly released; the pleasure consists in a passage into the contentment and quiescence of death. Is not orgasm instead the passage into the uncontainment and unrest of liquidity and vapour –

pleasure in exudations, secretions, exhalations? Voluptuous pleasure is not the Aristotelian pleasure that accompanies a teleological movement that triumphantly reaches its objective. Voluptuous pleasure engulfs and obliterates purposes and directions and any sense of where it itself is going. In the transubstantiations in the carnal substance, movements that do not terminate in quiescence or nirvana, voluptuous pleasure surges and rushes and vapourizes like the foam bursting in the sun as the sea sinks into the sands.

To be sure, blond hair represents for Thais as for Nietzsche the master race, candelight and wine represent *grand-bourgeois* distinction and raffinement, leather represents hunters and outlaws, diamonds represent security forever. But lust cleaves to them differently. Encrusting one's body with stones and silver or steel, polishing one's skin till it looks like marble, sinking into marble baths full of champagne or into the soft mud of rice paddies, feeling the ostrich plumes or the algae tingling one's flesh like nerves, dissolving into perfumed air and into flickering twilight, lust surges through a body in transubstantiation.

Libidinous eyes are quick, agile, penetrating, catching on to the undertones, allusions, suggestiveness of the act – responding to the provocation in the Janis Joplin number being done by a male Thai, its looks parries in the intercontinental sex duel. The eyes of lust idolize and fetishize the representation, metallize the crepe of the representation the performer has covered himself with, petrify in marble the powdered gestures of the face and arms, solidify the body in those gleaming belts and boots, liquifies the dyadic oppositions, vapourizes all the markers of *différance* into a sodden and electric atmosphere. About the materialization of these idols and fetishes, there is radioactive leakage; the castes, classes, cultures, nations, economies collapse in intercontinental meltdown.

Lust seeks not to represent the self to another representative; it seeks contact with organic and inorganic substances that function as catalysts for its transubstantiations. Lust is not the libido that transacts with the other as a representative of the male or female gender, a representative of the human species; it seeks contact with the hardness of bones and rods collapsing into glands and secretions, with the belly giggling into jelly, with the smegmic and vaginal swamps and effluvia, with the musks and the sighs. We fondle animal fur and feathers and both they and we get aroused, we root our penis in the dank humus flaking off into dandelion fluff, we caress fabrics, cum on silk and leather, we hump the seesaw and the horses and a Harley-Davidson. Lust stirs as far as does Heidegger's Care which extends to earth and the skies and all mortal and immortal beings in thinking building dwelling – muddying and making turgid the light of thought, vapourizing its constructions, petrifying its ideas into obsessions and idols, sinking all that is erect and erected back into primal slime, decreating all dwelling into the Deluge that rises.[7] It is lust that, in Tournier's novel *Friday*, overcame Robinson Crusoe in the araucaria tree:

> He continued to climb, doing so without difficulty and with a growing sense of being the prisoner, and in some sort a part, of a vast and infinitely ramified structure flowing upward through the trunk with its reddish bark and spreading in countless large and lesser branches, twigs, and shoots to reach the nerve ends of leaves, triangular, pointed, scaly, and rolled in spirals around the twigs. He was taking part in the tree's most unique accomplishment, which is to embrace the air with its thousand branches, to caress it with its million fingers.... "The leaf is the lung of the tree which is itself a lung, and the wind is its breathing," Robinson thought. He pictured his own lungs growing outside himself like a blossoming of purple-tinted flesh, living polyparies of coral with pink membranes, sponges of human tissue.... He would flaunt that intricate efflorescence, that bouquet of fleshy flowers in the wide air, while a tide of purple ecstasy flowed into his body on a stream of crimson blood.[8]

Lust is not a movement issuing from us and terminating in the other. It is the tree that draws Robinson, holds him, embraces him, caresses his breath with its million fingers. "The sea that rises with my tears" – obsessive line of a lovesong in Gabriel Garcia Marquez's novel *In Evil Hour*.[9] And it is the sea that rises in my tears. Lust of the sea, of the polyps liquefying the coral cliffs, of the rain dissolving the temples of Khajuraho, of the powdery gypsy moths disintegrating the oak forests, of the winter winds crystalliz-ing the air across the windowpanes.

Lust is not an intentional or appropriative movement; but does not lust throw one obsessively to the other? Is one not driven by lust into perma-nent association with others, that is, society?

There is a specific tempo of the surges and relapses of lust, there is a specific duration to transubstantiations. For the sugar to melt, *il faut la durée*. But the turgid time of the wanton contact is not the time extended by society. The associations that form society first establish an extended time in which the carnal pleasure of contact with another can be interrupted and resumed. This time is a line of dashes in which compensations for what is spent in catalysing another become possible, an extended time in which the water that is turned into wine and consumed can be turned back into water once again.

In society one associates with another – for portions of the other, for the semen, vaginal fluids, milk of the other.[10] The association first extends an interval of time in which one portion can be poured after the other. Transubstantiations become transactions, become coded, become claims, to be redeemed across time, claims maintained in representations. One associ-ates with another – for parts of the other, for the tusks of his nostrils, the fangs implanted in his ears, the plumes implanted in his hair of this lord of the jungle who has incorporated the organs of the most powerful beasts of prey into his own body; but the association extends a stretch of time in which the transfer of these detachable body-parts of his bionic body into yours can be delayed, a time in which the representation of self and the representation of the other forms. One associates with another – for prestige objects, for productive commodities, one transacts with representatives of oneself and of the other. In the association with another in which one transacts for prestige objects, for representatives of self and of the other, the association extends the infinite time of the libido, of desire which is desire for the infinite. A time to transact with the phallic objectives, the transnational corporation, the corporate states, the continents of which one is a representative.

The transaction itself, between representatives of the self, can be represented, in theatre. For example, in absolute theatre, transvestite theatre.

When, in the midst of social transactions, there is contact with the substance of the other, and lust breaks through, it breaks up the extended time of association with its clamorous urgency. But sometimes the extended time of society of itself disintegrates.

Lust throws one convulsively to the other; its surges and relapses break through the time of transactions to extend the time of transubstantiations. Shall we conceive of the transaction with representatives of self to function to postpone, control, exclude, suppress the surgings of lust? Does theatre – which represents society to itself, that is, represents the transactions with representatives of self – in its absolute form, transvestite theatre, travesty, parody, undermine, consume all our representatives of self, in an implosion of all our simulacra, leaving, as Baudrillard says, the absolute of death alone on the stage – or the naked surgings and relapses of lust?[11]

There is something not said in the absolute, transvestite theatre, where one dares everything. Is it transposing or releasing, subverting or trumpeting lust? That is its secret. The power to keep its secrets is the secret of its power.

Power flows in speech; when one transfers information to another, one supplies him with a possible programme for action. The determination of what is said, in what codes, to whom, and in what circumstances organizes channels of access to power about interlocutors. The one who can say can also not say. His silence is also a power.

The force in the walls of secrecy one can erect can function in many different ways. Secrecy can be a force that exalts and sanctifies ritual knowledge. It can be a force to maintain the identity and solidarity of a group. It can be a force that subordinates those to whom access to knowledge is denied. It can be a force that determines the division of labour. It can be a force to make intentions and instincts that circulate at large one's own. The established practice of reserve makes it hard to confront liars, and thus maintains a social space for different compounds of knowledge, fantasy and ritual behaviour. Secrecy can be a force to maintain a friendship on a certain level and in a certain style; I may choose not to reveal what I did last night not because I did anything that you should or would object to were I to explain the whole context, but rather because I choose to avoid a confrontational relationship with you, I value the affable and ingenuous tone of our interaction, where each of us spontaneously connects with what the other says. To lose face for a Thai is not simply to feel embarrassment; it is to feel loss of one's defining membership in overlapping groups and loss of the social attributes of position. The importance of keeping up appearances, and of the presentation of respectfulness, unobtrusiveness, calmness, of avoiding saying things in opposition to what is expected, does not only organize social interaction, but penetrates even into the psychological attitudes of Thais toward themselves. "This attitude may go so far as his not wanting to engage in a private self-analysis whose result might be inimical to his own self image."[12]

The walls of secrecy fragment our social identity. One is not the same person in different situations, in sacred and in profane places, in crowds and behind closed doors, in the day and in the night; one is not the same person before different interlocutors.

And within ourselves, walls of non-communication separate different and autochthonous psychic structures. In what psychoanalysis catalogued as multiple-personality disorder, two or more persons inhabit the same body. But when Freud identified the unconscious, an infantile and nocturnal self that does not communicate with the public and avowed self, he generalized the phenomenon of multiple-personality disorder, no longer a rare and aberrant case, but the case of each of us. Then one can drop the notion of "disorder"; a division of one's psychic forces, each system dealing with its own preoccupations, non-communicating with the others, may work quite well. Rather than deal with all her problems with the integral array of her methods and skills, the self-assured office manager closes off the rape-victim she also is and will be exclusively when she walks out of the office at night; the wall of sleep falls over our responsibilities of the day, and our infantile self is free to explore again the tunnels on the other side of the mirror.

Freud first explained the split in each of us by the concept of repression; the content of the unconscious would be produced by a censorship that represses representations from the conscious. But the concept of repression proves to be both theoretically inconsistent and vacuous. In order to repress a representation, the censorship would have to represent that representation; regression would be a contradiction in terms or an infinite regress. What is selected for repression is that whose expression is not to be exteriorized; the censorship the child installs within himself is an interiorization of the decrees of the father. But why does the father repress? Because he was repressed as a child. Another infinite regress. Freud soon saw that he was left with the fact that there is repression in the human species and the enigma of that fact. If we recognize the vacuous nature of the pseudo-explanatory concept of repression, we are left with these multiple psychic systems in our body, and walls of non-communication between them. These walls of secrecy function in multiple ways.

It is then too simplistic to suppose that the libidinous desire in us, which represents the self and makes the self a representative, which transacts with representatives of others who are representatives, functions to suppress, control or mask the lustful body surging and relapsing in its transubstantiations. The non-communication between them can function to maintain the identity and solidarity of one's libidinal representation of self, to exalt and consecrate it, it can function to establish a division of labour between libidinous desire and lust, each in its own sphere and time. It can function to maintain an intrapsychic space for different compounds of knowledge, fantasy and repetition compulsions.

There are politico-economic motives that enjoin us each to be individuals, enduring integral subjects of attribution and responsibility. The immense field of ephemeral insights, fantasies, impulses, intentions that link up in disjoint systems are forced to somehow form an individual whole in our one same body.

Our theories continue to conceive this whole either as an isomorphism between strata, a distributive organization of behaviours in distinct contexts, or a dialectical sublation of each partial structure and phase in the succeeding one. But these paradigms do not succeed in making intelligible our *personal identity*. The intrapsychic organization, whether isomorphic, distributive or dialectical, would have the form of a form of integration itself general, a distributive or dialectical law. It would give us the identity of a minor, a father, a person, subject of rights and obligations, a citizen, a chicano or a Wasp. But for each of us, our personal identity is not simply a molecular formula of continual knowledge and skills; it is a singular compound of fragmentary systems of knowledge, incomplete stocks of information and discontinuous paradigms, disjoint fantasy fields, personal repetition cycles and intermittent rituals.

We can conceive of our personal identity differently with the concept of inner walls of secrecy. It is one of the functions of walls of secrecy to maintain a space where quite discontinuous, non-communicating, non-reciprocally-sublating, non-coordinated systems can coexist. A space where episodic systems can exist, where phases of one's past and of one's future can be still there, untransformed and unsublated.

Desire is desire for the absent, for infinity; libidinous eyes are quick, agile, penetrating, catching on to the undertones, allusions, suggestive-nesses, cross-indexing. They are also superficial, they see the representation of a self and the self that is a representative. If they do not penetrate the wall without graffiti behind which lust pursues its transubstantiations, this wall may not at all function to exclude and to repress. It may function to maintain a non-confrontational coexistence of different sectors of oneself. One may value an affable relationship with the beast within oneself. One may not want to penetrate behind that wall, not out of horror and fear of what lies behind, but because one may choose to be astonished at the strange lusts contained within oneself. One may want the enigmas and want the discomfiture within oneself.

NOTES

1 Charles Baudelaire, *Oeuvres complètes*, ed. Claude Pichois (Paris: Gallimard, 1961), p. 1256.
2 Jean Baudrillard, *Seduction*, tr. Brian Singer (New York: St Martin's Press, 1979), p. 14.
3 Jacques Lacan, *Ecrits*, tr. Alan Sheridan (New York: W. W. Norton, 1977) pp. 72–7.
4 Gilles Deleuze and Félix Guattari, *Anti-Oedipus*, tr. Robert Hurley, Mark Seem and Helen R. Lane (New York: Viking, 1977), p. 338.
5 J. G. Ballard, *Crash* (New York: Vintage, 1985).
6 Jean-François Lyotard, *Economie libidinale* (Paris: Minuit, 1974).
7 Martin Heidegger, "Thinking building dwelling", tr. A. Hofstadter in Martin Heidegger, *Poetry, Language, Thought* (New York: Harper & Row, 1971), pp. 145–61.
8 Michel Tournier, *Friday*, tr. Norman Denny (New York: Pantheon, 1969) pp. 192–4.
9 Gabriel Garcia Marquez, *In Evil Hour*, tr. Gregory Rabassa (New York: Harper & Row, 1979).
10 Shirley Lindenbaum, "Variations on a sociosexual theme in Melanesia", in Gilbert H. Herdt *et al.*, *Ritualized Homosexuality in Melanesia* (Berkeley: University of California Press, 1984), pp. 337–61.
11 Jean Baudrillard, *Seduction*, tr. Brian Singer (New York: St Martin's Press, 1979), p. 24.
12 Daniel Wit, *Thailand – Another Vietnam?* (New York: Charles Scribner's Sons, 1968), p. 62.

8 Immanent death, imminent death

Reading Freud's *Beyond the Pleasure Principle* (1920) with Heidegger's *Being and Time* (1927) and *Metaphysical Foundations of Logic* (1928), though there's something in it for Aristophanes, too . . .

David Farrell Krell

David Farrell Krell is Professor of Philosophy at DePaul University, Chicago. He is one of the foremost interpreters of the tradition of continental philosophy represented by Nietzsche, Heidegger and Derrida, and he has extensively explored the possibilities of thinking "in the draught of their thought".

In his recent book *Of Memory, Reminiscence and Writing: On the Verge*, he depicts the way in which traditional metaphysical models for memory and reminiscence have collapsed. He poses the question of how mourning may be possible in this ruination, and suggests that the very breakdown enables an affirmation of a mirthful mourning, on the verge of a never-present past.

In this paper, arising from another recent book, *Daimon Life: Heidegger and Life-philosophy*, he extends these reflections through a consideration of mortality in texts by Freud and Heidegger. Through existential and "Dasein" analysis, developed respectively by Ludwig Binswanger and Medard Boss, Freud has been read from a Heideggerian stance, in an effort to free psychoanalysis from its supposed natural scientific and metaphysical moorings. Krell follows Derrida's reading of Freud in *The Post Card: From Socrates to Freud and Beyond* in reversing the current of this tide, figuratively posing Freud as a reader of Heidegger. He shows how Freud's speculations upon the death drive interrupt and interrogate Heidegger's formulation of "Being toward Death". In Heidegger's account death is forever *imminent*. For Freud, by contrast, death is an *immanent* tendency to reduce the quantity of the organism's excitation. By following the uncanny two-step of their speculations, Krell traces the path of the immanence/imminence of death in life – or what one might have to call *lifedeath*.

SELECT BIBLIOGRAPHY

Krell, D. F. *Intimations of Mortality: Time, Truth, and Finitude in Heidegger's Thinking of Being*, University Park, Pennsylvania: Pennsylvania State University Press, 1986.

—— *Postponements: Woman, Sensuality and Death in Nietzsche*, Bloomington: Indiana University Press, 1986.
—— *Of Memory, Reminiscence, and Writing: On the Verge*, Bloomington: Indiana University Press, 1990.
—— *Daimon Life: Heidegger and Life-philosophy*, Bloomington: Indiana University Press, 1992.

* * *

"What now follows is speculation", he begins in Chapter 4 of *Jenseits des Lustprinzips* (Freud 1982). As though his long detour through medicine and natural science – the detour he calls *psychoanalysis* – were coming to an end. Coming to an end in the speculative domain that in our own day has come to *its* end, the somewhat seedy domain of philosophy.

In the *Selbstdarstellung* of 1924–5, Freud said of even his most speculative writings, "I have assiduously avoided all approaches to philosophy proper [*die eigentliche Philosophie*]". He added that such avoidance was made easier for him by his "constitutional incapacity" for philosophy (1971: 87). Three decades earlier, in his letter to Fließ of 1 January 1896, the claim was quite different. Freud congratulated his friend for having advanced through medicine to physiology by taking medicine as a kind of "detour", conceding that his own use of the medicinal detour would ultimately conduct him back to his "initial goal", which, he confessed, was *Philosophie*.

Constitutional incapacity or skilful navigation of the detour? Final destination or initial goal? Progress or regress, innovation or restoration to an earlier state?

Later on in the *Selbstdarstellung* Freud makes another confession, perhaps a more ironic one: his speculations on society and religion, which served him as "yet another stage" (*eine weitere Bühne*) on which psychoanalysis could produce its kind of theatre, represent a "regressive development" in him (1971: 98). At all events, whether backward or forward, something *is* coming to an end in *Jenseits*. Here the coming to an end of a detour would be not a return to the highroad of life but the specular arrival of something we may have to call *lifedeath*. An arrival that could only be *imminent*, that is, always merely on the verge of coming to presence, and *immanent*, ensconced in the innermost interior of a fortress-like crypt. There *is* something cryptic about the detour, something catachretic. In the published version of the Freud-Fließ correspondence (Freud 1950) a bizarre typo alters the word "detour", *Umweg*, to "impassable path", *Unweg*. Fließ's deft way-around becomes a daft no-way. The printer might just as well have botched the whole thing and set the word *Holzweg*, meaning a timber track that leads nowhere, a *chemin qui mène nulle part*. Unless, of course, Freud really made no slip at all: perhaps he was trying to lead his friend, who was inclined to solar speculation, by the nose back to proper biological science and medicine. We would have to see the original letter in order to scrutinize the *m* of *Umweg* or the *n* of *Unweg*, on which the entire odyssey of psychoanalysis through medicine would depend. And even when we saw the extra stroke that makes of *n* an *m*, we still would not know whether it was a detour or a parapraxis. But enough of this cryptic philological limping along: it is time for the speculative leap – what Hegel called *der spekulative Satz*. **For whom is the funhouse fun? Perhaps for lovers. For Ambrose it is *a place of fear and confusion*.**

We are here in order to advance Freud's speculation. My own contribution will be obvious and rather flat, "frontal", in its theme: I shall ask whether the principle of immanent death in Chapters 5 and 6 of Freud's *Jenseits des Lustprinzips* is mirrored in Heidegger's existential-ontological interpretation of death in *Sein und Zeit*. As obvious as the question is, there is some risk in it, as there is in any frontal collision. For just as Freud abjures philosophy, so Heidegger demarcates existential analysis over against any psychological or biological speculation on death. To bring Freud and Heidegger together is to make a scene. A Lacanian scene: the unconscious, structured as a λόγος, both gathered and gathering to the overwhelming *truth* of being, to wit, unfulfillable desire. **To say that Ambrose's and Peter's mother was *pretty* is to accomplish nothing; the reader may acknowledge the proposition, but his imagination is not engaged. Besides, Magda was also pretty, yet in an altogether different way.** A Derridean scene: two cantankerous old grandfathers, *deux pépés*, PP × 2, who cannot decide whether they want to be radical revolutionaries or postal authorities of the Pleasure Principle. **You think you're yourself, but there are other persons in you. Ambrose gets hard when Ambrose doesn't want to, *and obversely*. Ambrose watches them disagree; Ambrose watches him watch. In the funhouse mirror-room you can't see yourself go on forever, because no matter how long you stand, your head gets in the way.** "To make a scene" is in German *Theater machen*, and this session of the conference promises something of the theatre, something of a scene. Lacan would welcome it, would relish its cruelties. Derrida, for his part, would discourage our making a scene. Not because Freud and Heidegger have nothing to do with one another, but precisely because, as they turn their backs on one another in a bootless *a tergo*, they have to do with one another more than with anything or anyone else. In "Spéculer – sur 'Freud' ", Derrida writes:

> Correspondence, here, between two who, according to the usual criteria, never read each other, much less met one another. Freud and Heidegger, Heidegger and Freud. We have embarked into a region where we navigate by this historic correspondence – and at bottom I am certain that these two "texts", indicated by these proper names but also, I am sure, overflowing them for reasons I am busying myself with here, are

preoccupied with one another, spending all their time deciphering one another, coming to resemble one another, as one ends up resembling what one excludes or the deceased in absolute mourning. They could not read each other – therefore they have spent all their time and exhausted all their energies in doing so. Let that go. There are a thousand ways to settle accounts with Freud and Heidegger, between Freud and Heidegger. Not to worry, it happens by itself, without our taking the slightest initiative.

(1980: 379–80, 357)

Derrida is right. Hence the rather obvious, flat, frontal nature of my own remarks on immanent, imminent death, however tenuous and laborious they may be. And yet. Derrida's own "Spéculer" picks up with the words, "Everything remains to be done", so that my own question may be given the go-ahead, encouraged to make a little scene about death. **We should be much farther along than we are; something has gone wrong; not much of this preliminary rambling seems relevant. Yet everyone begins in the same place; how is it that most go along without difficulty but a few lose their way?**

Let me begin with some Heideggerian theatrics, inasmuch as Freud's bobbin-on-a-string in the *fort/da* game at the beginning of *Jenseits des Lustprinzips* and his urbane invocation of Aristophanes at the end are so well known by now. Let me begin with a scene that Heidegger makes in his *Beiträge zur Philosophie*, written between the years 1936–8 but published only recently. The years 1936–8 themselves constitute part of a larger scene – Freud leaving Austria two months after the *Anschluß*, eight years after he is awarded the Goethe-Preis and five after the first burning of his books in Berlin – but I shall restrict myself to the scene of Todtnauberg, "Dead Meadow Mountain", where Heidegger during the years 1936–8 is spending more and more of his time. **Nobody likes a pedant.** This scene, the scene of the *Beiträge*, has at first blush nothing to do with Freud and the question of the immanence of death in life. Yet it does have to do with war. A war of words. Polemic. One of the most interesting aspects of the *Beiträge* is its juxtaposition of some of Heidegger's most inspired speculation – the "intimations" of beyng, the "futural ones", and "the last god" – alongside some of his most sardonic polemics. When we recall the strictures of *Was heißt Denken?* (1951–2) against polemic ("Every form of polemic fails from the outset to attain to the stature of thinking" [1954: 49]), then the violence of the repetitious, compulsive polemics is astonishing. For two reasons. First, the most strident polemics are directed against *Lebensphilosophie*, even though (or precisely because) Heidegger's ontology of Dasein springs in large measure from the soil prepared by Dilthey, Bergson, Simmel, Scheler and Nietzsche. Second, the energy exerted in such polemics (Freud would have spoken of their *Aufwand*) is so great that it somehow propels and energizes the most daring and delicate thoughts of the *Beiträge* – the history of beyng as abandonment of beings, the cleavage of beyng, and beyng's finitude. Heidegger's *thinking* in this work of 1936–8 I would designate as *paranoetic* thinking. Not paranoid thinking, not Schreber's *Denkwürdigkeiten*, but far more desperate than paranoid thinking: Heidegger's situation is more harrowing than Schreber's worst nightmares, inasmuch as Schreber knows where his God is, speculatively. Not paranoid, but *paranoetic* thinking: no being can serve as its noematic correlate, its tribunal or its ground. No *Seiendes*, and not even *Seyn*, which is a name for default, omission, nothing at all – the history of our epoch, for which even the name *nihilism* is non-essential. In paranoetic thinking, all names are lacking, no one is in charge, and every communication has to be p.p.'d. **There's no point in going farther; this isn't getting anybody anywhere; they haven't even come to the funhouse yet. Ambrose is off the track, in some new or old part of the place that's not supposed to be used; he strayed into it by some one-in-a-million chance, like the time the roller-coaster car left the tracks in the nineteen-teens against all the laws of physics and sailed over the boardwalk in the dark. And they can't locate him because they don't know where to look.**

Late in the *Beiträge*, Heidegger's polemic outdoes itself, producing a kind of theatre (1989: 65, 347). The polemic is directed against "theatrics" and "staging", *Bühne*, and it has eminent (if overdetermined) political implications. For the gigantism (*das Riesenhafte*) of National Socialism is the national-aesthetic expression of its machination (*Machenschaft*) and unbridled will-to-will. Such gigantism, which is all theatrics and staging, is all that is left of what Heidegger had recently been celebrating as the grounding and founding of a state. Politics of gigantism and colossal theatre – even though what is being discussed is the most speculative of Heidegger's themes, to wit, the way in which nonessence, disessencing and decomposition (*Un-wesen, Ver-wesung*) plague the essential unfolding of truth (*die Wesung der Wahrheit*):

> If truth unfolds essentially as the clearing of that which conceals itself, and if *nonessence* pertains to essence as a measure of the nullity of being, then would not the perversion of essence prate and prance [*sich breit machen*] in essential unfolding? Would it not do so precisely by distorting the clearing, dissimulating essence, driving distortion to the extreme by placing it at center-stage and in the limelight – all surface, all show? *Theatrics* – configuration of the actual as the task of the stage-manager!
>
> (65, 347)

For Heidegger such theatrics are immanent in the theatre of (un)truth, and in the section of the *Beiträge* called "The grounding", truth and untruth point back to the being-unto-death of Dasein. We would see this quite clearly if we worked through sections 201–2 of the *Beiträge* (65, 323–5), on *Da-sein* as *Weg-sein*, being-there as being-gone. While Freud's grandson and Heidegger agree *mutatis mutandis* about the character of the *da*, what playful Ernst calls *fort* the more earnest Heidegger calls the emphatic and even imperative *weg!* Being-there is always already being-begone, being-bygone. Without regard, one might almost say, but say very softly, *pianissimo*, **pp**, to the presence or absence of the mother. Study of these sections of the *Beiträge* and Chapter 2 of the *Jenseits* would link these remarks of mine on *Bühne* and paranoetic polemic to my proper theme, if one can say so, the theme of the immanence and imminence of death. Let the suggestion serve as the deed. **So far there's been no real dialogue, very little sensory detail, and nothing in the way of a *theme*. And a long time has gone by already without anything happening; it makes a person wonder. We haven't even reached Ocean City yet: we will never get out of the funhouse.**

For Freud's speculation, no insight is more compelling than the immanence of death in life. For Heidegger, no insight is more compelling than the imminence of one's own death. Let me turn now to Freud, rehearsing matters that are by now quite familiar.

The immanence of death in life: Freud is here profoundly influenced by the research and speculation of A. Weismann, himself one of the most important sources for E. Korschelt, Professor of Anatomy and Zoology at the University of Marburg – and a colleague of Heidegger's during the gestation period of *Sein und Zeit*. A genealogy embracing Weismann and Korschelt would enable us to link Freud and Heidegger in a way heretofore unsuspected: the two grandfathers might be brothers, at least as regards the idea of biologically immanent death.

For all theoretical biology and life-philosophy of the late nineteenth century, no speculation is more significant than that involving the immanence of death in life. As Georg Simmel puts it (in another work that Heidegger cites in *Sein und Zeit*), death is not the *Parzenschnitt*, not the thread of *Atropos* cut from above and outside the organism; death is not the extrinsic and contingent truncation of life introduced from the environment; death is not murder or being killed, *Getötetwerden*, but the culminating stage of organic development as such, life's essential unfolding, varying in its precise operation with each species yet always inherent in that species' life. The idea is so common today that it is difficult for us to experience its power in the way Simmel did when he exclaimed, "But this opposite of life derives from nowhere else than life itself! Life itself has produced it and includes it" (Simmel 1918: 101). And let us not abandon Simmel before reading the next paragraph of his text, for it suggests how influential the idea of immanent death as imminent death must have been for the existential-ontological analysis of birth and death, human being and finite time, in Heidegger:

> In every particular moment of life we *are* those who shall die. And that moment would be different if this determination had not been given us

as a dowry, if it were not somehow actual in us. Just as little as we are fully there [*da*] at the moment of our birth, inasmuch as something of us is being born continuously, so little do we die only in our last moment [*Augenblick*].

How much of the existential analysis is immanent in life-philosophy? Enough perhaps to explain Heidegger's polemic against it.

No sooner is the idea of immanent death born, however, than monstrous problems arise. If death is in some sense the τέλος of life, the essential unfolding of life as such, immanent in it and proper to it, then the very opposition of life and death becomes untenable, meaningless. One of the nagging doubts that Freud's 1895 "Project" (Freud 1950) had refused to confront **He envisions a truly astonishing funhouse, incredibly complex yet utterly controlled from a great central switchboard like the console of a pipe organ** was suggested by the very rubric *die Not des Lebens*, the exigency of life, considered as "primary process". Life emergent (but from what?) is in a perpetual state of emergency, "from the outset", inasmuch as the very means by which it secures its ascendancy constitute the gravest menace to it. Even in the "Project" that menace seems to come less from the outside, less from the penetration of the *Reizschutz* by unfiltered energy quanta, than from the internal dynamics of the system Ψ, the dynamics of trauma, hallucination and starvation. The system of life seems to be geared to auto-destruct.

By 1920, with *Jenseits des Lustprinzips*, Freud is invoking "inner drives", *Triebe aus dem Innern*, as the most formidable challenge to Fechnerian constancy. Yet even here his speculation does not really push the question of absolute constancy as stasis and stasis as death – the question of life-death. When in Chapter 5 Freud defines the drive as an indigenous compulsion in the animate organism to restore a former state (*ein dem belebten Organischen innewohnender Drang zur Wiederherstellung eines früheren Zustandes*: 1982: 3, 246), it is the intrinsic residence of the compulsion, *das Innewohnen*, the dwelling-within, *im-manēre*, that is most mysterious. It is the cryptic as such. For it pushes Freud's speculation, not *beyond* the PP, and not inside or outside it, but somewhere behind and beneath it. Exigent life is indigent; death is indigenous to it. From the outset to the end.

No, Heidegger would interject at this point, not to the bitter end, inasmuch as death is interpretable only as a possibility of Dasein, and as a possibility it can only be *imminent*. Freud would rejoin by agreeing that the abstract notion of time, the punctilious time of the time-line in the tradition that stretches from Aristotle through Husserl, is derivative of consciousness and secondary process, that it does not therefore suffice for speculation on lifedeath. From the outset to the end, Freud, like Heidegger, dreams of a more profound temporality, born of periodicity and a kind of rhythm. For his part, Freud is uncertain as to whether or not Heidegger's notion of *kairotic*, appropriate temporality remains punctilious. Heidegger would reply that the *kairotic* is only a stepping-stone to the far side of *ecstatic* temporality, time as the ἐϰστατιϰόν, but this sounds too oceanic to Freud's ear, and the two of them go back and forth on it interminably, full of mutual mistrust, as brothers often are, and should be, when they are speculators. In such a temporal scheme as Freud is dreaming of, which is itself rather oceanic, if the truth be told, neither the PP nor the so-called death drive (a pleonasm, inasmuch as Eros too, insofar as it *is* a drive contains its imminent, immanent death), neither a PP nor a beyond-the-PP are punctuated and available as evidence. Immanence itself is displaced, and imminence postponed, derailed onto the verge of each dimension of time. What would speculation on the verge be like?

To be sure, the entire speculation – on the pleasure and reality principles, the priority of the lifeless, the detour to death as the proper (*eigenen*) path of a specific organism, on the subordination of the partial drives of self-preservation, power and self-assertion to the immanent, ownmost possibility of return to the anorganic, and finally, the particularly unnerving speculation on the identity of lifeguard and psychopath, bodyguard and hit-man, angel and executioner ("*auch diese Lebenswächter sind ursprünglich Trabanten des Todes gewesen*": 3, 249) – the entire speculation, I repeat, hangs on the supposition of immanence: *Wenn wir es als ausnahmslose Erfahrung annehmen dürfen, daß alles Lebende aus* inneren *Gründen stirbt....* "If we may take it as an experience that admits of no exception that every living thing dies because of *inner* reasons ..." (3, 248). Never mind that this "inner", at least in the case of vertebrates, means no more than an invaginated exteriority, the spinal grey and the cortex of the brain being those exterior surfaces that house the deepest interiority of metaphysical man. Never mind that, because it is precisely those inner reasons, the putative immanence of death, that Freud himself purports to doubt in Chapter 6 of *Jenseits*:

> We have constructed a range of conclusions on the basis of a presupposition that all living things must die due to inner causes. We accepted the supposition without concern because it did not seem to us to be a supposition. We are accustomed to thinking this way – our poets confirm this tendency of ours. Perhaps we are determined to believe this supposition because it harbors some consolation.

Allow me to interrupt in order to highlight two strange aspects of Freud's doubt. First, what biological science regards as a major advance in its conception of death, the immanence of decline and demise, Freud now identifies as a customary, familiar idea, an old saw that "the poets" have seduced us into believing. Never mind that the final truth of Eros and Thanatos will be taken from the mouth of one of our oldest poets, and a comic poet at that, a comic poet figured by a very tricky philosopher writing a very tricky text. Second, when Heidegger develops the idea of the essential inherence in life of death, which he does in his lectures on theoretical biology in 1929–30, he professes the idea precisely *because* it is an idea of poets rather than biologists. The immanence of death in life is an idea of poets – and worse than poets: Heidegger cites an epistle of Paul and the apocryphal Book of Esra from the Old Testament to corroborate his biological meditation! – But to return to the passage from *Jenseits:*

> If one is oneself to die and to surrender to death those one loves most, then one would rather succumb to a merciless law of nature, to awesome Ἀνάγκη, than to a contingency one might have been able to avoid. However, this belief in the inner conformity to law [*die innere Gesetz-mäßigkeit*] of dying is perhaps no more than one of the illusions we have created "in order to bear the burden of existence".
>
> (1982: 254)

To be sure, in order to lend credence to his own suspicion of notions implanted in us by *poets*, Freud here cites *Schiller*. When it comes to tricky writers, Freud does not stand behind Plato – except in so far as plato (*sic*) stands behind Socrates. Yet no one who has studied Heidegger's existential-ontological analysis should evade the devilish point Freud is making. The very necessity that drives Heidegger to insist on appropriateness, resolve, openness to one's own finitude, readiness to assume the burden of an existence that is suspended over an abyss of nullity – this very necessity Freud reduces to a comfort and a consolation, as though the very backbone of fundamental ontology were invaginated superficiality, as though it were no more than what Heidegger in section 62 of *Sein und Zeit* calls "a factical ideal of existence", that is to say, an inherited idea about what existence *should* be, an idea and ideal that surreptitiously guide and thus mislead the entire analysis. Readiness for anxiety? Reticence and resolution? Guilt and conscience? Mere conjurings of a necessitous possibility designed to make the burden of contingency easier to bear.

I will not follow any further Freud's diabolical and daimonic text, so overdetermined, so merciless in its exposure of others' illusions, so scrupulous *and* blasé about its own contradictions and castles in the air. **I'll never be an author. It's been forever already, everybody's gone home, Ocean City's deserted, the ghost-crabs are tickling across the beach and down the littered cold streets. And the empty halls of clapboard hotels and abandoned funhouses.** Allow me to turn now to Heidegger's *Being and Time*, specifically to those pages that separate what Heidegger calls the preliminary sketch (*Vorzeichnung*) and the full concept (*voller Begriff*) of being-toward-death.

I want to make the transition by acknowledging my debt once again to Derrida's "Spéculer – sur 'Freud' ". Derrida's text derives from a seminar entitled "Life death", *la vie la mort*, in which it becomes clear that there is no getting beyond the pleasure principle (PP) to something one might properly identify as a death drive proper. In a text that functions "athetically", with no thesis but with countless "hypotheses", a text that proceeds by a singular drifting and diabolical limping, *er-hinken*, **"What are you limping for?" Magda inquired of Ambrose. He supposed in a husky tone that his foot had gone to sleep in the car. . . . How long is this going to take?** the very notion of propriety, along with the logics of opposition, contradiction and dialectic disperse. Derrida does not so much challenge the notion of the immanence of death in life – we have seen that Freud himself does that – as challenge the interiority to which immanence inevitably appeals. If the mirror-play of speculation toys with the demonic in Freud's text, with the uncanny eternal return of the daimon, with the drivenness of drives and compulsive repetition as essentially demonic, with the hopping devil of Freud's *Jenseits des Lustprinzips* as a whole, it is because the demonic enjoins an uncanny doubling of all its doubles and institutes an illimitable specular haunting. "Life Death", "Eros Thanatos", "Protector and Pallbearer", "quasi-immortality", "death-process" – these are less demonic than daimonic: they hover hermetically and hermeneutically in between all the identity poles, as Hermes hovers between heaven and earth, but also between earth and underworld.

When Derrida interprets the *fort* of the *fort/da* game as the emphatic *weg!* (be gone! be bygone! go bye-byes! bye!) he unwittingly underscores Heidegger's insistence in the *Beiträge* that *Da-sein* is *Weg-sein*, and not simply by way of opposition, contradiction, dialectic or paradox. However, the very propriety and identity that Freud's *Jenseits des Lustprinzips* undermines serves as the axis of Heidegger's fundamental ontology in *Sein und Zeit*. If *Freud's* text is daimonic, so too the δαιμόνιον to which Heidegger himself refers in his 1928 logic lectures will not leave intact the axis of appropriateness. For that axis is fixed in the slippery sockets of lifedeath. Discussing the detour that is self-preserving life, life maintaining itself by means of partial or component drives, Derrida worries about the "immanence" of the death that would be "proper" to a particular organism:

> The component drives [*Partialtriebe*] are *destined* to *insure* that the organism dies *of its own death*, that it follows its proper path toward death. That it arrives at death according to its proper pace [*eigenen Todesweg*]. That all the possibilities of a return to the inorganic that would not be "immanent" in it are kept at a distance from it [*weg!* we might say, *fernzuhalten* he says]. The nihilative pace [*pas*] must pass within it, from it to it, between it and itself. Thus the non-proper must be held at a distance, one must reappropriate oneself, one must cause to return [*da!*] unto one's death. One must send oneself the message of one's own death. . . . Not in order to keep oneself from death, or to maintain oneself against death, but only in order to avoid a death that would not revert to oneself, to cut off a death that would not be one's own or of one's own kind. In the detour of the pace, in the pace of the detour, the organism keeps itself from that other which might still steal

its death from it. It keeps itself from the other that might give it the death that, by itself, it would not have given to itself (for this is a theory of suicide deferred, or suicide by correspondence). . . . The drive of the proper would be stronger than life *and* death.

(1980: 378–9, 355–6)

Yet precisely this propriety – the drive of the proper – is undone in the Freudian text:

the most driven drive is the drive of the proper, in other words, the drive that tends to reappropriate itself. . . . The proper is the tendency to appropriate itself. Whatever the combinatory of these tautologies or analytic statements, they can never be reduced to the form S *is* P. Each time, in the case of drive, force, movement, tendency, or *telos*, a division must be maintained. . . . Heterology is involved, and this is why there is force, and this is why there is legacy and scene of writing, distancing from the self and delegation, sending. The proper is not the proper, and if it appropriates itself it is because it disappropriates itself – properly, improperly. Life death are no longer opposed in it.

(1980: 379, 356–7)

The immanence of lifedeath inaugurates interminable suspense, the inde- terminacy of a death that can only be the event of an uncertain future, an imminent death. The death drive *and* the PP operate by way of exappropri- ation; they belong to a domain that exceeds all oppositions and identities, "so that we no longer know precisely what we are saying when we say proper, law of the proper, economy, etc." (1980: 419, 393).

What must such exappropriation mean for a fundamental ontology that revolves about the appropriation of one's own (proper) being-toward- death? Section 50, "Preliminary sketch of the existential-ontological struc- ture of death", elaborates three decisive traits of death as the possibility of the sheer impossibility of being-there. Death is the *ownmost* (*eigenste*) possibility of Dasein. In the very first trait we hear the root of *Eigentlich- keit*, appropriateness. If existence is in each case my own, the possibility of death must be more proper to me than anything else. My own death, as the ownmost possibility of my being in the world, bears no relation (*Bezug*) to any other existence; death is (second trait) *non-relational* (*unbezüglich*). Ownmost, without relation, the death of Dasein is utter- most, outermost, *die äußerste Möglichkeit*. It cannot be surmounted or surpassed, cannot be overtaken or passed by; death is (third trait) *impass- able* (*unüberholbar*). Uncanny, this impassable possibility, driven by neces- sity. No wonder lucid analytical philosophers write articles and even books about Heidegger's obvious confusion of the Kantian modalities.

So much for the "preliminary sketch". Yet two more fundamental traits have to be added if we are to grasp the full existential concept of death. Section 52 counterposes "everyday being toward the end" and the full existential concept. The discussion, you will remember, has to do with the very certainty (*Gewißheit*) of death. Precisely this certitude, as Freud indicated, comforts quotidian Dasein. Death becomes the pendant to taxes. Heidegger's discussion of such equivocal certitude, conviction, taking-to-be-true and even apodicticity of evidence serves as a repetition of section 44, on "truth", the truth of an existence that is always simultaneously in untruth. Nowhere does Heidegger's project veer so close to its Cartesian legacy; nowhere does it repudiate that legacy so decisively. For the *certitude* of death (fourth trait) has something peculiar (*eigentümlich*) about it (1972: 258). No cogitation, no experience, no mental manipulation, no confrontation is equal to it. For the certainty of death is accompanied always by (fifth trait) "*indeterminacy* as to its when" (258). No, not merely accompanied. The fifth and final trait is not simply hooked onto the fourth, as the fourth is not merely appended to the first three. Impassable indeterminacy is the crucial determination of all the traits, the order of which now changes. Heidegger writes in italics the following definition of "the full existential-ontological concept of death". "*Death, as the end of Dasein, is the ownmost, nonrelational, certain and as such indeterminate, impassable possibility of Dasein*" (258–9). The third trait, *Unüberholbarkeit*, shifts now to fifth and final position. Or perhaps to the *fourth* and final position: are the traits of certitude and indeterminacy two or one? *Gewisse und als solche unbestimmte*: certain and, precisely as certain, indeterminate. One might object that indeterminacy as to the *when* of death does not render death as such indeterminate; however, the imminence of death, which as existential possibility is always still outstanding, renders problematic every form of immanence, including the immanence of death. The "peculiar" nature of death's certitude, the *Eigentümlichkeit* of indeterminacy as to its "when", displaces the propriety of precisely this most proper possibility. **This can't go on much longer; it can go on forever.** Heidegger will doubtless continue to insist on the reciprocal grounding of appropriate and inappropriate forms of existence. Yet the peculiar haunts the proper, undermines all the fundaments of fundamental ontology; the indeterminate imminent, which is a name for finite transcendence, τὸ δαιμόνιον, haunts all immanence. Existential certitude can never proceed as the firm footfall of confident interpretation. It can only limp along in the face of the overpowering, in the face of daimon lifedeath; it can only be what Heidegger himself calls an excessive demand and a phantasm, *eine phantastische Zumutung*. The imp of the perverse is always at home in such certitude. Which is perhaps why even nowadays *Sein und Zeit* is a difficult book to obliterate.

When immanence is displaced in *ecstasis* to an "outside itself" in-and-for-itself (329), what transpires? Let us speculate. Certitude seems to be held in suspension; it finds itself *on the verge*, where, in the end, naught nowhere was never found. It is a little like wandering through the mirrormaze at an amusement park, very much like being lost in the funhouse.

That is the title of a short story or brief text by John Barth (1967), and I have been reading it to you obsessively all the while I ought to have been pursuing pure speculation with Freud and Heidegger. **He wonders: will he become a regular person? Something has gone wrong; his vaccination didn't take; at the Boy-Scout initiation campfire he only pretended to be deeply moved, as he pretends to this hour that it is not so bad after all in the funhouse, and that he has a little limp. How long will it last?**

Two paces more, if you will allow. It is no surprise that Heidegger should lend himself to a speculation on the death drive. Yet can the full existential conception of death in any way be immanent in or imminent to Eros? How can it be, when Heidegger maintains the most stubborn silence concerning that area which Socrates, "the purest thinker of the West" (1954: 52), claimed to be his sole area of expertise – τὰ ἐρωτικά?

No doubt, Heidegger seldom invokes the daimon Eros by name – although see his remarks on τὸ ἐρασμιώτατον, "the superlatively rapturous", in the first of his Nietzsche courses. His Trakl essay of 1953 never conjures Eros, whatever it may say concerning the "discord of the sexes" and an envisaged return to a "gentler childhood", a "more confluent twofold". Where is there a spark of Eros in Heidegger to which a death drive could attach itself like a virus? Where in Heidegger is there any hope of contamination by an Aristophanic sneeze? **Naturally he didn't have enough nerve to ask Magda to go through the funhouse with him. With incredible nerve and to everyone's surprise he invited Magda, quietly and politely, to go through the funhouse with him. "I warn you, I've never been through it before," he added, *laughing easily*; "but I reckon we can manage somehow. The important thing to remember, after all, is that it's meant to be a *fun*house; that is, a place of amusement. If people really got lost or injured or too badly frightened in it, the owner'd go out of business. There'd even be lawsuits. No character in a work of fiction can make a speech this long without interruption or acknowlegment from the other characters."**

There is one place where Heidegger does discuss something like Eros. I mean the 1928 logic lectures, mentioned earlier, in the matter of τὸ δαιμόνιον. In these lectures Heidegger provides some guidelines for his "preparatory analysis" of Dasein. It is an analysis, he says, not of human beings but of *das Dasein*, a neutral and neuter-gendered phenomenon whose name guards the peculiar neutrality and indifference of what otherwise would be called *man*. As Derrida has emphasized, the very first thing toward which Dasein is proclaimed indifferent and with respect to which Dasein is declared essentially neutral is *Geschlecht*. Because Heidegger mentions "both *Geschlechter*", and because we assume that the sexes are two, and because this is a logic class, we infer that Dasein is neutral and indifferent *vis-à-vis* sexuality. Such neutrality is nothing negative, insists Heidegger, but is "the original positivity and puissance of essential unfolding", *die ursprüngliche Positivität und Mächtigkeit des Wesens*. **No reader would put up with such *prolixity*.** If the daimonic drivenness of drives in Freud has to do with power, mastery or at least coping, then we may surmise that Heidegger's nascent "metaphysics of Dasein" has indeed slipped into the speculative realm of Eros. That realm lies behind or beneath the ego of any egoism or of any isolated individual. Its isolation is metaphysical. (In the logic lectures, incidentally, it seems as though an idea were being daimonically driven to its speculative uttermost, simply out of curiosity, in some uncanny isolation.) At the heart of this penisolate realm is the primal font, *der Urquell*, from which all factical concretion flows. Factical concretion? Existences, like you and me, bodies concrescent, organisms assimilatory and erotized. (I am going too fast, I know, but it is a fast idea.) What are the dynamics of factical concretion? Factical concretion is – to speak an ancient language, a language Aristophanes knew and parodied – both condensation and rarefaction, both agglomeration and dispersion. Yet even if Heidegger is avowed the thinker of gathering, *Versammlung*, the two words he chooses in order to designate the dynamics of factical concretion are semination and dissemination, *Streuung* and *Zerstreuung*, literally, strewing and emphatic bestrewal or scattering. Strewing of what into what? That is hard to say. Emphatic bestrewal disseminates embodiment and thereby sexuality, which also enjoins a scattering or dispersal into space and into language, the language not of propositions but of prepositions.

Emphatic bestrewal sounds like something negative, even if *dis-* (from δύο, δυσ-) means doubly or utterly, and is essentially positive. *Zerstreuung* is an unfolding of facets, hence an aggregation of sorts. Scattering devolves upon an original semination, upon *Streuung* as such. Without even *whispering* the name *Aristophanes*, **Italics should be used *sparingly*** for that would cause *gastric upset*, **Italics mine,** *Heidegger writes:* "It is not a question of imagining some vast primal creature [ein großes Urwesen] that would have its simplicity split [zerspaltet] into many particulars" (26, 173). Rather, strewing is original multiplication; it is that which allows multifaceted, manifold being; *Zer-streuung* is therefore the ultimate modality, the necessitous possibility of all actual possibles.

However, the dynamism that projects Dasein into a dual sexuality inaugurates the never-ending scene of the drive or drives that constitute the mating process (*die gattungshafte Einigung*: 175), which for Heidegger as for Hegel drags on into wretched infinity. The dynamism of a driven or strewn Dasein produces a scene – a polemical scene – in which the narrowing, compelling, obscuring and obfuscating of *other* possibilities (the possibilities of the *other*, the *other sex*, for example) is the rule. Heidegger wonders aloud why our being-with-one-another has to be "compressed [*gedrängt*] into this particular factical direction in which other possibilities are left in the shadows or remain altogether closed [*abgeblendet werden oder verschlossen bleiben*]" (175). Multiplication, even of one by two, yields dispersion. Assimilation or gathering yields disaggregation. Concentration yields distraction. *Streuung* yields *Zerstreuung*. The emphatic *Zer-* is daimonic, it is the ζα of ζωή, the very force of lifedeath, and it is unstoppable. It blasts every contact barrier and obliterates the stores of all cathexis; it restores the delirious reign of chaos and extravagant expenditure.

Streuung ought to have been life alone, and *Zerstreuung* death. Yet Heidegger's putative dualism is as futile of Freud's. "From the outset", boasts Freud in Chapter 6, "our conception was a *dualistic* one, and today it is so more keenly [*schärfer*] than ever before". *Jenseits* is full of "sharp distinctions", if only in order that Freud may take a swipe at Jung's libidinal "monism". Yet how bizarre are Freud's sharp distinctions, forever trying to balance an equation consisting of two unknowns, "life" and "death", presuming they are two (*3*, 266); how full of bravado and *miserere* is his limping text: "We are coming under suspicion of having tried all the while at any price to escape from an embarrassment" (263). **A long time ago we should have passed the apex of Freitag's Triangle and made brief work of the *dénouement*; the plot doesn't rise by meaningful steps but winds upon itself, digresses, retreats, hesitates, sighs, collapses, expires.** Earlier in Chapter 6 he calls his conception of the life of drives (*Triebleben*) an "exquisitely dualistic conception" (258). *Exquisit dualistisch. Exquisit* means either "exceptional" and "profoundly thought-through" or "contrived", "belaboured". It also means a painful examination, and refers to the excruciating pain of torture, the exquisite pain of the dentist's drill. Freud's speculation is *exquisitely* dualistic, unable to withstand the pain yet incapable of collapsing into supine monistic immanence. For the lifedeath of drives is as far beyond beings as being ever was, and the thinking that broaches it can only be exquisitely paranoetic.

Recall, finally, that for the Heidegger of the early Freiburg period, especially between the years 1919 and 1923, factical life is essentially ruinous, or as he says, *ruinant*. To resist such *Ruinanz* he posits a *Gegenruinanz*, a homologue to Freud's *Gegenbesetzung*, the effort to stem psychic trauma. Neither Freud nor Heidegger dreams of an effortless existence. *Die Not des Lebens* is for both *die Not-wendigkeit*, the exigency of life is the turning and turning of need, and the mysteries of primal repression and primary process are mysteries of being, whether one thinks being as ruinance, care, destitution or calamity of beyng.

To be sure, the journalist in us is ready by way of *dénouement* to reduce both Heidegger and Freud to some determinate *Zeitgeist*, some nice niche in the pan-German Ideology. Yet I wonder whether, once we have finished speculating on the two of them as though we were the stage-managers of the world-historical *Bühne*, their crypts will gape once again and they will rise to haunt us with things we thought we knew and had under control by now, things still secret even after they have been utterly disclosed, things both homey and monstrous at once, things both within and without our ken, both canny and uncanny – in a word, a word beloved of both

Freud and Heidegger, things *unheimlich*. If death is immanent in life precisely because it is ever imminent, we will never feel at home with these two old grandpapas who never speak to one another, these two irascible heroes and daimons, these guardian angels and godfathers of lifedeath, these two grand *pépés*. **He wishes he had never entered the funhouse. But he has. Then he wishes he were dead. But he's not. Therefore he will construct funhouses for others and be their secret operator – though he would rather be among the lovers for whom funhouses are designed.**

p.p.

BIBLIOGRAPHY

Barth, John (1967) "Lost in the Funhouse", in *Lost in the Funhouse*, Garden City, New York: Doubleday.

Derrida, Jacques (1980) *La carte postale de Socrate à Freud et au-delà*, Paris: Aubier-Flammarion. See esp. pp. 378–9; 419.

Freud, Sigmund (1950) *Aus den Anfängen der Psychoanalyse*, ed. Ernst Kris, New York: Imago. This volume contains both the letters to Flieβ and the "Project". See esp. p. 152.

—— (1971) "*Selbstdarstellung*", *Schriften zur Geschichte der Psychoanalyse*, ed. Ilse Grubrich-Simitis, Frankfurt am Main: Fischer Taschenbuch Verlag, originally published in 1925, no. 6096. See esp. p. 87.

—— (1982) *Jenseits des Lustprinzips (Beyond the Pleasure Principle*, originally published in 1920), in *Studienausgabe, Band III: Psychologie des Unbewußten*, Conditio humana, Frankfurt am Main: Fischer Verlag, pp. 213–72. (Contains the editorial material of the English *Standard Edition of the Complete Psychological Works of Sigmund Freud*, London: Hogarth Press, 1975.)

Heidegger, Martin (1954), *Was heißt Denken?* Tübingen: M. Niemeyer. See esp. pp. 49 and 52.

—— (1972) *Sein und Zeit*, 12th edn, Tübingen: M. Niemeyer, a reprinting of the seventh edition (1953). See esp. sections 50 and 52.

—— (1978), *Metaphysische Anfangsgründe der Logik im Ausgang von Leibniz*, in *Gesamtausgabe*, vol. 26, from the year 1928. Frankfurt am Main: V. Klostermann. See esp. pp. 173–5.

—— (1985) *Phänomenologische Interpretationen zu Aristoteles: Einführung in die phänomenologische Forschung*, in *Gesamtausgabe*, vol. 61, from the years 1921–2. Frankfurt am Main: V. Klostermann. See esp. Part III, chap. 2.

—— (1989) *Beiträge zur Philosophie (Vom Ereignis)*, in *Gesamtausgabe*, vol. 65, from the years 1936–8. Frankfurt am Main: V. Klostermann. See esp. pp. 323–5; 347.

Nietzsche, Friedrich (1980) Notebook M III 1, Spring–Autumn 1881, from the *Nachlaß: Sämtliche Werke, Kritische Studienausgabe*, ed. Giorgio Colli and Mazzino Montinari, Berlin and Munich: W. de Gruyter and Deutscher Taschenbuch Verlag. Vol. 9, pp. 441–575.

Simmel, Georg (1918) *Lebensanschauung: Vier metaphysische Kapitel*, Munich and Leipzig: Duncker und Humblot. See esp. chap. 3, "Death and immortality".

9 The word of silence

William Richardson

With his monumental study: *Heidegger: Through Phenomenology to Thought*, **William Richardson**, Professor of Philosophy at Boston College, has played a crucial role in introducing the philosophical work of Martin Heidegger into the English-speaking world. In the 1970s his interests, however, turned decidedly in the direction of psychoanalysis. He trained as a Lacanian analyst in Paris, and with John Muller he wrote a lucid introduction to Lacan's *Ecrits*. The present paper is deeply lodged within the various orientations of Heidegger and Lacan, as Richardson explores the issue of silence as a fundamental element of analysis. He shows how philosophy may supply a more adequate understanding of the realities of clinical practice than much analytic theory. By attending extensively to actual case material, Richardson elucidates different forms of silence and their varying function in the analytic situation. He then makes way for Heidegger's account of the ability to be silent as one of the conditions for authentic human speech as opposed to, for instance, hearsay or chatter. Silence or stillness becomes the very foundation of the spoken word and hence of the world according to Heidegger. This "ringing stillness" testifies to an otherness which is similar to what Lacan sought to explore under the sign of the unconscious in the analytic situation. Richardson argues that Lacan's reading of the Freudian unconscious as "structured like a language" cries out for a philosophical foundation much better supplied by Heidegger than by Lacan's own recourse to linguistic and mathematical formalism. In order to substantiate the depth of language, Richardson carefully guides the reader to appreciate a rootedness of our language in the tradition of Greek philosophy.

SELECT BIBLIOGRAPHY

Richardson, William, *Heidegger: From Phenomenology to Thought*, The Hague: Martinus Nijhoff, 1963.
—— and Muller, J., *Lacan and Language: A Reader's Guide to "Ecrits"*, New York: International Universities Press, 1982.

* * *

Recently, a psychoanalyst friend reported a case he was treating in which the silence of the analyst played a significant role. It was as if the whole analysis rested on a base of silence. It recalled to him certain passages in the work of Martin Heidegger, whose book, *What Is Called Thinking?* (1968), he had read many years before. The book had spoken to him about thinking, and speaking and keeping silent. Since he knew that I had a certain interest in Heidegger, he proposed that we reflect upon the case together and present it as a collaborative effort to our professional peers: he would supply the clinical data, I would extrapolate upon it in Heideggerian fashion, and we would invite our colleagues to help us evaluate the success or failure of the experiment. I propose here to share with the reader my part of the bargain.

This friend, though intellectually very gifted, had in no sense a "philosophical" mind. What, then, fascinated him in Heidegger? In that particular work Heidegger reflects on the Greek words for thinking: *legein* and *noein*. *Legein* (verb; noun form – *Logos*), according to Heidegger, originally meant a laying together in the Open and collecting into unity what had been dispersed (one recalls Monet's paintings of haystacks). Only much later did the word come to mean explicitly "to think" and "to speak" in the sense that we use those words today. But when the analyst invites the analysand to lie down on the couch and say whatever comes to mind, isn't that a *legein*? And if *noein*, in Heidegger's reading, originally meant "to accept" or "to take under one's care", is not the analyst's engagement to listen a commitment to take this *legein* under his care, to shelter, protect it and give it a place and a time to be? Is not psychoanalytic work, as such, a *legein* and a *noein* of this kind? And isn't it a process of revelation through which *a-letheia* comes about? And it includes a certain discreet silence: "perhaps language demands a just silence more than precipitate speech", Heidegger wrote (1977: 223). At any rate, this is what was to be reflected upon, and the reflection that I offer here. I propose to summarize briefly the essentials of this clinical case; then to review Heidegger's conception of language with attention to the role that silence plays in it; finally to return to the case and offer some personal animadversions.

Karl was a 32-year-old physician when he came into analysis – a bachelor and overt homosexual. The reasons that led him to analysis were as follows: (1) a certain inhibition in talking and writing; (2) a difficulty with confronting persons in authority (such as Dr Hofrat, his superior); (3) his incapacity to deal with his "drives" – their "pettiness ... or [their] mortal danger"; (4) his entrapment in an oppressive but loving relationship with his mother who appeared to be a powerful, dominating, constantly chattering woman in contrast to a totally silent and almost paralysed father – whose silence Karl came to consider a frozen and irreversible symptom of neurosis as well as a sign of contempt for his son; (5) his failure of an oral examination in psychiatry, although he had always been a very bright student – the sort of anti-social act of which Winnicott writes and to which Masud Khan refers in his well-known article on "Silence and communication" (cited Khan 1974: 171). It was this obvious act of rebellion that precipitated the analysis.

As for Karl's family background, both parents were still alive and he had one sister (older by six years), the divorced mother of an 8-year-old child. The family had included the mother's sister, Aunt Donna, who had died of cancer four years earlier. In the preliminary interview, the analyst was struck, on the one hand, by the contrast between the stiffness of Karl's body, the almost total absence of gestures, the immobile expression of his face, and, on the other, the extreme elegance of his speech, which was that of a written text rather than of oral speech – all the more surprising because one of his complaints was that he was unable to write. Karl ended his last preliminary interview by stating that he thought that three years of analysis would suffice, that he had made financial arrangements only for that length of time, and then that would be it. The analyst greeted this with total silence and ended the interview abruptly.

During the first three years of the analysis, the analyst kept almost completely silent. For Karl, this silence was of the same kind as that of his father. It was felt to be contemptuous, an obstinate refusal to consider him as a possible object of desire, or even as a human being worthy of any kind of attention at all. At the same time, there was a clear imaginary transference that wanted the analyst to be his *alter ego*, his ideal ego, the one he believed to have been deeply repressed by the influence of his silent father.

In the beginning, Karl spoke little about his father. He was much more talkative about the mother and her father, whom she respected highly. He had been a butcher and for some unknown reason had gone bankrupt during the childhood of his daughters. After his wife died, the two daughters cared for him in his senility, along with a younger brother who died of uremia in his teens. Karl's mother always presented her father as the ideal of strength and masculinity in contrast to Karl's own father, her taciturn and almost paralysed husband. Karl adored his mother and was fascinated by her inexhaustible stream of talk. As soon as she came home (she worked daily for the father in his restaurant), she would create around Karl an imaginary world of fantasy and fairy tales. Every evening until he was 13 or 14 he would sit silently on her lap, both of them in a rocking chair, and she would invent these stories for him.

But he also felt the weight of her controlling personality and he would seek refuge in the mother's sister, Donna, his aunt, a sympathetic woman, who, along with distance from his mother, would give him some genuine affection as well as reassurance when he was depressed by the total indifference of his father. As for girls, Karl had never been attracted to them. A solitary boy, he had few friends and began to have homosexual fantasies in his teens. When he went up to the university he started to act them out, sometimes quite promiscuously, even violently. He stopped having random sex before beginning analysis, however, because of his intense fear of AIDS.

During these first three years, the patient built up his world of maternal imagos, and the analyst maintained his silence. It is possible that the patient interpreted the analyst's silence as similar to his own while listening to his mother's chattering – another form of mirroring identification, putting the analyst in the position of the other – the other in the mirror, namely himself. From the analyst's point of view, the silence served three functions: (1) the first was to avoid being caught up in the imaginary, specular relationship that Karl did his best to establish between the two of them; (2) the second was to sustain Karl's demands by listening to them without yielding to them; (3) the third was to let Karl feel the analyst's presence when, for example, he would suddenly stop talking. Thus Lacan: "the most acute feeling of the presence of the analyst is bound up with the moment when the subject can only remain silent, that is to say when he even recoils before the shadow of demand" (1977: 255). The silences during parts of some sessions, however, were tense and heavy and led the analyst to think that they had nothing to do with his father's silence but rather with that of someone on whom Karl had been intensely dependent at a very early age. These were all the more noticeable in contrast to the brilliance of his imaginary world, peopled by his mother's fantasies.

The first period of the analysis culminated in a dream toward the end of the third year of treatment: Karl and the analyst were watching a fantastic show with Madonna on stage dressed as Marie Antoinette. He described in great detail the production, which was like an instantiation of the imaginary world he had reconstructed during the previous three years. Marie Antoinette's sister, Elizabeth, was also on stage. The analyst was sitting in silence; he was watching both the show and Marie Antoinette herself walking to her death in an incredibly beautiful costume. The executioner could be seen in a shadowy corner of the stage, and Karl described in detail the complex network of glances at work among the characters – the game of looking and being looked at. This led the analyst to ask what was under, or behind, the beautiful costume, and Karl answered in a puzzled tone: "a maliferous body". The analyst was struck by the unusual word, "maliferous", and echoed it back to him in an inquiring tone. But Karl kept silent and became very tense.

Shortly after this dream Karl announced that his three years were up and that he would finish the analysis at the end of the month. He felt "much better", etc., and "thank you very much". The analyst answered: "Well, you have finished something, but you decided to put an end to the analysis before you even began. Now that you have reached *your* end, perhaps you can really begin the analysis at last." Several sessions of total silence followed, but Karl decided to continue.

Thus began the second phase of the analysis. All at once the whole analytic atmosphere changed. Karl stopped interpreting the analyst's silence as an imaginary one, i.e., as contemptuous and despising, and took it to be rather a supportive, i.e., in the analyst's view, a symbolic one. When he resumed speaking, he said he could now walk toward the analyst naked, with his maliferous body. "Both our silences were finally in tune", the analyst observed, "even if they were different in function."

The stage of the maternal imagos had suddenly vanished; even the low monotony of his voice changed into a more raucous and choppy tone. He began with great difficulty to (re)discover a new version of his father. If Karl's father had indeed been a silent man, and if he was now almost paralysed, he had been both active and industrious when Karl was very young. He would do a lot of things about the house: he would repair things and even build with his own hands furniture, cupboards, toys, etc. Very slowly – at about the time that Karl himself started to do handiwork around his own new apartment – Karl began to remember with uneasy and uncertain words, intertwined with embarrassed and halting silences, that when he was very young, even before he was 4, his father would show him how to do things with his hands. He would sustain the achievements of his son by his attentive presence, and approve of them in silence. This for the analyst recalled another passage from Heidegger:

> We are trying to learn thinking... [Thinking] is a craft, a "handicraft". "Craft" literally means the strength and skill in our hands.... The hand's essence can never be determined, or explained by its being an organ which can grasp. Apes, too, have organs that can grasp, but they do not have hands.... Only a being who can speak, that is, think, can have hands and can be handy in achieving works of handicraft.

> But the craft of the hand is richer than we commonly imagine.... The hand reaches and extends itself, and receives its own welcome in the hands of others.... The hand designs and signs, presumably because human being is a sign. Two hands fold into one, a gesture meant to carry humans into the great oneness. The hand is all this, and this is the true handicraft.... But the hand's gestures run everywhere through language, in their most perfect purity when man speaks by being silent. (1968: 16–17)

By learning this handiwork from his father, Karl, as the analyst saw things, discovered the Name-of-the-father through the doings-of-the-father, in so far as they were part of his silent language. Here, for the therapist, was the wisdom of Heidegger: "The hand's gestures run everywhere through language, in their most perfect purity precisely when man speaks by being silent." Not only did Karl discover how to use his hands as a speaking being, *un parlêtre* (Lacan), but in the analysis he learned to put into words the doings-of-the-father. It is worth noting that during this time his writing inhibition was lifted. The analyst's silence, which now was experienced as a supportive one, allowed him to rediscover the silent language that took place very early in his life between his father and himself. But at the same time he also discovered a fundamental and deadly silence in his mother as well.

It was a dream that led to a third phase of Karl's analysis: Karl entered a catacomb, the catacomb known as the "Tomb of the saint". His aunt was the saint. She was in a coffin which was closed, and Karl's mother was sitting totally mute, apparently lifeless, nearby. Her absolute muteness protected the secret of the dead saint.

The saint turned out to be less Karl's aunt than his grandmother, and beyond her the great-grandmother, whose name was "Antoinette". The name Antoinette brought back the earlier dream and the signifier "maliferous", which the analyst now pronounced as "mali" – "ferous". Now Karl transformed it into two words of which "maliferous" was the condensation: "malediction" and "ferocious". These two signifiers gave rise to two distinct chains of associations that led to unveiling the secret of the saint.

The name "Antoinette" brought back a memory. Karl had heard that his maternal great-grandmother gave birth to twenty-five children, but eighteen of them died at almost the same time during the epidemic of "Spanish influenza" at the end of World War I. For him this indicated a malediction attached to Antoinette and her offspring, transmitted through the maternal lineage, of a predisposition to malignant tumours: cancer of the breast. The maternal grandmother had died of this, likewise Aunt Donna, and about this time Karl's sister discovered that she, too, had cancer of the breast. Yet total silence had been kept about this malediction in the family, presumably as a means to avoid confrontation with death. You will recall Freud's observation: "We have shown the unmistakable tendency to shove death aside, to eliminate it from our life. We have tried to cover it over with silence" (1915: 289).

There was another aspect to the secret of the saint, suggested by the signifier "ferocious". Even in the earlier dream, the executioner could be seen in a shadowy corner and seemed "ferocious". Karl had said that the hangman was a butcher before his life disintegrated. Apparently he would not only sell meat but would personally slaughter the animals for the shop – a "ferocious" butcher. This led to a memory of the father killing in the restaurant a "ferocious" rat that had frightened him with its sharp eyes. Karl associated with amusement to his uncontrolled fear of his boss, Dr Hofrat; then to rat holes, those seedy bars with dark back rooms where he could have heavy sex and indulge in sadistic practices in the dark. Then back again to the grandfather's butcher shop and memories of his mother telling him how the grandfather would kill rats with an axe, wearing a "ferocious" smile. Karl tried to question his mother about the grandfather, but she became vague and strangely silent. After some investigations of his own, Karl discovered that when the grandfather collapsed he had gone through a period of extremely destructive behaviour, slaughtering animals cruelly, and then, after his wife's death, slaughtering his daughters' animal pets in the house. Finally, considered a threat to his children, the grandfather was hospitalized for criminal insanity. This, then, was the secret of the saint. This was what the mother had been depressed about and masked with her brilliant chatter. This was the deadly depression that Karl, as her male child, had been forced to share and against which he was expected to defend her.

Karl decided not to mention to his mother what he had discovered. He kept silent on the subject, but his silence was intended to protect her muteness and prevent her from falling into the horror, which, as the analyst saw it, she had foreclosed. The analyst, silently again, agreed with Karl's decision, for it allowed him to shift away from his mother's control, though he went on listening to her chatter, for he was aware of what abyss of horror it covered over.

There are many kinds of silence in this segment of an analytic process: there is the enigmatic silence of the father, the traumatic silence of the mother, the silence of Aunt Donna about her malediction, all conjoined in the silence within Karl himself that was locked up in a vault of darkness that was his basic symptom. Add to this the silence in Karl that is in every analysand: the silence of opposition, resentment, fear, etc. – those mysterious blockages to full speech that constitute what we call "resistance". Finally, there is the silence of the analyst, deliberately chosen, strictly disciplined, conscientiously sustained. The first of these is essentially destructive, the second obstructive – both negative in their effect on Karl. This negative silence that pertains to his pathology I shall refer to simply as "pathological". The third silence is constructive in its effect, liberating, restorative and healing – this is the focus of attention here.

If we turn now to Heidegger for a context in which to think this therapeutic silence, we must go back to long before the analysis of *legein/ noein* in the later years to his first major work, *Being and Time* (1962a). It is common knowledge, of course, that Heidegger's question there was "What is the meaning of Being as different from beings?" where "beings" are "whatever is" and "Being" whatever lets them be (i.e. manifest) and present themselves as what they are – the "is" of "what is". It is common knowledge, too, that he chooses as the phenomenon *par excellence* for analysis that being who must know what "is" means, since "is" is an essential part of its daily speech, i.e., human being (Dasein). This he analyses as Being-in-the-World, first examining the meaning of World, then what it means to be "in" such a World. Being-in the World involves several different components: one lights up the world like a searchlight (he calls it "understanding"); another discloses in an affective way Dasein's relatedness to other beings (he calls it "disposition"); both components being weighted down by the burden of Dasein's inescapable finitude (he calls this Dasein's "fallenness"). Besides these two components, Dasein has a third: the capacity to articulate what is disclosed to it in Language. This structural component Heidegger calls *Rede*, normally translated "discourse" but itself translating the Greek *logos*. To retain the force of the Greek, I propose to anglicize the Greek and call it "logos". Dasein's built-in capacity to articulate language, then, is the structural component of "logos".

This is what we must examine more closely. If we consider the World as a Matrix of Meaning, then the World itself would be the totality of whatever can be articulated, hence the articul-able, while actual speaking would be the articula-tion of meaning. In that case, the structural component of "logos" should be thought of as articulate-ness, the "existential/ ontological" dimension of speech (Heidegger 1962a: 204, 214). This structure involves two modalities: being attentive (*hören*) and being silent (*schweigen*). One can be attentive either to the other (*hören auf*) or to oneself. Attentiveness to the other implies the entire structure of Dasein as with other Daseins in-the-World. In fact, the disclosure of the World to Dasein takes place only when the experience is shared, and there is genuine communication (*Mitteilung*): this is the foundation of all discourse, most especially the psychoanalytic one (163, 217). To listen to oneself is to listen to the call of conscience inviting one to be one's true self, to achieve one's truth.

But the second modality of Dasein's "logos" consists in being silent, and it is this that is of interest here:

> Who in talking with another remains silent may "make something understood", i.e., develop an understanding more authentically than he who is never short of words. Speaking a great deal about something does not offer the slightest guarantee that thereby understanding is advanced. On the contrary, talking extensively about something covers it up and brings what is understood to a sham clarity – the unintelligibility of the trivial [this is not exactly the case of Karl's mother, but her loquacity certainly was, at the very least, a cover-up]. But to keep silent does not mean to be [completely] dumb. On the contrary, if a man is [completely] dumb, he still has a tendency to "speak". Such a person has not proved that he can keep silence; indeed, he entirely lacks the possibility of proving anything of the sort. And the person who is accustomed by nature to speak little [Karl's father, perhaps?] is no better able to show that he is keeping silent or that he is the sort of person who can do so. He who never says anything cannot keep silent at any given moment. Keeping silent authentically is possible only in genuine discourse. To be able to keep silent, *Dasein* must have something to say – i.e., it must have at its disposal an authentic and rich disclosure of itself. In that case one's reticence [*Verschweigenheit*] makes something manifest and does away with "idle talk" [*Gerede*]. As a manner of engaging in discourse, reticence articulates the comprehensibility of

Dasein in so primordial a fashion that it gives rise to the power to be attentive that is genuine and a being-with-others that is transparent.

(1962a: 208, 164–5)

In a word, then, silence is a form of articulate-ness, a modality of "logos", to the extent that it lets-be-seen in interchange with another what there is to understand. Under the best of circumstances, silence of this order is an antidote to the perverse effects of Dasein's fallenness upon its use of language, e.g., when it loses itself in "idle talk" (*Gerede*) – what Lacan calls "empty speech".

But the picture is not yet complete. For if the structural component of Dasein called "logos" retains the sense of that-which-lets-be-seen/heard, it also retains its affiliation with truth under the guise of revelation (*alētheia*). The relation between truth and being is a classic one, of course, and Heidegger singles it out for special attention both in *Being and Time* and later in an essay "On the essence of truth". The normal meaning of truth, namely of some kind of conformity between subject-judging and object-judged is valid enough as far as it goes, but it presupposes a more fundamental level of truth that makes this access between subject and object possible. For Heidegger, this more fundamental truth is the disclosure of the World in and through Dasein. As itself this disclosure (*Erschlossenheit*), Dasein is said to be "in the truth". But this disclosive process that is Dasein is profoundly finite, hence "fallen". As a result:

> To *Dasein*'s state of Being belongs *falling*. First of all and for the most part *Dasein* is lost in its "world." ... That which has been uncovered and closed off by idle talk, curiosity and ambiguity.... Beings have not been completely hidden; they are precisely the sort of thing that has been uncovered, but at the same time they have been disguised. They show themselves but in the mode of seeming-to-be. Likewise what has formerly been uncovered sinks back again, hidden and disguised. *Because Dasein is essentially falling, its state of Being is such that it is in "untruth"....* In its full existential-ontological meaning, the proposition that "*Dasein* is in the truth" says equiprimordially that "*Dasein* is in untruth".

> (1662a: 264–5, 221–2).

The emergence of truth, then, though a liberation from darkness (-*lēthē*) remains trammelled by the abiding shadows that filter through every revelation, and the same negativity contaminates every functioning of *legein/* speech as well – yes, and of silence, too. All that obstructive silence that we call "resistance" has its ground in Dasein's untruth. This, too, in Heidegger's terminology, would be the ground of what Lacan calls *méconnaissance*.

How does Heidegger put all this together? Let it suffice to say that "logos", as the call of conscience, is an invitation to Dasein, uttered in silence, to assume itself or authorize itself as what it is, i.e., as endowed with a privileged access to Being but trammelled by finitude, the most dramatic form of which is the limit of its own death. To acquiesce to all that is to achieve "authenticity" in a gesture that Heidegger calls "resoluteness" (*Entschlossenheit*). In Lacanian language, the analogue might be the subject's acceptance of "symbolic castration".

All that has been said so far concerns the role of language in Dasein, when this is conceived, however imprecisely, as somehow analogous to the subject of psychoanalysis. When one speaks of the "other" in this context, the sense is always that of the other "subject", as in the transference situation. But the meaning of "other" shifts for Heidegger in the 1930s – it's the famous "turning" (*Kehre*) in his thought, where his quest for the meaning of Being goes through a sea-change in which the focus shifts from Dasein as a propaedeutic to the Being-question to Being itself, from "logos" as a structural component of Dasein that makes all articulation possible to Being itself as the *Logos*, Aboriginal Language, where silence will again have a unique function. After the turning of the 1930s, Being/*Logos* becomes the Other.

The shift takes place, however, not through a meditation on Being as *Logos* but on Being as *Alētheia*/non-concealment. Starting in 1930, Heidegger re-examines the truth-problematic of *Being and Time*, but when he considers the untruth that is proper to truth, he thinks of it as the *-lēthē that somehow precedes the a-lētheia* (unconcealment) so that the disclosive process is not simply searchlighted by Dasein but of itself reveals itself to, simultaneously concealing itself from, Dasein. In effect, there are two modalities of concealment/untruth: the first he calls "mystery", where the concealment conceals itself (1977b: 132–5); the second he calls "errancy" (*Irre*), and this is how he describes it:

> The errancy though which man strays is not something which, as it were, extends alongside man like a ditch into which he occasionally stumbles; rather errancy belongs to the inner constitution of the *Dasein* into which historical humanity is admitted.

> Errancy is the essential counter-essence to the primordial essence of truth. Errancy is the open site for and ground of *error*.

> Every mode of comportment has its mode of erring. Error extends from the most ordinary wasting of time, making a mistake and miscalculating, to going astray and venturing too far in one's essential attitudes and decisions.

> By leading him astray, errancy dominates man through and though.
>
> (1977b: 135–6)

The process by which beings emerge into truth, then, is contaminated through and though by untruth which lies at the foundation of the untruth (*méconnaissance*) of Dasein as described in *Being and Time*. What is important is that the same situation prevails when he comes to think of Being as *Logos*, Primordial *Legein*, the Other that speaks us. Twenty years later he will say that *Logos* withdraws in the beings it reveals, e.g., in the words that are just brought to expression. This means that there is a "not" in every word, behind which Being as *Logos* retreats. This constitutes the domain of the un-said, immanent in everything that is said (as Lacan, say, finds such an unsaid in the said of Freud). We recognize here the essentials of Being-as-mystery. But the negativity of Being in language is such that it not only remains as such, withdrawing into words, but it dupes human being into disregarding and distorting it:

> That is to say, [*Logos*] plays in such a way with our speaking process that it gladly lets our language wander astray in the more obvious meanings of words. It is as if humans had difficulty in dwelling authentically in language.
>
> (1968: 118, 83)

The same contamination that accounts for the negativity of truth accounts now for the corruptibility of language, and all the ruses of silence that tend to subvert the revelation of truth now sabotage the function of speech. This is why in the psychoanalytic process every revelation of truth is contaminated by untruth, why Lacan remarks: "the man who in the act of speaking breaks the bread of truth with his fellows [also] shares the lie" (1966: 379).

It was not until the "Letter on humanism" (1947) that the general public read the famous phrase, "Language is the house of Being" (1977a: 193), and again, "language is the language of Being as clouds are the clouds of the sky" (1977a: 242). Actually Heidegger had struck the metaphor at least ten years earlier in commenting on Rilke:

> Being measures itself out as its own confines [*Bezirk*] that thereby are confined [*temnein, templum*] in such fashion that it comes to presence in the word. Language is the confine [*templum*], i.e., the house of Being.... Because language is the house of Being, we gain access to beings in such a way that we constantly go through this house. When we go to the spring, when we walk through the woods, we always already go through the word "spring", through the word "woods", even when we don't utter these words or think about anything linguistic.

As a consequence of all this, the nature of silence will be affected, too: "Perhaps... language requires much less precipitous expression than proper silence. But who of us today would want to imagine that his attempts to think are at home on the path of silence?" (1977a: 223). Silence, then, is a modality of the thinking of Being. Henceforth, silence will become more and more central to the experience of language, now more and more obviously the Other of Dasein. I shall here nest together a series of texts with a view only to their coherence. The theme of silence emerges under the guise of three different words: "Silence" (*Schweigen*), "reticence" (*Verschwiegenheit*) and "stillness" (*Stille*). It may be experienced by either the poet or the thinker as each strives to be attentive to (*hören*) and respond to (*entsprechen*) the call that comes from Being itself to be articulated. For according to the way Being's call is heard or overheard, the response can be one either of saying or of silence (see 1956: 35).

Let us begin with the poet. The clearest formula comes in Hölderlin's poem, "As When Upon a Day of Rest". Here Being is experienced by Hölderlin as the Holy. He belongs to the Holy, and his very heart is that centre within him where his own most proper essence gathers to a fullness in the "stillness of his belonging-ness within the compass of the Holy" (1944: 69). The poetic experience is conceived as the breaking of day. Prior to it, all is darkness, but then "Lo, the dawn has come!" Thus the poet cries out as the Holy discloses itself to him. But the cry is a calling out to what is already in ad-vent. It is the Holy itself that determines what the poet is to say, whose stillness becomes word through the poet's song, so that "the Holy [not only] bestows [the poet's] word [but] passes itself into this word" (1944: 74). It is thus that the poet's silence is broken. Stillness, then, precedes the spoken word and passes into it.

In commenting on Stefan George's *Ein Winterabend*, the same structure becomes even more explicit: "Language speaks.... Humans speak to the extent that they respond to language. To respond is to attend [*hören*]. [Responding] attends to the extent that it is an attendant of [*gehört*] the hail of stillness" (1971b: 210).

Being calls to humans, then, out of stillness. It is noiseless, yet not without resonance: "The soundless gathering call, by which [language] moves the world-relation on its way, we call the ringing of stillness. It is the language of Being" (1971b: 108).

The "ringing of stillness", then, is the silence of Being out of which language emerges for humans. Notice how clearly this parallels a remark about silence made by Theodor Reik: "We ought to suppose that silence is essential, and that the word is born of silence as life is born of the inorganic, of death. If our life here is only a passage, our speech is only a fugitive interruption of eternal silence" (cited Nasio 1987: 24 n. 1).

> Language speaks as the ringing of stillness. Stillness stills by the carrying out, the bearing and enduring, of world and things in their presence. The carrying out of world and thing in the manner of stilling is event of appropriation that takes place as the dif-ference. Language, the ringing of stillness, is, inasmuch as the dif-ference takes place. Language goes on as the taking place or occurring of the dif-ference for world and things.
>
> (1971b: 207).

Stillness presides over the events that appropriate the different epochs of history (1950: 342; 1957: 91; 1962b: 47). And if the stillness of Being passes into the song of the poet, it has a slightly different function for the thinker. For the thinker may be inclined to preserve the silence rather than break it:

> The highest form of thoughtful saying consists in this: not simply to be reticent in saying what is properly to be said, but to say it in such a way that it is uttered in not being said: the saying of thought is a keeping silent. This [kind of] saying corresponds to the deepest essence of language, which has its origin in silence.
>
> (1961: I, 471).

But the best way to get a sense of what would be an appropriate dialogue in Heidegger's terms would be to follow him through the long discussion with a Japanese professor concerning the nature of language. Too diffuse to repeat here, it wanders freely from subject to subject – associating, reflecting, recollecting, hesitating, leaping – always circling about the fundamental question: what do the Japanese mean by language? Together they listen to the Other and attend to what is articulated through them and finally emerges as a kind of answer. For the Japanese, language means: *koto ba*, where *ba* means the leaves or petals of a blossom, and *koto* means "the appropriating event of the luminous message of grace" (1971a: 45). Together they listen to the stillness of the Other and bring it into words. Such a dialogue for Heidegger proceeds *from* language, and there is "more silence than talk. Above all, silence about silence" (1971a: 52).

How does all this add to my colleague's understanding of the analytic process which took place between him and Karl? If we measure this process by the paradigm of the classical Freud, Heidegger has little to say indeed. Introduced to Freud late in life by his Swiss psychiatrist/friend, Medard Boss, Heidegger was totally unsympathetic with Freud's effort. He took Freud to be attempting to explain the human phenomenon by chains of efficient causality and, in the face of gaps in conscious experience, simply postulated another psychic cause, the unconscious, to account for them. But if we understand human being as Being-in-the-world, the whole notion of psychic causality is rendered superfluous and superseded by a vision more profound and more comprehensive of what it means to be human. Any notion of an unconscious is completely gratuitous. But if one does not stay with the classical Freudian paradigm, if one claims that what Freud discovered in the unconscious was not an unbroken chain of psychic causality but the hidden power of speech, and that the unconscious is structured not like a thermodynamic machine but rather like a language, what then? This, indeed, is the hypothesis of Lacan, this is the hypothesis out of which my friend's question arises. You can understand, then, why his turn to Heidegger was quite plausible. But how far can Heidegger take him along a genuine Lacanian path?

To begin with the paradigm for the analytic situation is not to be found in the free-wheeling dialogue with the Japanese professor. Analysis is simply not a mutually shared exchange between two equal partners in an open wide-ranging search for truth. A better analogue for the analyst might be Hölderlin, the poet, where he waits through the night for the coming of dawn, so that through his attentive response he may help the significant word come to articulation. Normally, however, the process is not quite that romantic.

To be sure, a certain analogy between the two men is obvious: the primacy of the Other of language over human being. "Language speaks. Human being responds", said Heidegger. For Lacan, language – the subject of the unconscious – speaks the subject. For Heidegger, the poet (here analyst) – waits in silence for the significant word like the coming of dawn. For Lacan, the analyst's silence leaves the word to the Other of speech.

> The analyst intervenes concretely in the dialectic of the analysis in playing the dummy [as in the bridge], in taking the position of a cadaver, as the Chinese say, whether by his silence where he is the Other with a capital "O", or by nullifying his own resistance where he is the other with a small "o".
>
> (1966: 430)

Such silence indeed is in the mode of speech. When the analyst responded in silence to the announcement that Karl's analysis would last for only three years, this did not mean only that he made no noise but that he kept silent *"in place of* a reply" (Lacan's emphasis, 1966: 351). Thus the function of the analyst's celebrated neutrality consists precisely in leaving the word to the Other of Language:

> It is to this Other beyond the other that the analyst leaves room by the neutrality through which he makes himself *ne-uter*, neither one nor the other of the two [subjects] who are there, and if he remains silent, it is to leave the word to [this] Other.
>
> (1966: 439)

That is why "silence ... is not something simply negative, but has a value beyond speech. Certain moments of silence in the transference represent in the sharpest form the apprehension of the presence of the Other as such" (1975: 313).

The task of the analyst as *legein* is to let-be-seen/heard the truth of the analysand, with and through his inevitable untruth/*méconnaissance*. When the negative transference during the first phase, in which Karl experienced the analyst's silence as his father's presumed contempt, shifted to a positive transference in the second phase when silence was experienced as support, the change came about by reason of a shared presence, to be sure, but it came to pass in Karl, not in the analyst. Rather it was *through* the analyst's silence as *legein*/letting-be-seen/heard that it took place. It was the silence that constituted the *Mitteilung*, the communication, between them.

Again, Karl began slowly, painfully, haltingly to articulate his early memories of how his father had at one time, through a profound yet basically benevolent silence, taught Karl the craft by which he built things with his hands and shared with Karl the secret of how one can speak by being silent. Whether this was enough, as the analyst himself would claim, to constitute what Lacan calls the "paternal metaphor" and inscribe in the boy at once both the "Law of the Father" and the "interdiction" of the mother, is a question that cannot be examined here, but what is clear is that the analyst's silence has permitted him to break the silence of his own distorted relationship to the father, and liberate him into a first flickering moment of truth.

This step achieved, the same attentive *legein* of the analyst makes possible the dream about the secret of the saint. When the great-grandmother's name "Antoinette" emerged, the analyst's intervention is not a signifier of his own but merely the echo of Karl's idiosyncratic signifier, "maliferous". The rest takes place in Karl. The malediction of hereditary cancer and the ferocity of his mother's buried memories had somehow fused in him to help constitute the inarticulate blackness of his symptom – his own "pathological" silence from which the analyst's silence helped to free him. In Heideggerian language, Karl's pathology was a form of *-lēthē* that through the exercise of *legein* would slowly become *a-lēthes*, i.e., revealed in its truth, as true. In Lacanian language, Karl's pathology would be called the Real in him. The task of analysis would be to bring it to representation through the Imaginary and the Symbolic. In both cases the process consists in a *legein*, a letting-be-seen/heard, the paradigm for which is the analyst's own silence. One might even say that the goal of analysis is to transform the silence of pathology into the silence of attention, leaving the analysand free to be the poet of her life according to the measure of her gifts.

Am I conflating Heidegger and Lacan here in a kind of cheap reductionism? Certainly not! There is no way to reduce one to the other without destroying both. Heidegger's Other, Being as Aboriginal *Logos*, is radically different from Lacan's Other, the Symbolic Order, for the Symbolic Order, a notion he takes from Lévi-Strauss, is essentially a scientific concept; it pertains to the order of beings, Aristotle's *onta*. In Heideggerian terminology it is completely ontic, just as the play of signifiers (e.g., the echoes of "Antoinette", the associations to "maliferous/malignant/ferocious") is a purely ontic game. The Symbolic Order itself that supplies a structure for these signifiers is indeed "ultimate" in the order of beings, corresponding to Heraclitus' "many" (*panta*), but ontic nonetheless. For Heidegger, *Logos*, as the Aboriginal *Legein*, is in his terminology an "ontological" phenomenon, in the dimension of Being, corresponding rather to Heraclitus' "One" (*Hen*).

But this does not make Being a kind of meta-language – some Other of the Other in the sense of a meta-symbolic (likewise ontic), a notion that Lacan has repudiated more than once. The Symbolic Order remains ultimate in the order of spoken language; *Logos* would be ultimate in the order of Being, the gathering gatheredness that lets the Symbolic Order *be* what it is. It is the ontological difference between them that makes this possible, the difference that emerges out of the primal stillness: "Language, the ringing of stillness, is, inasmuch as the dif-ference takes place. Language goes on as the taking place or occurring of the dif-ference for World and things" (1971b: 207).

What, then, do I claim? My claim is that Lacan's interpretation of the Freudian unconscious as "structured like a language" desperately needs a philosophical base that mathematical formalism and all the topology in the world cannot give him. Else why does a Lacanian analyst, French-born, French-bred, French-educated, trained as a Lacanian and enriched by twenty-five years of clinical experience, turn to Heidegger to help him understand what he does? Furthermore, my claim is that Heidegger does have something to offer him.

My first reason for saying this is that the conception of Being as the Aboriginal *Logos* that emerges out of the ringing of stillness "inasmuch as the dif-ference takes place" accounts for the ontological dimension of an otherwise purely scientific notion of the Symbolic Order, with all the disadvantages that that implies.

My second reason is that the conception of human being as Being-in-the-World with other Daseins is a way to think the analytic situation more broadly and comprehensively than is possible now. How this conception might accommodate the perspective called for by James Hillman in this volume is too large an issue to address within the constraints of the present context. In the perspective of the material as presented, however: if a devout Lacanian can talk about silence as a way to let Karl feel his "presence", and if Lacan in turn can say that "certain moments of silence in the transference represent in the sharpest form the apprehension of the presence of the Other as such", then Heidegger's conception of Dasein gives us a way to think the presence of analyst to patient and patient to analyst in the presence of a "presencing" World in a non-metaphysical way.

I am sensitive, of course, to Derrida's objections to the word "presence" in this context and cannot address them further here. What is crucial is to conceive of the analysand as a de-centred subject that comes-to-presence and recedes-from-presence in the dynamic unity of time – a self, then, a "social agent" (in Gayatri Spivak's terminology). Such a subject would be able to respond to a call of the Other, hence would be a radically responsible being, and in that sense capable of functioning as the so-called "ethical subject", however pressing the need for the examination of its own genealogy, however much the terminology itself may need deconstruction. The analytic process, then, would be essentially a *legein* that includes the

modality of silence, rendering possible the transformation of the analys-
and's pathological silence into an attentive one that listens for the word of
the Other that is still to be uttered.

Finally, Heidegger offers us a way to talk about truth in psychoanalysis,
not as a verification of validity claims but as revelation that never completely emerges from darkness and includes its own untruth. That is why
"the man who in the act of speaking breaks the bread of truth with his
fellows [also] shares the lie". But the *legein* that lets this truth be seen is
a liberation from darkness. The fundamental mystery of psychoanalysis,
that both Freud and Lacan observed but neither could explain by his
theory, Heidegger offers a way to understand: the "talking cure" cures,
psychoanalysis heals, because it sets us free – in truth!

Can we claim all this for Karl? Surely some provisional truth appeared
in terms of his relation both to his father and his mother. That more work
still remains to be done appears from the dream which begins the fourth
("perhaps final", in the analyst's estimation) phase of the analysis:

> A man who owns a Rolls Royce buys two sweaters for several thousand
> dollars in a shop kept by two women. Karl decides to buy one at a
> much cheaper price. The two women wonder whether they asked him
> to pay too high a price or not. Karl leaves the shop with his new
> sweater. He meets his cousin Elizabeth; she is radiant and he is moved
> by her beauty and her carnal vivacity. But as he examines his bill he
> realizes he has paid too much. The women have charged him a 20 per
> cent tax instead of 5 per cent, four times too much. He goes back to
> the shop to get a refund. The women are gone. A man is standing
> by the cash register. As Karl is about to complain, he suddenly realizes
> that the part of his bill where the tax was written is missing. He
> therefore has to face the biting sarcasm of the man and he wakes up
> furious and frightened.

Is this progress? I leave that to the judgement of others. My only claim
here is for the validity of the analytic method conceived as *legein*, even in
– perhaps especially in – the silence of the analyst. Herein lies, I submit,
the only ground for psychoanalytic hope.

BIBLIOGRAPHY

Freud, S. (1915) "Our attitude towards death". *Standard Edition* 14; pp. 289–300,
London: Hogarth Press, 1957.
Heidegger, M. (1944) *Erläuterungen zu Hölderlins Dichtungen*, Frankfurt: Klostermann.
—— (1950) "Der Spruch des Anaximander", in *Holzwege*, Frankfurt: Klostermann,
pp. 296–343.
—— (1956) *Was ist das – die Philosophie?* Pfullingen: Neske.
—— (1957) *Der Satz vom Grund*, Pfullingen: Neske.
—— (1961) *Nietzsche*, 2 vols, Pfullingen: Neske.

—— (1962a) *Being and Time*, tr. John Macquarrie and Edward Robinson, New York: Harper & Row. First published 1927. German edition: *Sein und Zeit*, in *Gesamtausgabe*, vol. 2, Frankfurt am Main: Klostermann, 1977.

—— (1962b) *Die Technik und die Kehre*, Pfullingen: Neske.

—— (1968) *What is Called Thinking?* tr. F. D. Wieck and J. G. Gray, New York: Harper & Row. First published 1954.

—— (1971a) *On the Way to Language*, tr. A. Hofstadter, New York: Harper & Row. First published 1959.

—— (1971b) *Poetry, Language, Thought*, tr. A. Hofstadter, New York: Harper & Row.

—— (1977a) "Letter on humanism", tr. F. A. Capuzzi and J. G. Gray in *Basic Writings*, ed. David F. Krell, New York: Harper & Row, pp. 189–242.

—— (1977b) "On the essence of truth", tr. J. Sallis, in *Basic Writings*, ed. D. F. Krell, New York: Harper & Row.

Khan, M. (1974) *The Privacy of the Self*. London: Hogarth Press.

Lacan, J. (1966) *Ecrits*, Paris: Editions du Seuil.

—— (1975) *Le Séminaire: Livre I: Les écrits techniques de Freud*, ed. J. A. Miller, Paris: Editions du Seuil. First published 1953–4.

—— (1977) *Ecrits: A Selection*, tr. A. Sheridan, New York: Norton.

Nasio, J. (1987) *Le Silence en psychanalyse*, Paris: Rivage.

10 *The Sandman* looks at "The uncanny"

The return of the repressed or of the secret; Hoffmann's question to Freud

Nicholas Rand and Maria Torok

Nicholas Rand, Professor of French Literature at the University of Wisconsin-Madison, and **Maria Torok**, a practising French analyst and theoretician, are collaborating on a reassessment of the conceptual status and genesis of psychoanalysis in their forthcoming book *Questions to Freudian Psychoanalysis*. Maria Torok is best known for her works *The Wolf Man's Magic Word: A Cryptonymy* and *The Shell and the Kernel: Renewals of Psychoanalysis* which were both co-authored with the late philosopher-analyst Nicolas Abraham, and have been translated into English with introductions by Nicholas Rand. In these books Abraham and Torok formulate theories of psychic functioning that insist on the particularity of any individual's life story, the specificity of texts and the singularity of historical situations. The new concepts illuminate psychic structures of secretly perpetuated multiple identities (incorporation and crypt), they identify the psychological implant in us of our ancestors' secrets (phantom) and they introduce methods for the recovery of disintegrated meaning (cryptonymy). Abraham and Torok's theories of intrapsychic secrets and interpersonal silence cast new light on mourning, melancholia, manic-depressive psychosis, fetishism, obsessive behaviour, anorexia and psychosomatic afflictions. Nicholas Rand has carried the investigation of psychic concealment into literary criticism, the problem of political ideology, as well as translation studies with a book of essays entitled *Le Cryptage et la vie des oeuvres: Du secret dans les textes*. His brand of criticism posits that texts are at once the unwitting generators and the analysts of their own secrets. The present paper is an example of how a psychoanalytic reading may proceed when the importance of secrets is given due attention.

The theoretical and clinical scope of the idea of "family secret" is elaborated in section V of *The Shell and the Kernel*.

SELECT BIBLIOGRAPHY

Abraham, N. and Torok, M.: *The Wolfman's Magic Word: A Cryptonymy*, tr. with an introduction by N. Rand and with a foreword by J. Derrida, Minneapolis: University of Minnesota Press, 1986.
—— *The Shell and the Kernel: Renewals of Psychoanalysis*, ed. and tr. N. Rand, Chicago: University of Chicago Press, 1994.

* * *

As is well known, Freud introduced the concept of the uncanny into psychoanalysis in 1919 and used *The Sandman* as a prime illustration for his definition. We propose to reverse the order of Freud's approach, interpreting Hoffmann's tale first and proceeding to deduce the nature of the uncanny from it. This will produce changes because *The Sandman* departs significantly both from Freud's interpretation of it and from his general conception of the uncanny. Our intent is not to criticize Freud's theory of the uncanny, only its applicability to *The Sandman*. Moreover, we think the designation uncanny describes aptly the emotional atmosphere of Hoffmann's text, even though the source of the uncanny feeling in the story differs from the one Freud posited. The crux of our argument can be summarized briefly: Freud sees in *The Sandman* an example of the frightening return of a repressed infantile complex (castration); we perceive the return of a family secret. Our reading not only entails a new psychoanalytic definition of the uncanny but has implications for the study of Freud's works in general. The reading points to a discrepancy between Freud's detailed lexical account of the word "uncanny" in German (at the beginning of his essay) and his independent theory of the uncanny. Furthermore, we find that the psychological substance of *The Sandman* is in accord with the meanings of the German word *unheimlich* (uncanny) as listed by Freud, but not with his interpretation of them in terms of his theory of the return of the repressed. These findings raise a host of other issues we can only mention here. What kind of significance should we attach to potential inconsistencies and methodological paradoxes in Freud's work? How important is it to note that Freud chose to exemplify his theory of the uncanny with a literary text that arguably does not corroborate it? Why is it useful to conjecture that Freud may have selected *The Sandman* for a reason different from the one he stated or even intended?[1]

I

In "The uncanny" Freud uses dictionaries to present us with an aesthetic problem as related to linguistic usage. Freud proposes a methodological choice:

Two courses are open to us at the outset. Either we can find out what meaning has come to be attached to the word "uncanny" in the course of its history; or we can collect all those properties of persons, things, sense-impressions, experiences and situations which arouse in us the feeling of uncanniness, and then infer the unknown nature of the uncanny from what all these examples have in common. I will say at once that both courses lead to the same result: the uncanny is that class of the frightening which leads back to what is known of old and long familiar. How this is possible, in what circumstances the familiar can become uncanny and frightening, I shall show in what follows. Let me also add that my investigation was actually begun by collecting a number of individual cases, and was only later confirmed by an examination of linguistic usage. In this discussion, however, I shall follow the reverse course.[2]

The thesis of Freud's essay is clear and convincing, but its sometimes tortuous progress is much less so. With its unordered sequence of examples (taken from literature, everyday life, the beliefs of primitive peoples and the various stages of Freud's own psychoanalytic theory), the essay often gives the impression of being unsystematic and yet it manages to cohere around a central idea: the disquieting return of the long-ago repressed. The concept of something familiar having been repressed allows Freud to combine, under the rubric of the uncanny, structures of infantile psycho-sexual development and archaic forms of human mental organizations.

> We have now only a few remarks to add – for animism, magic and sorcery, the omnipotence of thoughts, man's attitude to death, involuntary repetition and the castration complex comprise practically all the factors which turn something frightening into something uncanny.
>
> (p. 243)

Freud equates two types of recurrence here, one deriving from repressed infantile psychosexual sources, the other from early phases in the mental evolution of humankind, the so-called animistic conceptions of the universe that, according to Freud, still survive in modern civilizations under the guise of irrational beliefs in things like magical powers, the evil eye, demonic influences, the double, spirits, ghosts and haunted houses. These two types of causes, which Freud places at the root of the uncanny, have in common the unexpected return of something that should have been overcome, by repression or civilization, but has not been. Finally, although Freud is somewhat reluctant to regard simple involuntary repetition (for example the unintentional return to the same spot during a walk) as a pure instance of the uncanny, the idea of a "repetition-compulsion" fits squarely within his general model of the recurrence of archaic features. Just as the fear of castration, the double, haunted houses, etc. refer, in Freud's estimation, to early, obsolete phases of infantile or collective human mental development, so too repetition-compulsion is allegedly a primal form of human psychic organization – the "death drive" (a psychic representative of the more general Freudian idea, expounded in *Beyond the Pleasure Principle*, according to which the primeval origin and ultimate end of life is inanimation, that is, death). In short, all Freudian instances of the uncanny spring from the untoward return, after the fact, of familiar but unacknowledged infantile psychosexual or archaic mental forms that, despite appearances, have not been fully outgrown, mastered or repressed.

This bare bones outline of Freud's theory of the uncanny throws into relief an anomaly in his essay. *The Sandman*, used by Freud to bolster his general argument, defies his main thesis that the uncanny derives from the disturbing return in adult life of the familiar but repressed infantile castration complex. Freud concludes his analysis of *The Sandman* as follows:

> We know from psycho-analytic experience . . . that the fear of damaging or losing one's eyes is a terrible one in children. Many adults retain their apprehensiveness in this respect, and no physical injury is so much dreaded by them as an injury to the eye. . . . A study of dreams, phantasies and myths has taught us that anxiety about one's eyes, the fear of going blind, is often enough a substitute for the dread of being castrated. . . . We may try on rationalistic grounds to deny that fears about the eye are derived from the fear of castration, and may argue that it is very natural that so precious an organ as the eye should be guarded by a proportionate dread. . . . But this view does not account adequately for the substitutive relation between the eye and the male organ which is seen to exist in dreams and myths and phantasies. . . . All further doubts are removed when we learn the details of their "castration complex" from the analysis of neurotic patients, and realize its immense importance in their mental life. . . . We shall venture, therefore, to refer the uncanny effect of the Sand-Man to the anxiety belonging to the castration complex of childhood.
>
> (*SE 17*, pp. 231–3)

It is understandable that Freud might want to find a literary affirmation of his idea of the uncanny as based on the infantile castration complex. However, *The Sandman* categorically defeats that attempt. In fact, we shall go so far as to say that Freud's analysis does not deal with Hoffmann's tale. Despite Freud's warning, "I would not recommend any opponent of the psycho-analytic view to select this particular story of the Sand-Man with which to support his argument that anxiety about the eyes has nothing to do with the castration complex" (p. 231), we will question the relevance of substituting the penis for the eyes in *The Sandman*. The eyes do in fact play a major role, but for a different reason. They symbolize the hero's thwarted attempt to see, to inquire, to discover. Injury to the eyes is a crucial element in *The Sandman*, but it needs to be understood figuratively as a lack of insight followed by the loss of reason. The hero's madness is due to his inability to gain insight into the murky affairs of his own family.

The feeling of the uncanny arises because the hero was never able to obtain the vital knowledge others withheld from him. *The Sandman* deals with the lasting effects of secrecy in the family, a secrecy that, unfathomable and ultimately devastating to a child, disrupts the intimacy and familiarity of the home. We value Freud's methodological principle of linking the manifestations of psychic turmoil to causes lying beyond the sufferer's immediate reach. But we do not always confirm the Freudian content of these causes, the repression of sexually-oriented desires, fantasies, the Oedipus complex and castration. Our primary aim here is to produce – with the freshness of an initial encounter – a psychoanalytic reading of *The Sandman* that follows step by step the fictional life and psychic events of the protagonist without recourse to established Freudian doctrine.[3]

II

> Gentle reader, nothing can be imagined that is stranger and more extraordinary than the fate which befell my poor friend, the young student Nathanael, which I have undertaken to relate to you. Have you, gentle reader, ever experienced anything that totally possessed your heart, your thoughts, and your senses to the exclusion of all else? Everything seethed and roiled within you; heated blood surged through your veins and inflamed your cheeks. Your gaze was peculiar, as if seeking forms in empty space invisible to other eyes, and speech dissolved into gloomy sighs. Then your friends asked you: "What is it, dear friend? What is the matter?" And wishing to describe the picture in your mind with all its vivid colors, the light and the shade, you struggled vainly to find words. But it seemed to you that you had to gather together all that had occurred – the wonderful, the magnificent, the heinous, the joyous, the ghastly – and express it in the very first word so that it would strike like lightning. Yet, every word, everything within the realm of speech, seemed colorless, frigid, dead.[4]

Nathanael's story unfolds in this eerie and bewildering atmosphere. Hoffmann combines the diabolical (as we know it in Goethe, Tieck and Jean-Paul) with the evocation of mental derangement. His is a tale of possession by the devil, according to the old terminology, a possession rendered the more unusual as the hero himself attempts to search out the source of his disturbance. Nathanael writes to Lothar, his closest friend and his fiancée's brother.

> Something horrible has entered my life! Dark forebodings of some impending doom loom over me like black clouds which are impervious to every ray of friendly sunshine. I will now tell you what happened to me. I must tell you, but the mere thought of it makes me laugh like a madman. Oh, my dearest Lothar, how can I begin to make you realize,

even vaguely, that what happened a few days ago really could have so fatal and disruptive an effect on my life? ... You will surmise that only associations of the strangest kind that are profoundly entangled in my life could have made this incident significant.... In fact, this is the case. I will, with all my strength, pull myself together and calmly and patiently tell you enough about my early youth so that everything will appear clearly and distinctly to your keen mind.

(pp. 93–4)

The woes of the university student Nathanael begin on the day, 30 October at noon to be exact, when a barometer dealer, Coppola-Coppelius, enters his room, only to leave it under a threat of being kicked down the stairs by Nathanael. This incident is followed by others, all of which underscore Nathanael's madness. He later composes and reads a poem to his beloved fiancée Klara who cries out upon hearing it: 'Nathanael, my darling Nathanael, throw that mad, insane, stupid tale into the fire" (pp. 109–10). The poem shows Coppelius destroying the couple's happiness.

He portrayed himself and Klara as united in true love but plagued by some dark hand which occasionally intruded into their lives, snatching away incipient joy. Finally, as they stood at the altar, the sinister Coppelius appeared and touched Klara's lovely eyes, which sprang into Nathanael's own breast, burning and scorching like bleeding sparks. Then Copelius grabbed him and flung him into a blazing circle of fire which spun round with the speed of a whirlwind and, with a rush, carried him away.

(p. 108)

Some time after his return to the university, Nathanael

was writing to Klara when there was a soft tap at the door. At his call, the door opened and Coppola's repulsive face peered in. Nathanael was shaken to the roots.... Coppola, however, came right into the room and said in a hoarse voice, his mouth twisted in a hideous laugh, his little eyes flashing piercingly from beneath his long, grey eyelashes, "Oh, no barometer? No barometer! I gotta da eyes too. I gotta da nice eyes!" Horrified, Nathanael cried, "Madman, how can you have eyes? Eyes?" But Coppola instantly put away his barometers and, thrusting his hands in his wide coat pockets, pulled out lorgnettes and eyeglasses and put them on the table. "So, glasses – put on nose, see! These are my eyes, nice-a eyes!" Saying this, he brought forth more and more eyeglasses from his pockets until the whole table began to gleam and sparkle. Myriad eyes peered and blinked and stared up at Nathanael, who could not look away from the table, while Coppola continued putting down more and more eyeglasses; and flaming glances crisscrossed each other ever more wildly and shot their blood-red rays into Nathanael's breast.

Overcome by an insane horror, Nathanael cried, "Stop, stop, you fiend!"

(p. 112)

At the end of this scene Nathanael buys a spyglass from Coppola. Forgetting that the dealer is still in the room, Nathanael seizes the spyglass and fixes his gaze in fascination at Olympia, supposedly the daughter of the physicist Spalanzani, a friend of Coppola's.

> For the first time now he saw her exquisitely formed face. Only her eyes seemed peculiarly fixed and lifeless. But as he continued to look more and more intently through the glass, it seemed as though moist moonbeams were beginning to shine in Olympia's eyes. It seemed as if the power of vision were only now starting to be kindled; her glances were inflamed with ever-increasing life.

(p. 112)

Having always kept his daughter secluded, Spalanzani organizes a ball for her début in society. Nearly all the university students are invited. Everyone finds her walk stiff and measured, her voice high-pitched, bell-like, almost shrill. Many of the guests make up their minds about Olympia's doll-like bearing and behaviour. Nathanael is her only and rapturous admirer to the point that: " 'Do me a favor, brother,' Siegmund said to him one day, 'and tell me how it is possible for an intelligent fellow like you to have fallen for that wax-faced, wooden puppet across the way?' " (p. 112). Nathanael's love does not listen to reason and knows no bounds until the day when he goes to Spalanzani's house to ask Olympia to marry him.

> While still on the stairs he heard a singular hubbub that seemed to come from Spalanzani's study. There was a stamping, a rattling, pushing, a banging against the door, and, intermingled, curses and oaths: "Let go! Let go! Monster! Villain! Risking body and soul for it? Ha! Ha! Ha! Ha! That wasn't our arrangement! I, I made the eyes! I made the clockwork! Damned idiot, you and your damned clockwork! Dog of a clockmaker! Out! Let me go!" The voices causing this uproar belonged to Spalanzani and the abominable Coppelius. Nathanael rushed in, seized by a nameless dread. The professor was grasping a female figure by the shoulders, the Italian Coppola had her by the feet, and they were twisting and tugging her this way and that, contending furiously for possession of her. Nathanael recoiled in horror upon recognizing the figure as Olympia's. Flaring up in a wild rage, he was about to tear his beloved from the grasp of these madmen when Coppola, wrenching the figure from the professor's hand with the strength of a giant, struck the professor such a fearful blow with it that he toppled backwards

over the table on which vials, retorts, flasks, and glass test tubes were standing – everything shattered into a thousand fragments. Then Coppola threw the figure over his shoulder and with a horrible, shrill laugh, ran quickly down the stairs, the figure's grotesquely dangling feet bumping and rattling woodenly on every step. Nathanael stood transfixed; he had only too clearly seen that in the deathly pale waxen face of Olympia there were no eyes, but merely black holes. She was a lifeless doll. Spalanzini was writhing on the floor; his head and chest and arm had been cut by the glass fragments and blood gushed from him as if from a fountain. But he summoned up all his strength: "After him, after him! What are you waiting for! Coppelius – Coppelius has stolen my best automaton. Worked at it for twenty years – put everything I had into it – mechanism – speech – movement – all mine. Damn him! Curse him! After him! Get me Olympia! Bring back Olympia! There are the eyes!"

And now Nathanael saw something like a pair of bloody eyes staring up at him from the floor. Spalanzani seized them with his uninjured hand and flung them at Nathanael so that they hit his breast. Then madness racked Nathanael with scorching claws, ripping to shreds his mind and senses.

"Whirl, whirl, whirl! Circle of fire! Circle of fire! Whirl round, circle of fire! Merrily, merrily! Aha, lovely wooden doll, whirl round!" With these words Nathanael hurled himself upon the professor and clutched at his throat.

(pp. 119–20)

Apparently cured after a long illness, Nathanael plans to marry Klara, his long-time fiancée. During a noon-hour walk they climb up the bell tower of the town hall to admire the surrounding landscape.

> Suddenly, Nathanael takes out Coppola's sypglass from his pocket. Then there was a convulsive throbbing in his pulse. Deathly pale, he stared at Klara; but soon streams of fire flashed and spurted from his rolling eyes. He roared horrendously, like a hunted beast, leaped high into the air, and bursting with horrible laughter, he shrieked in a piercing voice, "Whirl wooden doll! Whirl wooden doll!" And seizing Klara with superhuman strength he tried to hurl her from the tower.

(p. 124)

Klara's brother hears her cries of despair and rushes to her rescue. Nathanael remains in the tower, leaping up in the air and shouting.

> A crowd gathered quickly, attracted by the wild screaming; and in the midst of them there towered the gigantic figure of the lawyer Coppelius, who had just arrived in town and had come directly to the market place. Some wanted to go up and over-power the madman, but Coppelius laughed and said, "Ha, ha! Just wait; he'll come down on his own."

And he looked up with the rest. Nathanael suddenly froze, leaned forward, caught sight of Coppelius, and with a shattering scream of "Ah, nice-a eyes, nice-a eyes!" jumped over the railing.

Nathanael lay on the pavement with his head shattered, but Coppelius had vanished in the crowd.

(p. 125)

This is how Nathanael's story ends. The meaning of his possession by Coppelius is not communicated explicitly in the tale, but the clues Nathanael himself provides about his childhood allow us to reconstruct the cause of his illness. His first recollection concerns the incomprehensible changes he noticed periodically in his father's behaviour. Normally devoted to his family and eager to see his children happy, Nathanael's father would at times withdraw from their circle, wrapping himself in rigid silence and clouds of smoke so that the entire family "would swim in fog" (p. 94). On such evenings, Nathanael's mother would be very sad and hurry the children off to bed, saying that the Sandman was coming.

And at times I really did hear something and as my mother led us away, I asked her: "Oh, Mama, who is this nasty Sandman who always drives us away from Papa? What does he look like?" "My dear child, there is no Sandman," my mother answered. "When I tell you that the Sandman is coming, it only means that you are sleepy and can't keep your eyes open any longer, as though someone had sprinkled sand into them."

(p. 94)

Not satisfied with his mother's reply and wanting to find out who disturbs the family's quiet existence, he continues to ask questions. His sister's nurse tells him.

"Oh, dear Thanael," she replied, "Don't you know that yet? He is a wicked man who comes to children when they refuse to go to bed and throws handfuls of sand in their eyes till they bleed and pop out of their heads. Then he throws the eyes into the sack and takes them to the half moon as food for his children, who sit in a nest and have crooked beaks like owls with which they pick up the eyes of human children who have been naughty."

(p. 95)

Still dissatisfied with the answers he is given about the frightening phenomenon, Nathanael decides to investigate the mystery on his own.

I was old enough to realize that the nurse's tale of the Sandman and his children's nest in the half-moon couldn't be altogether true; nevertheless, the Sandman remained a frightful specter; and I was seized with utmost horror when I heard him not only mount the stairs, but violently tear open the door to my father's room and enter. Frequently, he stayed away for a long time; then he came many times in succession. This continued for years, and I never got used to this terrible phantom. My image of the horrible Sandman grew no paler. His intimacy with my father occupied my imagination more and more. An insurmountable reluctance prevented me from asking my father about him; but if only I – if only I could solve the mystery and get to see this fantastic Sandman with my own eyes – that was the desire which increased in me year by year.

I could tell one evening from my father's silence and my mother's sadness that the Sandman was coming. I pretended, therefore, to be very tired, left the room before nine o'clock, and hid in a dark corner close to the door. The front door groaned. Slow, heavy, resounding steps crossed the hall to the stairs. My mother hurried past me with the rest of the children. Softly, softly I opened the door of my father's room. He was sitting as usual, silent and rigid, his back to the door; he didn't notice me. I slipped quickly behind the curtain which covered an open cupboard in which my Father's clothes were hanging. Closer, ever closer resounded the steps – there was a strange coughing, scraping, and mumbling outside. My heart quaked *with fear and expectation.* Close, close to the door, there was a sharp step; a powerful blow on the latch and the door sprang open with a bang! Summoning up every drop of my courage, I cautiously peeped out. The Sandman was standing in the middle of my father's room, the bright candlelight full on his face. The Sandman, the horrible Sandman, was the old lawyer Coppelius who frequently had dinner with us!

(pp. 95–6, our emphasis)

The Sandman here is not a fiction designed to get cranky children to sleep, as the mother claims; nor is he a brutal goblin, as the nurse would have Nathanael believe. The Sandman possesses a definite and recognizable reality. He is a person Nathanael knows well, the lawyer Coppelius. The mother and the nurse tried to soothe the child's anxiety by deceiving him. Nobody frightful is coming to see father, it is only that children refuse to go to bed. "When I tell you that the Sandman is coming, it only means that you are sleepy and can't keep your eyes open, as though someone had sprinkled sand into them" (p. 94). To speak, in the context of Nathanael's questions, of someone who throws sand in children's eyes until they bleed and jump out is tantamount to revealing, as in an involuntary slip of the tongue, what one is actually doing: throwing dust in the child's eye in order to prevent him from finding out what the real situation is. His mother and the nurse wilfully mislead Nathanael, telling him in effect: you may be worried about the frightful things going on in the family, but none of it is meant for children; don't try to find out, go to sleep; terrible things happen only in fairy tales.

Who is this Coppelius then, whose dealings with the father are to be concealed from the children.? He is a repulsive man, especially hateful toward children. "Mother seemed to loathe the repulsive Coppelius as much as we did; the moment he appeared, her gaiety, her lightheartedness, and her natural manner were transformed into dejected brooding" (p. 97). Despite everybody's displeasure, Nathanael's father is devoted to Coppelius.

> Father behaved toward him as if he were a superior being whose bad manners must be endured and who must be humored at any cost. Coppelius needed only to hint, and his favorite dishes were cooked and rare wines were served.
>
> (p. 97)

The father not only tolerates the awful Coppelius, but is his accomplice, even resembling him when Nathanael discovers the two of them from his hiding place.

> "To work!" Coppelius cried in a hoarse, jarring voice, throwing off his coat.... My father opened the folding door of a wall cupboard, but what I had always believed was a cupboard was not. It was rather a black recess which housed a little hearth. Coppelius went to the hearth, and a blue flame crackled up from it. All kinds of strange utensils were about. God! As my old father now bent over the fire, he looked completely different. His mild and honest features seemed to have been distorted into a repulsive and diabolical mask by some horrible convulsive pain. He looked like Coppelius.
>
> (pp. 97–8)

Nathanael's beloved father is associated with the activities of "a horrible and unearthly monster who wreaked grief, misery, and destruction – temporal and eternal – wherever he appeared" (p. 97). The child tries to explain his father's secretiveness, a secretiveness somehow bound up with the repulsive Coppelius. But Nathanael will not succeed. He will never be able to grasp the nature of his father's murky business with Coppelius. Shortly after Nathanael's own ill-fated attempt at spying, his father is killed in an explosion provoked by Coppelius, taking his secret to the grave. When Nathanael tried to observe the two men, he was unable to understand anything. In fact he was able to experience no more than his own thwarted attempt to see.

> It seemed as if I saw human faces on all sides – but eyeless faces, with horrible deep black cavities instead. "Give me eyes! Give me eyes!" Coppelius ordered in a hollow booming voice. Overcome by the starkest terror, I shrieked and tumbled from my hiding place to the floor. Coppelius seized me. "Little beast! Little beast!" he bleated, baring his teeth. He dragged me to my feet and flung me on the hearth, where the flames began singeing my hair. "Now we have eyes, eyes, a beautiful

pair of children's eyes!" he whispered. Pulling glowing grains from the
fire with his naked hands, he was about to sprinkle them in my eyes.

(p. 98)

Nathanael's fear that he might actually see the terrible thing everybody
wants to keep from him turns into a chilling hallucination about his own
eyes. And sure enough, all of Nathanael's subsequent hallucinations and
ravings revolve around the eyes: to begin with, his poem showing Coppelius who makes Klara's eyes spring into Nathanael's breast; then Coppola,
the eyeglass and telescope dealer whose dazzling wares blind Nathanael as
though a heap of bloody eyes had been thrown on the table; Olympia's
initially lifeless eyes and mysteriously scorching gaze; the violent quarrel
between Coppelius and Spalanzani during which the physicist flings the
puppet's bloody eyes at Nathanael, shrieking that they had been stolen
from him; finally, the scene in the tower when Nathanael cries out desperately after having noticed Coppelius with Coppola's spyglass: "Ah, nice-
a-eyes, nice-a-eyes!" (p. 125). All these instances of delirium focus on the
eyes. But what kind of eyes? These are eyes ripped out of their sockets,
dazzling and dazzled, mystified, inert and lifeless; in short, these eyes are
deprived of the power of sight, they are denied insight and the capacity
to discriminate. Nathanael would like to see, he hides in his father's room,
hoping to detect his secret machinations with the Sandman, but as he is
about to discover what they are doing, he falls prey to a negative hallucination that deprives him of his sight, strips him of his senses and eventually
his sanity. His bold search is thwarted there just as his questions had been
mocked by his mother's and the nurse's devious answers: there is no
Sandman, only an evil goblin who mistreats children. (We may note in
passing how closely Nathanael's hallucination in his father's study parallels
the nurse's implied threat: if you try to look, you'll be blinded.) His
mother and the nurse distracted the child's attention, they prevented him
from looking or gaining insight into his father's dubious activities. However, the two women unwittingly hinted at something in their manner of
speech. The expression they use "to throw sand in someone's eyes" (*Sand
in die Augen streuen*) is the German equivalent for the English "to throw
dust in someone's eyes", meaning to mislead, to dupe or trick. (Similarly
the dustman is a variant Anglicism for the Sandman.) Wanting to mislead
the child, wanting desperately to keep the worrisome reality from him, the
mother and the nurse inadvertently hint at some form of deception or
fraud: "handfuls of sand in the eyes." Is this to be taken as an unintended
insinuation about the father's activities with Coppelius? We definitely think
so. This suspicion can be confirmed by other elements in the tale.

The doll Olympia is used to suggest the idea of fraud openly, at first in
connection with her eyes, then her movements and voice. Siegmund is
speaking to Nathanael.

She seems to us – don't take this badly, my brother – strangely stiff and soulless. Her figure is symmetrical, so is her face, that's true enough, and if her eyes were not so completely devoid of life – the power of vision, I mean – she might be considered beautiful. Her step is peculiarly measured; all of her movements seem to stem from some kind of clockwork. Her playing and her singing are unpleasantly perfect, being as lifeless as a music box; it is the same with her dancing. We found Olympia to be rather weird, and we wanted to have nothing to do with her. She seems to us to be playing the part of a human being, and it's as if there really were something hidden behind all of this.

(p. 117)

The trickery will be clear to all when, following Nathanael's fit of madness in Spalanzani's house, Olympia's real nature is exposed.

Spalanzani was forced to leave the university because Nathanael's story had caused a considerable scandal and because opinion generally held that it was an inexcusable deceit to have smuggled a wooden doll into proper tea circles, where Olympia had been such a success, and to have palmed it off as a human. In fact, lawyers held that it was subtle imposture and considered it felonious.

(p. 120)

We believe that the fake Olympia parallels the father's and Coppelius's secret machinations. This is why Nathanael becomes irrationally attached to Olympia; she is the embodiment of the dust thrown in Nathanael's eyes. Tricked first by dusty answers, then by his own fear of discovering the forbidden family secret, and finally dazzled by Coppola's distortive spyglass, Nathanael's eyes see nothing but illusion. While his friends see through the fraud, Nathanael remains blinded. His witless infatuation with the puppet his fellow students suspect to be a fake shows Nathanael in the situation of his childhood. He is dazzled with the blindness forced upon him by his parents and the nurse. As in his childhood, Nathanael is again kept from knowledge others possess.

The Sandman suggests the source of the hero's mental anguish by linking it to his family's uncanny secretiveness, a secretiveness embodied for the child in the mysterious Sandman and his own father's unexplained double nature in the manner of Dr Jekyll and Mr Hyde. The child suspects some clandestine manoeuvres in the family and yet his inability to define them only serves to heighten the uncanny feelings of terror in him. Those who know, the mother and the nurse, do all they can to divert his attention, to daze him with the threat of actual blindness: take care because the evil Sandman night throw handfuls of sand in your eyes so that they will pop out all bloodied. By means of this rather ungraceful ploy, the adults derail the child's earnest search, leading him into the mysterious realm of the unreal, the fantastic, the marvellous and the diabolical. The father's death puts a tragic end to the child's inquiries and, at the same time, serves to underscore the disastrous character of the unrevealed family secret. Under these circumstances the child's preoccupation with the unapproachable family mystery can only reappear surreptitiously under the guise of an obsession with the diabolical figures of the Sandman, Coppelius-Coppola – the fiendish embodiments of an inexorable destiny. The mysterious Coppelius-Coppola, the bane of Nathanael's life at the university and the apparent cause of his mental demise, symbolizes the impossibility of bringing to light an enigma, the very enigma that threw Nathanael's family into disarray before actually destroying it, just as Nathanael's own life is shattered in the final scene.

From the psychoanalytic viewpoint, Hoffman's story is aptly called *The Sandman* because the name of this character refers to Nathanael's lot and the family secret haunting him. The Sandman is neither a goblin who scares children nor a monster who destroys the happiness of lovers; he stands for a name that suggests the situation of twofold deceit in which Nathanael lives. The Sandman plays out the dust thrown in the eyes; his name points to some fraudulent activity in the family and, at the same time, to its being covered up before the child. Furthermore, the Sandman represents the devastating metaphor that constitutes the unthinkable stuff of Nathanael's hallucinations: there is foul play in the family and the adults throw dust in my eyes so that I should not be able to see it.

III

Freud is not intent on interpreting Hoffman's text. Undoubtedly, Freud left that task to his readers. He himself appeals to the authority of well-established psychoanalytic insights:

> We know from psycho-analytic experience, however, that the fear of damaging or losing one's eyes is a terrible one in children. Many adults retain their apprehensiveness in this respect, and no physical injury is so much dreaded by them as an injury to the eye. . . . A study of dreams, phantasies and myths has taught us that anxiety about one's eyes, the fear of going blind, is often enough a substitute for the dread of being castrated.
>
> (p. 231)

Freud is interested here in the allegedly indubitable relation between the fear of castration and the fear of losing one's eyes. "All further doubts are removed when we learn the details of their 'castration complex' from the analysis of neurotic patients, and realize its immense importance in their mental life" (p. 231). Freud wishes to defend the symbolic equivalence between the eyes and the penis, even if it is at the cost of losing sight of Hoffmann's tale. Rather than analyse *The Sandman*, Freud uses it as a weapon against his potential detractors: "I would not recommend any opponent of the psycho-analytic view to select this particular story of the

Sand-Man with which to support his argument that anxiety about the eyes has nothing to do with the castration complex" (p. 231). To dispute the interdependence of the fear of losing the eyes and castration is not our primary aim. Whether or not this is true in general makes no difference to Hoffmann's tale. Despite Freud's statement to the contrary –

> Elements in the story like these, and many others, seem arbitrary and meaningless so long as we deny all connection between fears about the eye and castration; but they become intelligible as soon as we replace the Sand-Man by the dreaded father at whose hands castration is expected.
>
> (p. 232)

– we feel *The Sandman* is coherent without the idea of castration.

It seems to us at times that Freud actually created a fiction of his own in discussing *The Sandman*. An example will suffice. In Hoffmann's tale Nathanael's father dies in a mysterious explosion during an evening work session such as he had had for many years with the lawyer Coppelius. Nathanael does not see the explosion, he simply hears it from his room. Yet in support of the castration complex, Freud asks: "Why does Hoffmann bring the anxiety about the eyes into such intimate connection with the father's death?" (p. 231). Hoffman's tale provides no such connection. It is curious that Freud's account should include such contradictions and equivocations. Another case in point is the idea of the split father-imago and the parallel role of the puppet Olympia. Freud makes the relevance of castration dependent on the ambivalent father-imago, split, according to him, into a good and a bad one. The bad father-imago is supposedly symbolized by Coppelius, the good one by Nathanael's own father who intercedes to save his eyes. From what follows in Freud's account, it would appear that the good father dies at the hands of the castrating bad father as an expression of Nathanael's own repressed death-wish against his evil father-imago. The idea of repression serves to jumble the roles and to create for the reader a veritable psychoanalytic imbroglio. Instead of the bad father-imago, who should have been killed, the good one is destroyed. Having been wished dead, the bad father does away with the good one. Freud continues:

> Coppelius is made answerable for it. This pair of fathers is represented later, in his student days, by Professor Spalanzani and Coppola the optician. The Professor is himself a member of the father-series, and Coppola is recognized as identical with Coppelius the lawyer. Just as they used before to work together over the secret brazier, so now they have jointly created the doll Olympia.
>
> (p. 232)

In keeping with the split paternal imago previously proposed by Freud, one of these new father substitutes should be deemed good, the other bad.

Yet these attributes disappear from Freud's analysis as if they had never been introduced. At this point Freud is interested solely in the idea of two fathers, since this allows him to assert that Spalanzani and Coppola, Olympia's "fathers", are the reincarnations of Nathanael's split father-imago. Logically, Olympia would then have to function as Nathanael's *alter ego.* "This automatic doll can be nothing else than a materialization of Nathanael's feminine attitude towards his father in his infancy" (p. 232). In Freud's fiction Olympia personifies a dissociated complex of Nathanael's and mirrors a narcissistic form of love, since "the young man", fixated upon his father by his castration complex, becomes incapable of loving a woman" (p. 232). There is nothing inherently implausible in this episode of Freud's psychoanalytic fiction, even if it is rather far-fetched in relation to Hoffmann's tale. But did not Freud say a moment ago that the castrating father constantly interfered with love and not only divided Nathanael from his beloved Klara, but also destroyed "the second object of his love, Olympia the lovely doll"? (p. 231). There is a confusion here in Freudian terms. Olympia must be either the representation of Nathanael's dissociated narcissistic complex or his object of love. In other words, either Olympia is a personified expression of Nathanael's own feminine attitude toward his castrating father in childhood or else she is the young man's external object of adult love on the same level as Klara. Whatever power the concept of castration may have in Freudian psychoanalysis, it cannot help equate a real flesh-and-blood object of adult love with the regressive projection of an infantile Oedipal position onto a lifeless doll.

These equivocations are due to Freud's desire to see Hoffmann's tale fit his castration model. Yet the effect is exactly the opposite; the inconsistencies serve to underscore the disparity between *The Sandman* and Freud's account of it.

Injured, blinded or lifeless eyes are omnipresent in *The Sandman* and they symbolize the sheer inability to see – nothing else. Freud's parallel between the eyes and the penis is extraneous to Hoffmann's story. In prescribing this equation Freud diverts attention from the eyes as the organ of sight and the metaphor of insight; he obscures the tragedy of thwarted understanding. Nathanael's true fear (as manifested in his first hallucination) is that he will have his eyes plucked out because he is trying to pry into his family's secret. Inexorably, Hoffman's tale stages the misadventure of the eyes, the plight of blocked understanding. No more is needed to grasp fully the hero's suffering.

Despite numerous disparities in his argumentation, Freud privileges Hoffmann's tale in "The uncanny". Why? Freud's presentation of *The Sandman* follows closely upon his discussion of the linguistic usage of the German words *heimlich* and *unheimlich*. If we read the dictionary entries Freud provides side by side with *The Sandman*, an astonishing convergence between the two occurs: they share the idea of secret. In our view, this meeting between the words and *The Sandman* explains, albeit covertly,

Freud's inclusion of the short story in his essay as well as his misinterpretation. It is as if, through his misreading of the story, Freud gave his readers free reign to interpret it for themselves.

The word *unheimlich* or uncanny actually appears several times in Hoffmann's tale but here it is more relevant to concentrate on the possible connections between Nathanael's story and the meanings of the word. Nathanael's childhood is marked by the intrusion of a troubling mystery, the secret collaboration between his beloved father and the repulsive Coppelius. Periodically, a "dense cloud" surrounds the father's activities and keeps him at an uncomfortable distance from his children. Nathanael is harrowed by the uncertainty surrounding his father: is he a kind man or the willing accomplice of the "demon" Coppelius? The fog spread about him – and made ever more dense by the dusty answers of the mother and the nurse – slowly overtakes Nathanael and unhinges his reason. Nathanael is the victim of family life overcome by a secret forever concealed. The secret's insidious presence haunts him throughout his life. He is trapped by silence, a permanent lack of communication, in short, by his inability to speak to anyone about his painful distrust of his father. As a result he could never lay to rest the grief he felt over his father's sudden death or murder. The mysterious circumstances of the explosion killing his father undoubtedly deepened Nathanael's suspicions while heightening his overall sense of bewilderment.

The twofold meaning of the uncanny in German can now be linked to *The Sandman*. The opposite senses contained in the word *heimlich* (meaning both "familiar, intimate, belonging to the home" and "secret or hidden") describe quite aptly Nathanael's paradoxical family situation. The familiarity and intimacy of the home in which the child normally feels at ease are upset by his father's mysterious behaviour. Something secret and impenetrable is happening in the family behind the child's back. Nathanael's obsession is thus due to a haunting sense of the *unheimlich*. The secret pervading the family makes the intimacy of his own home chillingly foreign to him.

Returning to Freud's initial definition, we find that he presents the uncanny as a process in three successive stages. Something that has long been familiar to someone individually or to humans collectively (a desire, a fear, a belief, etc.) is overcome or repressed and thereby removed from active consciousness. When years later and despite repression, this formerly familiar thing returns, we no longer recognize it; as a result it provokes in us a sense of the uncanny. Perfectly plausible and highly suggestive as an independent idea, Freud's breakdown of the uncanny into a three-tiered sequence does not, however, correspond to *The Sandman*. Hoffmann shows us the case of a family infiltrated by a secret which rendered it disturbingly unfamiliar to one of the children. Here the uncanny does not arise because someone no longer knows that he repressed his infantile complexes or the scattered remnants of our common stock of animistic beliefs. Rather, the uncanny overwhelms the hero because, even as he lives in its midst, his family is wilfully concealing secrets from him. The uncanny owes its upsetting and frightful effect to a thoroughly paradoxical simultaneousness. What we consider to be the closest and most intimate part of our life – our own family, our own home – is in fact at the furthest possible remove and the least familiar to us.

The twofold meaning of the word *heimlich* – belonging to the home, familiar *and* hidden or secret – defines the contradiction the child must endure in a family with secrets. Labouring under the oppressive weight of their family's secret, children are often victims of unrelenting emotional chaos, most likely also experiencing numerous crises of indecision: they doubt the veracity of their own suppositions and even observations. With respect to their own inmost conjectures and experiences, these children are frequently plagued with bewildering confusion, a painful sense – precisely of the uncanny. Due to covert manoeuvres to which they are not privy, children can become virtual strangers in their own homes. They are consumed with doubts and ruminations that can lead to madness such as Nathanael's in *The Sandman*.

Under more favourable circumstances children will bury their unanswered questions and as adults will draw from them the singular and mysterious vigour of their creativity. Are we justified in conjecturing that this latter scenario applies to Freud? Only further research can confirm or invalidate our hypothesis. At this stage of our thinking, it seems to us that Freud's interpretation of *The Sandman*, as an example of the return of the repressed, is both a symptom and a reassuring compromise, shielding him from his own unwittingly endured traumas. The Sandman, the tormenting stranger in the home, is ultimately no stranger at all – the uncanny is but the disguised return of something already familiar. Yet this comforting idea is punctured by *The Sandman*, Hoffmann's "question" to Freud. Is the uncanny the return of something we ourselves have repressed or of the secrets our own family permanently keeps from us?

NOTES

1 These queries derive in part from our long-standing interest in a possible connection between Freud's psychological theories and his unwittingly endured traumatic experiences. If convincingly shown, the connection could shed psychoanalytic light on the genesis of Freudian theories and interpretative strategies. Samples of this ongoing research project can be found in N. Rand and M. Torok's "Questions à la psychoanalyse freudienne: La rêve, la realité, le fantasme", *Les Temps Modernes* vol. 48, no. 549, (April, 1992), 1–31, tr. "Questions to Freudian psychoanalysis: Dream interpretation, reality, fantasy", *Critical Inquiry* vol. 19, no. 3; "The secret of psychoanalysis: history reads theory", *Critical Inquiry* vol. 13, no. 2 (Winter 1987), 278–86; M. Torok, "What is occult in occultism: between Sergei Pankeiev – Wolf Man and Sigmund Freud", in N. Abraham and M. Torok, *The Wolf Man's Magic Word: A Cryptonymy*, tr. N. Rand (Minneapolis: University of Minnesota Press, 1986); "A Remembrance of things

deleted: between Sigmund Freud and Emmy von N", in N. Abraham and M. Torok, *The Shell and the Kernel: Renewals of Psychoanalysis*, ed. and tr. N. Rand (Chicago: University of Chicago Press, 1994).

2 "The uncanny", in *The Standard Edition of the Collected Works of Sigmund Freud* (London: Hogarth Press), pp. 217–56, p. 200. Further references to this work will appear in the text.

3 We feel that, in this instance, Freud's attempt to apply previously established concepts in a new context leads to a fundamental discrepancy between his theories and the literary text under consideration. The recent scholarly literature on "The Sandman", mindful of Freud's "The uncanny" or not, is considerable. We cite only a selection of those works that indicate directions of inquiry germane to ours. The various authors' premises, approach and focus are quite different from our own, yet isolated points of contact can be established in each case. Helene Cixous's "Les noms du pire: Lecture de l'*Homme au sable*", in *Prénoms de personne* (Paris: Seuil, 1974), pp. 39–99; "Le double e(s)t le diable: L'inquietante étrangeté de l'*Homme au sable*", in Sarah Kofman, *Quatre romans analytiques* (Paris: Galilée, 1973), pp. 135–81. Françoise Meltzer, "The uncanny rendered canny: Freud's blind spot in reading Hoffmann's *Sandman*" and Bernard Rubin, "Freud and Hoffmann: *The Sandman*", both in S. L. Gilman (ed.), *Introducing Psychoanalytic Theory* (New York: Brunner/Mazel, 1982), pp. 205–39; E. F. Hoffmann, "Zu E.T.A. Hoffmann's *Sandmann*", *Monatshefte*, vol. 54 no. 5 (1962), 244–50. Others have questioned Freud's interpretation of *The Sandman* on various grounds, most notably Harold Bloom *Agon: Towards a Theory of Revisionism* (New York: Oxford University Press, 1982); M. V. Jones "*Der Sandmann* and 'The uncanny': a sketch for an alternative approach" *Paragraph*, vol. 7 (March 1986), 77–101; S. Milner, *Freud et l'interpretation de la littérature* (Paris: SEDES, 1978).

4 *Tales of E.T.A. Hoffmann*, ed. and tr. L. J. Kent and E. C. Knight (Chicago: University of Chicago Press, 1972) p. 105. Further references to this work will appear in the text.

11 The pleasure of therapy

Charles E. Scott

Charles E. Scott is Edwin Erle Sparks Professor of Philosophy at Pennsylvania State University and a leading figure in continental philosophy.

In his recent book *The Question of Ethics: Nietszche, Foucault, Heidegger*, Scott argues that ethics is a way of thinking and judging that has come into question as philosophers have confronted the suffering and conflicts that have arisen out of our traditional systems of value. Scott traces the successive problematizations of ethics in the work of Nietzsche, Foucault and Heidegger. At issue for Scott is the possibility of a type of thinking that puts in question the values that give meaning to our thought and actions, a process that he identifies as one of self-overcoming.

In the following paper, Scott adopts such a stance toward the subject of therapy. In his *History of Sexuality*, Foucault marks out the differing formation of the ethical subject in the regulation of the body and its pleasures. He argues that psychoanalysis was the final outcome of a process of the transformation of sex into discourse and a locating of the truth of the subject in desire, a process that was inaugurated by Greek and Roman practices and refined by the Christian confessional. For Scott, the unravelling of traditional forms of subjectification through self-mastery paradoxically releases a new experience of pleasure, one that may be found to occur in therapy itself, and one that is outside the perimeters of identity and selfhood.

SELECT BIBLIOGRAPHY

Scott, C. E., *The Language of Difference*, Atlantic Highlands: Humanities Press International, 1987.
—— *The Question of Ethics: Nietzsche, Foucault, Heidegger*, Bloomington: Indiana University Press, 1990.

* * *

Disciplined training transforms animal nature into human nature.

(Kant, *Über Pädagogik*)

This dismemberment, the properly Dionysian *suffering*, is like a transformation into air, water, earth, and fire ... we are therefore to regard
the state of individuation with the origin and primal cause of all suffering, as something objectionable in itself.

(Nietzsche, *The Birth of Tragedy*)

The curious blending and duality in the emotions of the Dionysian
revelers reminds us – as medicines reminds us of deadly poisons – of
the phenomenon that pain begets joy.

(Nietzsche, *The Birth of Tragedy*)

PLEASURE WITHOUT SELF[1]

We speak of the work of therapy. Can we speak also of its unworking, of
its not doing, its idleness, its pleasure, its silence in the endless flow
of words? Speak not of a conversation with the unconscious or the translation of the unconscious or the embodying of the Dionysian but speak
of no work at all and no words at all, of nothing to be known, sublimated,
worked through or worked out? Can we speak of the pleasure of therapy?
A pleasure that belongs neither to a self nor to a soul, but to itself? Speak
of pleasure's pleasing in therapy?

Can we speak of a self that in its moments begins not only in the
possibility of its absence, but begins in its past absence, begins not only
in remembrance but in forgetfulness, begins not solely in retrieving itself
but in relinquishing its constructions, constructions that are so intimate to
it that their loss means opening beyond distinctions?

I speak of the pleasure of therapy with the thought that in the losses of
self that occur in therapy something takes place that relieves the time-
space of selfhood, unburdens an identity, places speaking beyond its speech
and recollections, and gives nothing to be said or used, but gives something
like pleasing that is strange to the self in the self's suspension. Something
untreated and untreatable comes to pass, something unworkable, something
without health or disease, something other to self-relation: something like
pleasure. Not mindful or soulish or one. The pleasure of no one. Unpos-
sessed, unconcerned, unregarded. Perhaps beyond self-touch and chains of
signifiers. Perhaps outside of imaginative grasp. The pleasure of therapy.
Far beyond the principles of pleasure.

In speaking of therapy I speak also of the burden, the unpleasure of the
self. Not that the self lacks its satisfactions: its myths of origin and destiny,
its meaning – above all its struggle for meaning. Nor do I wish to demean
the self. I do not wish to deny the self's satisfactions. But I wish to speak
of pleasure that does not belong to the self, pleasure to which the self

cannot belong, pleasure which can concern the self, but which the self excludes by a distance that measures the self's limits, measures its lack of the pleasure of unidentity, egolessness, spiritlessness, soullessness. Do I speak of nothing at all?

I speak of non-belonging when I mention unworking and non-treating. The non-belonging of not being either this or that in being both this and that: of not being either citizen or friend in being both citizen and friend, of not being either therapist or theorist in being both therapist and theorist, of not being either self or body in being both self and body. I speak of non-belonging when I speak of the evacuation of spirit as subject and desire as object, when I speak of pleasure without spirit and without objectivity. Not to belong: not to be a work, not to be working, not be of a subject or for a subject, not to be sub-ject, not to be of ob-ject. To lack debt, judgment, concept and value: not to belong – not to be a self or for a self. And yet to be?

We are many in ourselves. Many voices, many histories that converge in us. Although one or two voices may organize the others in a semblance of unity and co-operation, our dreams and lapses show us some of the many that we are and the exteriority to them of a singular identity. It would be too much to say that singularity is imposed upon us. Perhaps it grows from us. Or by processes of disciplined abandonment, elimination and recognition we come to hear ourselves in a voice, like a rope, that is woven from many strands into a singular theme that must be sealed at the ends to prevent unravelling. And this rope excludes unfixed strands that will not fit or would make the weave too thick. Or some of the strands are of other and unfitting stuff. So we in our identities are like a limited community, one, usually, that does not know itself, but is bound together silently and by training with fixations, anxieties, memories, needs, expectations. A community that needs *not* to know its full cacophonous variety in order to affirm its commonality. A group of contesting voices making a burden of sounds that contest without singularity – voices that constitute our singularity – giving us multiple striving and heritages and giving witness to the death of singularity in all of its moments. Do we not, in the singularity of our identity, wish a triumph over this death, wish an ego arising from its own perpetual ashes, wish a rightness that overrides the many contesting voices of our self?

The self may be idealized in the image of a communion, a community that tends toward fusion, a unified immanence of the self's interests and trajectories. In this ideal we ask what kind of self organizes the best community: an open self that hears many voices? A good self that obeys the highest values? A spiritual self that ascends within itself to the highest voices? A moderate self that tempers the extremes in its domain? A confessional self that bears witness to all that it hears? Each kind of self will have its own satisfactions, and the therapist may well attend to the interest of the particular self in order to allow it its autonomy as it seeks its fulfilment. A fulfilled self in the ideal of a communion is like a satisfied, benevolent sovereign. Only a threat to its sovereignty will make it angry.

Why do I speak of the pleasure of therapy? In therapy there may happen, regardless of the theoretical orientation of the therapist, a falling apart of the subject and an attunement not only to the release of will's control, but to the pleasure of being indeterminate in the midst of all determinations, of being non-representable in the midst of all representations, of no desire in the midst of directed desires, of not being totally male or female, of being no who in who one is, of being something inactive in our activity, of being neither variant nor invariant, neither one nor many: attunement to being other to the circumspection of subjectivity, other to the limits of subjectivity, other to the polarity of self and other. A pleasure of being nothing that can be fragmented or fulfilled, carne or incarnate. A pleasure in being unspeakable. And yet coming to speech and departing from it. The pleasure of not being one, the pleasure of the division between being and not being. The pleasure of non-belonging.

The pleasure of therapy is proximate to a breakdown of the "psyche" in its process of coming to know itself: the breakdown of the certainty of self-knowledge, of the self's experience of itself. The pleasure of not belonging to one's attachments and self-identifications. The disaster of this pleasure takes place in the depths of the self's order and gives no hope for its return. It takes place in the passing of speakable satisfactions.

In the pleasure of therapy we are before the alterity of terminations without closure, such terminations as the loss of the self's constructions and their work, the exposure of no identity in the boundaries that traverse our many voices, the termination in alterity of the self's obsession with being a self, the termination of being a self: we are speaking of a "sense" proximate to the lifting of something heavy or to the falling of the self's satisfaction. Pleasure in tears and mourning, pleasure without satisfaction, pleasure other to the self's satisfactions that accompany the self's life. This pleasure is not like passion. It is like openness that lacks categories and subjectivity, that lacks a line of termination. I believe that it cannot be affirmed by the self except in its loss. I would like to say that it is unimaginable energy, that it gives life. But by that wish I speak in my self's desire. Is my self's desire proximate to this pleasure? Only as the desire loses its force.

I wish to speak of a pleasure that does not satisfy the self, a pleasure that can be neither true nor false, one that begins in a space where the self finds its ending. This would be a space where one comes to disappear without satisfaction. The self would have no language for marking and specifying the pleasure, a place where pleasure comes to disappear. It would be an unhuman pleasure, foreign to us, without a "we", one that awakens us to the passage of our work and transformation, one that satisfies none of the normal conditions of our lives. Yet I am driven to use a normal word – pleasure – and to suggest its abnormality. An abnormal pleasure that gives us to wonder if we are satisfied by something that is not pleasure as though pleasure were not known, as though it led to something that "we" cannot know in our consensus of satisfactions.

Can we be led in therapy to despair in our satisfactions, in the accomplishments of strength and the force of insight? Are we led to this ending, to the limits of this language, by an enticement beyond our powers to live well and normally with each other? Are we led to pleasure's pleasing outside of the fixtures by which we know ourselves to be as we are? I speak of a "movement" of pleasure, without work, one that moves like a dream through satisfactions and accomplishments, moves like desire might move in an element that is foreign to it, like desire that is at ease with its need as flowing water that knows no source and moves without a goal, not hungry water that wants to fulfil itself, but water that flows until it ceases to flow, drops until dropping closes on itself. It is like a "movement" that does not seek itself but without seeking pleases. Always nearing with no place primarily to be.

Perhaps I speak of a lost pleasure. We might give it a myth from outside of itself, the myth of a mother, for example, who is close without distance, holding us so closely that touch vanishes in the absence of a self to be touched. Perhaps we protect ourselves from pleasure by an imagined recall of umbilicalled attachment without a discernment of distance or reach, a pleasure of sleeping awakeness that fuses dream and perception, an origination of quiet, total sufficiency. Perhaps we believe that without the divisions of self and language only the fused mother pleases. Perhaps pleasure's pleasing makes us unfaithful to our humanity and to our common bonds of identity. Perhaps we carry such unfaithfulness in us and find satisfaction in remembering this foreign longing as though it came of time before we were cut off from a dream of non-human silence in closeness. Perhaps our work is to give more distance to this unreachable fusion, to speak of it, signify it and quiet its draw. Perhaps the work of our language and therapy is to give more division, to divide the division, to satisfy our severed, severing language by a discipline of attention to our separateness. Perhaps we can undeceive ourselves in a constellation of myth and belief that frees us from the mother of our lives, restores us to good sense and masters the lure of pleasure outside of ourselves. Or could that be a treachery in ourselves, a caution against non-signification, a refusal of something inhuman in ourselves, a denial of risk that is close in the divisions of our lives? Perhaps it is a caution against unburdening ourselves, against the self's termination.

SPEAKING OF THE SELF'S BURDEN

I have spoken of pleasure without self in such a manner that the self comes to appear as a burden to itself. This suggests not that the self should relinquish itself, should become other to itself, should deny itself, but that the self constitutes a limit in its life. Self-fulfilment – fullness of self – gives burden as well as satisfaction. I have suggested that part of the self's limit is found in naming its other. If it names its other the unconscious, for example, it re-enfolds its other into itself. That is part of its burden, its self-perpetuation. If it attempts to make the pleasure of which we speak its own, the self loses it. We wonder at what the self loses in being itself, in naming and knowing its other.

Foucault's genealogy of the ethical self is suggestive in our context, not because he speaks of the pleasure of therapy, but because he presents an option for understanding the self's burden to itself. In his last trilogy, Foucault interprets our obligatoriness as a formation in a process of fragile self-attentiveness, as a construction in a lineage of problems arising from the body's desire. It is a lineage of division from body that gives us to know what we mean when we say *self* and *body*. We come to know what these words mean in this lineage, but our knowledge is not without burden and doubt and non-necessity. Perhaps an aspect of the self's burden is found in repeated attempts to overcome the burden of self-doubt, its non-necessity.

Our issue for the moment is the self's burden to itself. My suspicion is that the self cannot avoid being a burden to itself and that its satisfactions and its work constitute this burdening. I shall develop this suspicion in relation to Foucault's genealogy of the ethical self's development. The burden of the self to itself is found in its divisions from what cannot be self-like. In Foucault's genealogy the issue is the body's pleasures, which, for the ethical self, are kept outside of the self's care for itself by projects of self-mastery. For us the issue is focused by the self's falling apart and opening to an alterity to which it cannot belong and which accompanies without suffering the self's suffering. It is like pleasure in the sense that a life goes on without measure or sense in the self's ending. I do not speak in this paper of the body's pleasures, but Foucault's genealogy, in speaking of the formation of the ethical self in relation to the body's pleasure, allows us to see the possibility that in its self-care the self is heavily burdened by a time of self-conservation and by a need for continuous self-formation. Possibly, as the self falls apart in therapeutic work – in spite of therapy's fit with an obsession for self-conservation and self-formation – possibly an unburdening takes place that opens with seeming disaster to what we are calling the pleasure of therapy.

Foucault's genealogical study of sexuality is a study of "the modes according to which individuals are given to *recognize* themselves as sexual *subjects*".[2] This is not a conceptual analysis, but an account of

> the *practices* by which individuals were *led* to *focus* attention on themselves ... as *subjects of desire*, bringing into play between themselves ... a certain *relationship* that allows them to discover, *in desire, the truth of their being*, be it natural or fallen.[3]

The practices in question lend and provide focus for individuals. The focus is on themselves. *Subjects* of desire are not found in desiring, but in *relationships* to desire in which the self forms itself by separating itself from the life of desire. Desiring, then, is at a distance from the subject of desire, and this distance is structured by many relations of power which the subject exercises in the form of disciplines and practices, each of which has its own lineage of interest and leverage. The subjectivity of desire is found in a relationship to desire, and Foucault found that in the relationships that developed in our lineage, desire in its distance to the subjects who were to govern it was recognized as the truth of our being. Hence, truth, desire, power and a certain fragmentation among them are all implicated in his study of the formation of ethical subjectivity. We note at the beginning that the *subject* of desire, i.e., this subjectivity and manner of being a self, is not structured primarily by desire or a force of will, but by a circulation of powers that emerge as individuals are formed within given circumstances. This circulation of powers stands over against the life of desire in the development of the ethical subject. The subject is defined in part by its regulation of desire and by its self-maintenance before the force of desire. The energy of the ethical subject is other to the energy of desire and finds its identity in both self-control and control of the dangerous other. The subject, rather, takes its *form* of movement from *problems* that have to be faced because of the values and purposes that are found in the relations at hand and that raise new issues to be met. It is formed by coping, solving and resolving: by the development of values and practices that satisfy its fundamental interests as well as avoid what threatens its power of self-control and communal survival.

The areas of circulations of powers are found in the relationships, foci, recognitions, discernments and practices that make up subjectivity in relating to desire. Practices give attentiveness; attentiveness defines a certain manner of relating to one's body and the bodies of other people, and the relation produces a body of knowledge and truth. This particular complex of practices, attentiveness, relation, knowledge and truth is called sexuality, and we will see that sexuality composes a moral subjectivity, that the moral subject is a way of relating to the body's desires, and that the early ethical self's life is a process of continuous struggle to maintain itself in relation to the force and danger of desire.[4]

Foucault does not begin his work on sexuality and the self with repression or the interdiction of desire, given his wish not to universalize sexuality and approach his topic as though something universal and natural for all people is denied or diverted. He makes the self-caring self and the problems generated by self-care his centre of attention in order to give accessibility to the historical character of sexuality. His perception is that sexuality began to develop out of individuals concerned in ancient culture for the health of their bodies. Problematization – confronting problems and developing practices to address those problems in a complex flow of powers – and not repression is thus his point of emphasis as he gives a genealogy of individuals concerned for health in Greek and Roman culture. His concept of power as a circulation of assertions and resistances in social and cultural relations, rather than power as an essence that takes a variety of forms – that concept of circulation in relationships is central to his genealogical project. These relations are fluid and continuously encountering their own limits before changing circumstances: subjects are always in crisis because of flows of events that are not unlike a river's multiple, fluid trajectories. We are unsteady creatures in our identities, not because we repress our true natures and not because we have our true natures repressed for us by our parents, our leaders or our culture. We are unsteady in ourselves because we are relational in who we are and our relations are formed in lineages of problems whose transformations have produced other problems as well as identities made in relation to other problematizations. Our selves are questionable not because we have fallen from something pristine, essential and pre-established but because lived questions and answers that raise other lived questions give us to be as we are. To be a self is always to have something to preserve and solve and avoid.

Foucault's genealogy exposes a surface freedom that accompanies the fragmentations that run through our historically produced selves, the freedom of being also on the margins as well as in the centre of the dominant relationships and truths that give us the ability to recognize ourselves. Within his work we cannot say what selves *are*. We can speak of this or that kind of self that is formed in this or that lineage of subjection. But we stand outside of the reality question concerning selves as we follow the lineages that have produced the range of the "who's" that we can be. We find our selves fragmented and resisting fragmentation as we follow the development of regulations, practices and truths that make self-regulations possible and as we discern what our bodies have become for us, how our pleasures take place, how, indeed, much that has been pleasurable has been made unspeakable and unknowable, how we imprison our bodies, discipline our desires, insure our souls, exclude other bodies and empower our knowledges. As we encounter ourselves belonging to a lineage of subjection, and as we make the encounter in a genealogical ethos that comes to knowledge of itself by accounts of its own lineage, as we encounter ourselves in an ethos of fragmented freedom, we both care for ourselves and problematize the caring that regulates us. We problematize care for the selves that have come in question by following their lineage as Foucault's genealogy extends the care of self in his account of the dangers of self-care.

We are dealing with a freedom of fragmentation, a freedom that comes from individuals' not belonging *essentially* to anything, a freedom that comes from not being *essentially* any one, a freedom that accompanies the differences that constitute a lineage of loose alliances, relations of resistance and mastery and confederations of fluid interests – a freedom that accompanies the lineages that give us to be as we are. This freedom of fragmentation traverses the problems that arise from transformations out of other problems – it is the element of problematization. It names people's ability that arises in specific circulations of power to look again, say yes or no, experience danger in the midst of security, and hold in question the firmest of principles and established practices. It allows knowledges and practices to fall apart or to mutate with other knowledges and practices. This freedom is not anything in particular, cannot be used or directly addressed, and does not belong to subjects, although on Foucault's terms, it enables genealogy to be done. Rather, freedom means fragmentation in the structures that identify selves. It is a Dionysian factor that gives selves to be always in question, particularly at junctures of greatest certainty. The self is given to struggle against its ability to form and care for itself as it gives itself forms of health and well-being by which it knows itself and judges itself to be more or less true to itself. Its freedom means that in coming to itself – in belonging to itself – it also does not belong to itself. To arise as a self is to court the disaster it most fears: the disaster of falling apart.

This language of freedom sticks to the surface of events and offers us no satisfaction. Even the fractures of which it speaks and the local satisfactions that it permits lack a language of incandescent mystical infusion, or participation in emptiness. It is not transcendent or transcendental, this freedom. It is not exactly a capacity or a vapour, not a ghost or a trace of something. It is merely non-connections among connected things that means non-belonging – non-belonging to which we cannot belong: a broken surface of circulations in which individuals are at a distance with themselves and with all other things. Neither love nor strife are its meaning. It has no face and no nature.

The subjection process – the process of making moral subjects – is complex. On the one hand the word *subjection*, in the context of Foucault's work, refers to the emergence and unfolding of the subject who measures, regulates and knows desire. On the other, the word suggests mastering, compelling and obligating, and it is by subjection that the ethical subject has come to be. We have seen, however, that subjection in this context does not mean repression or interdiction by a higher authority. It refers, rather, to a process of discipline by which individuals give themselves a particular self-relation and come to be the selves that they are. On the basis of this at first largely individual *ascesis*, later religious, governmental and institutional regulations and methods of normalization developed. What are some of the relations that empowered the emergence of the subject of desire – the ethical subject – and that have come through multiple moral mutations to be our selves?

In his discussion of *aphrodisia* – of the "acts, gestures, and contacts that produce certain forces of pleasure"[5] – Foucault identifies a dynamic relation of desire, act and pleasure that forms the "texture" of ethical experience in the late classical period. It is not concupiscence or the inherent evil of desire. *Aphrodisia* names a texture of ethical experience that is both natural, and because of the pleasure's intensity and acuteness, is subject to excess. *Excess* means elevation of a pleasurable force above more important things, such as the soul's "highest" activities or the responsibilities of citizenship.

In addition to the problem of excess, there are the problems generated by the sexual roles played by individuals. In the Greek context, role is identified in terms of activity and passivity. Activity is relegated to men and is closely associated with being a free citizen as distinct to being a slave or a woman. And passivity is associated with women and slaves. This means that the formation of moral subjectivity emerged *within* an active-passive polarity in which the active male's privilege is complete. Passivity meant being an object of activity, and this created problems not only regarding women's pleasure, but also regarding the identity of the receptive male. Within the classical context, the passive object was a giver of pleasure for whom the experience of pleasure was not a primary concern.

Within this context of *aphrodisia*, which Foucault identifies as the substance of ethics in the late classical period and as the interplay of natural forces that became unnatural by virtue of their power and pleasure, I will note only two of the three areas of problematization that he raises and then turn to the care of self in order to focus on the emerging form of the early ethical subject that established the paternity for western ethical subjectivity which constitutes one of the self's major burdens.

Enkrateia: self-mastery, self-control. The *attitude* in relation to oneself that is necessary to an ethics of pleasure and which was manifested through the *proper use* of pleasures is termed *enkrateia*. The word designates the domination of oneself by oneself and the effort this domination demands is also designated by the word. Self-mastery establishes an attunement with one's need for balance and moderation in an effort to avoid ill health and suffering and to bring to realization the unique nature and beauty of the human soul. Self-mastery indicates an agonistic relation in which one fights against many pleasures and desires and cultivates a combative attitude toward pleasures. One must subdue the temptation to excess on the part of "inferior" appetites (*inferior* means appetites shared with animals). This is a struggle against *enslavement* by inferior passions. It is not that they are bad, but their ascendancy and dominion is destructive of the best part of a man. Ethical conduct thus includes a battle for superior power.

In this battle against the dominion of inferior desires, one does battle with oneself. The enemy is one's body. One's body, not an alien power, is the object to be mastered. One sought victory by oneself over oneself *in* the body's desires. Self-rule, self-mastery, and not self-renunciation or purification or integrity were the goals.

Self-mastery is like a governance of the soul, an internal state that is organized by the authority of right principles. Training and discipline are thus necessary and provide the structure of *askēsis* that will enable an individual to subject all that is inferior to whatever is superior. One had to know the dangers, attend carefully to himself and transform himself. The goal is to face privations without suffering and to reduce every physical pleasure to nothing more than the satisfaction of needs: a natural economy that would produce a life of proper satisfaction. We should note that governing oneself and governing others have the same form. Self-govern-ance leads to civic leadership. There is a transfer of power from the governed self to the governed other. But this transfer came naturally from the right measure of self-governance. Self-mastery was an end in itself; its means were its goal. There was no distinction between the act of the self and ethical conduct.

Freedom and truth. *Sophrosyne* (moderation and prudence), is made possible by *Enkrateia*. Is is characterized by freedom, not by purity or innocence. Freedom by self-mastery and self-domination is the classical goal. The opposite to freedom is enslavement of the self. One sought, for example, freedom from the force of pleasures. This freedom thus meant power over oneself: "a power that one brought to bear on oneself in the power that one exercised over others."[6] If one were under the control of others, one would not find *sophrosyne* in himself or herself. In that case one simply obeyed. But if one achieved self-mastery, one could make moderation and prudence the measure of one's relation to those under his authority. The test of this virtue is when one curbs his appetite with those over whom he has power. Such a person was truly free, a freedom, we have noted, which places the self at odds with its ability to be a self that falls apart.

This active freedom was known as "virile". The truly free individual commanded what needed commanding, coerced what was not capable of self-direction and imposed reason on what was wanting in reason. This kind of activity was definitive of a free man's proper relation to himself and others. Domination, hierarchy and masculine authority were thus aspects of a free man's proper measure. Although a woman could be in a certain sense free, she would need to be like a man in that freedom. To have strength of character, she would need dependence on male virility and hence on a man. And immoderation was known then to derive from a passivity that relates it to femininity and was thus unsuited to males. The independence needed for self-virtue and the virility necessary to attrac-tive males were thus problems for this ethos, and out of these problems different relationships between husbands and wives and men and boys developed.

Sophrosyne necessarily accompanies a certain form of knowledge: "*one could not form oneself as an ethical subject in the use of pleasure without forming oneself at the same time as a subject of knowledge.*"[7] Logos must have supremacy and regulate behaviour and the individual must have a sense for proper timing and measure in the application of rules and prin-ciples. The individual must know himself in such a way that his essential relation to what is true is clear to him. Such truth, however, is outside of his own being and selfhood. There is no inclination to turn to the self to know the truth of the self: "... it is important to note that this relation to truth never took the form of a decipherment of the self by the self, never that of a hermeneutics of desire.... The relation to truth was a structural, instrumental and ontological condition."[8]

One of the implications of this account is that within the structure of the ethical subject there is a privileging of assertiveness and virility that radically privileges males in western culture. A question that I can raise but not answer is whether ethical subjectivity continues to disengage people from non-active values, the values of touch for the sake of touch, hearing without assertion, the gentle qualities of animality such as non-judgmental nurturance, nestling, gathering, licking, grace of movement and quiet compatibility with an environment. Are need for dominance, predisposition to competition and drive for self-protective selfhood at the heart of ethical subjectivity even after centuries of transformations such that efforts for goodness and justice, silently, almost unthinkably, cultivate the traditionally male characteristic of assertive virility? Is the *ecstasis* of victory, that elevation and exhilaration that come with overcoming obstacles and bringing to completion a project of domination, part of what ethical conduct must mean? Does the activity of ethical conduct include a translation of ancient male conduct? Do we demean in ethics a side of our lives that has been branded passive and thus given to enslavement by the elevation of activity as an excellence in self-fulfilment?

When Foucault gives an account of the care of self[9] he is giving an account of the emergence of a different way of being in the Graeco-Roman ethos: the emergence of a self that is formed in relating to itself by caring for itself. The structures of this way of being are fateful for us in the sense that a capacity for internal reference is coming to be that makes itself its objectifying project. From this capacity we may expect a lineage in which the self is a problem to itself, in which the *governance* of selves is extremely important, in which mastery and a high degree of assertiveness are primary values, in which knowledge of the self's desires and satisfactions is necessary for good conduct, in which care and control are closely associated, and in which truth, control, privilege and knowledge are affiliated. Most important of all, perhaps, is that the subject who knows and judges Foucault's work is in this lineage, that both the authorship and readership of this genealogical claim are of the studied lineage. In developing genealogical knowledge of a lineage and also being a part of this lineage we need not only find that we are not connected to something outside of our history to which we are bound in our self-relations. We as genealogical knowers also find that we are not the selves that non-genealogically we know ourselves to be. In referring to itself genealogically the self refers to a lineage that is not like the selves we know in our modern truths, and yet the genealogical knowledge that interrupts traditional self-knowledge is also in the lineage of care for self, for as we have seen, resistance to totalization and domination are strong motives in Foucault's work, and self-objectification is a major part of his genealogical project. The self's burden is clearly a part of Foucault's account of the formation of ethical subjectivity.

This is a strange situation. In the form of caring for itself in genealogical knowledge, the self – the subject of ethical knowledge as well as the subject of moral practices – finds itself to be other than the moral principles that it follows and other than the desire that it regulates. It finds itself also to be other to itself. In the tradition of the majesty – Foucault says the *glory* – that the moral self classically assigned to itself as the moderate subject of self-knowledge, it – the self – now finds, by genealogical knowledge, that it is a product of complicated processes of subjection behind which there is no selfhood to be realized and no locale of non-historical truth to give it ontological support. It comes to be only by the energy and manner of its self-care. In its power structure the self does not even belong to the force of desire and thus often finds self-satisfaction in the denial of desire and pleasure. But it also knows that it is harmed by totalization, that it is not made for enslavement and that the liberty that it seeks is without a model or a generative form. Formless freedom. A fragmented self. Care now without a home for nurturance or a guide for truth. A self whose dreams of a transcendent guide and of a propriety that opens to truth and freedom now finds that such dreams come of circulations of powers that mask a structure of dissymmetrical control. It isn't bad, remember. But it *is* dangerous, and the danger is to itself as well as to others. Danger is never avoided by the self, and its life depends on how it replaces one danger with another.

The ascetic ideal which plays so obvious a part in the formation of the ethical self is found on Foucault's account in a mistrust of pleasures in the late classical period. They can abuse the body and the soul and must be contained by a *well-disciplined regulator* and by *practices of containment*: Foucault emphasizes specifically marriage and disaffection with the spiritual meaning of love for boys. Pleasures can weaken the body, distract the soul, disperse the body's and soul's interaction. *Containment indicates strength and is paired against dissolution.* The development of an obsession with unity and unfragmented wholeness for the self is clearly anticipated by the emerging ideal of desire controlled by truth and administrated by an agent of vigilant self-knowledge.

The making of self-relation *vis-à-vis* desire required *specific practices* whereby habits and identity are formed. *These practices produced a self-knowledge which was lived as an identity.* One needed regularly to test himself to see if he could *do without unnecessary* things and remain constant and independent in himself. The Epicureans, for example, carried out disciplines of *abstinence* to show how a more stable satisfaction could be found when one needed only the most elemental things. The Stoics, on the other hand, prepared for privation without disturbances by absencing themselves from all attachments.

Practices of *self-examination* accompanied the disciplines of abstinence. One looked into himself, reviewed his actions and words, sifted through the day's moments, scrutinized and judged what he had done and not done. Learning honest and true self-judgment was an important part of caring for oneself, and to find satisfaction, not in experienced pleasures, but *in the process* of self-examination was crucial to becoming a true self. One learns how to conduct oneself and which rules to follow when one becomes a critical spectator of oneself. The goal is not to reject oneself or to cultivate guilt, but to become a serene judge of what is best to do by coming to know oneself by thorough and complete self-disclosure in reference to reason and transcendent truths.

A third practice is one of *thinking about what one thinks*. The individual "steadily screens representations, examines them, monitors them, and sorts them out. One is like a night watchman, in the words of Epictetus, 'who checks the entries at the gates of cities or houses' ". This is a practice of attitude whereby all thoughts and representations are examined and evaluated. One wants to find which are valid and which are untrue. Nothing should be privileged that is shallow or misleading. Looking behind the scenes of thought for their basis and merit is necessary if one is to care for himself. Only what is consonant with the self's freedom and rationality may be entertained, and thinking about one's thoughts in practical self-reflection is an important discipline. Thought's self-objectification is part of the cure for wayward people who do not know who they are rightfully to be in the world. We note again this movement into the primacy of the self in order to know oneself properly in relation to others.

Foucault calls the general principle for these practices *conversion to self* (as distinct to detaching oneself from oneself, or the discipline of genealogical critical thought). *Epistrophe eis heauton* is the phrase that Foucault uses to think through the process of conversion to self. It means attention paid to a person or thing, regard, wheeling about, reaction, twisting-turning about: turning to self with regard to the self. This turn demands attention to what does not enslave one to what is untrue and passing. It expects freedom from the everyday, from curiosity, momentary absorption and hence from the body's search for intense and engrossing pleasure. Seneca says:

> The soul stands on unassailable grounds if it has abandoned external things; it is independent in its own fortress; and every weapon that is hurled falls short of the mark. Fortune has not the long reach with which we credit her; she can see none except him that clings to her. Let us then recoil from her as far as we are able.

One is to "belong to himself" in the sense of possess oneself by self-mastery, i.e., one is to be one's own slave and master according to true knowledge. One answers to oneself and is free from preoccupations of the external world. In conversion to self one is to possess oneself without anxiety, fear or hope. Self-possession is an end in itself. This is the change the development of which Foucault wants to follow: the self forms itself as an ethical subject that replaces, as far as ethics is concerned, all authorities in the world and comes to its identity as it knows and brings to bear universal principles of nature or reason. Because the self is frail and subject to disease and dispersion, self-knowledge grows in importance:

> the task of testing oneself, examining oneself, monitoring oneself in a series of defined exercises makes the question of truth – the truth concerning what one is, what one does, and what one is capable of doing – central to the formation of the ethical subject. . . . The end result of this elaboration is still and always defined by the rule of the individual over himself. But this rule broadens into an experience in which the relation to self takes the form not only of domination but also of an enjoyment without desire and without disturbance.[10]

An absence of pleasure is at the core of self-conversion by *uses* of pleasure. The distance of pleasure and desire is not meant by the word *jouissance*, although it means used as well as enjoyment, possessing pleasure and being in the possession of pleasure. *Jouissance* has the sense of simultaneous secular, spiritual, bodily and mental involvement as pleasure. The word refers us to a body of pleasure, an earthy inclusion without an implied mysticism. *Jouissance* is not without meaning – indeed it is saturated with meaning in the sense of having pleasure and mind together at once. But it lacks the essence of having meaning *in* a regard for something that stands outside of the meaning's structure. *Jouissance* does not occur as representation or as object of use or possession. This immediacy, this fullness of pleasure is lost in the distance of the self's usage. *Subjection* means a loss of pleasure by a mastery of pleasure. By subjecting pleasure and desire to the interests of a discipline of good health, the subjects of desire gain their determination and lose that indeterminateness that occurs in *jouissance*. The subject of desire comes to possess pleasure and desire, thereby losing them by mediating them. This self gives pleasure a space that is not of pleasure, but is of an *ascesis* that has its own space and time. The body's space and time of pleasure are lost in the space and time of a mastering agency. The body might know pleasure in a way that gives its own words and sounds as it bodies itself toward *its own* absence. It might undergo pleasure's pleasing in a heightened mortality, a fragile passing, an intense and deathly movement which bring together living and dying without a clear division, providing a passage that comes of itself as it leaves itself, enriching and sickening, without practical foresight, threatening disaster as it touches the deepest flow of life, giving everything and losing it in the gift, leaving behind exhaustion and only a possibility of return. Insecured vibrations of touch, febrile flesh without the transcendence of self-projection, without the anxiety of the self's time.

The subject of desire knows of such fullness in a *movement of abandonment*. In order to preserve pleasure it abandons the region of *jouissance*. *Jouissance* uses in the senses of engages fully and indulges. The subject of desire uses in the sense of converts pleasure to the service of something that is outside of pleasure. When we recall that the antonyms of pleasure are anger, pain, injury and displeasure we can see that Foucault is showing, in an elaboration of Nietzschean resentment, that the ethical self emerges in a movement that takes pleasure away from itself, a movement that angers and hurts while it fulfils a different body of intentions. The ethical self finds *its* satisfaction in a loss of pleasure. I believe that *this* movement shows one of the dangers embedded in the ethical subjectivity: it is made in a non-verbal antagonism between itself and the *force* of pleasure, a structurally dictated suspicion of *jouissance* that not only makes a language of *jouissance* impossible but constructs a disinclination regarding pleasure's pleasing and an inclination toward satisfaction in the severance of body from proper meaning and value. Does this mean that the tendency to universalize and totalize has as part of its destiny a demeaning of the body in the self's "highest" interests and pursuits? Does an angry and antagonized body find revenge in selves that are twisted from their own bodies and the bodies of others in the pursuit of conquests and control? Does the distanced body angrily give suffering in the self's pursuit of a proper measure? Would we have a different compassion if we were free of the control of those values that find satisfaction in victory at the expense of pleasure's pleasing, values that seek to overcome the death that lets pleasure be?

The problem that Foucault is uncovering is that the ethical subject displeases itself in satisfying itself, that it angers its life in attempting to satisfy it, and that it endangers its life by the offence that it makes as it attempts to give itself a proper life. This danger is at the core of his suspicion that fascism and cruelty indwell the best intentions of ethical responsibility.

Our attention is drawn by the burden of selfhood that is highlighted in its lineage. Not only is the self dangerous to its own life in its disciplined separation from the desire that is its truth, its life is also a process of continuous care by reference to itself and its creations. In the context of this paper I am suggesting that the pleasure of therapy is non-representably discernible as the self-relational structure breaks down, as the burden is unburdened in the self's dying. The pleasure is not the body's *jouissance*. It is other to the names that we have including, of course, the name that I have used. It might be closer to mourning than to responsibility.

MOURNING: GAINING A LOSS

The time of mourning is not quiet. Even if something quietly passes away instead of being torn violently from us, mourning gives the sounds of wounding loss. The loss seems to come from outside of the mourner: something other is lost in its otherness, and at first it becomes in its loss so other that it implodes, dissolves into itself beyond touch, and leaves in the place of its alterity nothing. Or leaves something like an empty space – another alterity – where once something dwelled. Something with which we found ourselves in relation. Something other that was in our lives. In the language of these remarks, something that was in ourselves as other to ourselves. And now this one becomes nothing and is retained as traces of experience that might give pleasure in the suffering of annihilation.

The other's implosion happens to and in the self, not like something represented or something observed to which we respond, but like a desire in a living thing, like a tear that exposes organs and flesh without protection. Mourning, which is sometimes called a process of healing, gains the loss by making the loss its own, making the loss into an organ of the self-organism. We might locate pleasure there: in gaining the loss, in the self's self-repair, we might find a strange pleasure that brings a death to life as a death. Not resurrection, but the coming of the grave. And by that grave the self is able to laugh again, to go on, to feel healthy again in the world's possibilities. The self is resurrected from its grave.

But I am moving too rapidly for mourning. I shall pause at the tearing. In the wounding loss the self is opened beyond itself. Its terrible burden includes an unburdening. Not the unburdening of the lost other, but an unburdening of the self's presence to itself, its interminable conversation with itself, its constant, silent projections. *In* the loss, the self loses itself. It dies to itself in tearing interruption. Does this suffering in mourning as the imploded other leave nothing of itself behind: does this suffering include pleasure? Certainly not a satisfaction of the self. In this moment one is closer to torture without the deception of ecstacy that nerves, insane from torment, may produce as a final gift. The self in the freshness of its loss is without satisfaction. But as the individual buckles, is bent by pain and gives voice to something lost and irreplaceable, is there pleasure beyond the self in the unburdening and wounding? I do not mean a masochistic pleasure of undergoing pain. I mean something like *jouissance* beyond the self, like possibility's granting or like something left open, like something the self will not know, something that gives the wound to be in the wound's abandonment of the self's texture.

This coming of pleasure might be like the passing among us of an unseen god. Odysseus says of Circe:

> While we were on the way to our ship in sorrow and mourning, Circe had got there before us and left fastened near the ship a black

ram and ewe. She slipped past us easily. Who could set eyes on a god if he did not wish it, going this way or coming that way?[11]

Odysseus and his companions were in sorrow and mourning because they had to go before the dead to find how they could return home. Circe walked unseen through their crowd to give them animals whose sacrifice would bring forth the terrifying dead. Their heavy hearts were unrelieved by her passing and her gifts: Circe's gifts brought them closer to the dead. She gave them no satisfaction or relief from their dread. In not freeing them from their sorrow she set them toward the occasion that would lead them toward Ithaca and that would also lead most of them to their deaths. Silently, imperceptibly passing through them, giving them an opening to the dead. Letting them be sent to fatal dangers: this "radiant goddess" bestowed on them a blessing-curse that removed no vulnerability but let them pass visibly beyond the stationary satisfaction of her dangerous island. They were blessed by the danger of passage through a place of no humans, a place beyond human feeling, a place of madness and awful foresight, a place of transition that gave life out of Hades' grave – and that gave also new occasions to die.

Such passage looks less like object-identification or regression to narcissism than it appears in an element of radical alterity in which an individual is torn from its identity and falls, as it were, into a danger that has accompanied invisibly its satisfactions and comforts, moves it beyond itself without motion or human emotion, converts visibility into invisibility and leaves it to open, freeing possibility and its stern necessity of danger and calamity.

What a strange thing. To undergo the voicelessness of death, the ephemeral radiance of a blessing goddess, her elusiveness, the deathless danger of her hospitality, the arising of new adventure and occasion for bravery – soul-stretching encounters – and, passing through the sorrow and mourning of losing the known, finding again that to arise anew is already to move toward losing the surge of returning life. Turning through mourning to new life. Turning through living to mourning. Do we speak of therapy's pleasure?

The pleasure of therapy does not provide the ecstacy of a body's singular enjoyment. It takes place as the self is unburdened – in the pain of unburdening as self-relation fails, as its self-attentiveness and obsessive self-concern are stilled and the self's unburdening gives way to the unself of the individual's life. The space of this pleasure is like a boundary that separates names and identities without itself having either name or identity. It is like a space before an identity closes, a space that cannot be encompassed by a story, a spacing in the self's absence. *In* the boundary's space one is "abandoned to the absence of boundaries"[12] to which nothing can belong.

This is not a flow of energy or a place of gathering, hardly a clearing for things, but more like a silence before something begins or more like lostness without threat. This pleasure is without the burden of selfhood, without caution or distance regarding anything. It is without ethical care or rational structure. It seems to be silently and indiscriminately with the self, to be through the body. The pleasure of therapy is without the self's disturbances.

If we assume that the self and its many aspects come to be in lineages, whether or not we accept Foucault's genealogy, and if we assume that the self is intensive, self-limiting, always self-concerned – in a word, burdened by taking care of itself – then we may expect that exposure of its lineages will make possible changes in its being. The self is a way of knowing, a highly structured, trained and influenced kind of being. Its own self-relatedness appears to come of disciplines of self-concern – Foucault's genealogy, for example, does far more than give an account of ethical practices. It shows the formation of inner self-relatedness as it develops from and grows apart from public mirroring. As we live through the collapse of certain self-relations in the exposure of the lineage of these self-relations, the pleasure of therapy is like an opening out of this lineage, as other to the lineage. It is like indeterminateness proximate to the struggles of self-determination, like an other to determination, without comfort or condemnation, like a peace that has come at a terrible price, but a peace that nonetheless offers silence without offering only death.

I believe that Freud was wrong in his estimating that death is forecast in the wish for stillness and that life is essentially motion and disturbance. That might be accurate regarding the self and its anxieties. The pleasure of therapy, however, comes with those experiences in which the self undergoes its deathliness. It is probably most discernible in the self's deaths. But this pleasure takes place without concern in proximity to both death and life at once. And when a person becomes attuned to it it is like the appearance of Circe whose seeming blessing is also like condemnation because it is essentially neither. It is merely the voice of a god who cannot be totally understood, but only interpreted, and it comes from outside our self's narrative. To be without a self seems impossible. To live as though one were totally a self is to be divided from much else that is one's life. To think the pleasure of not-self and to be self with not-self is probably the distinct struggle of our lineage. It is a struggle, I believe, that might alter the lineage by a silence that our lineage has repeatedly lost by investing it with the self's words.

NOTES

1 By *self* I have in mind a historical, thoroughly social formation that represents itself to itself and that represents whatever it encounters representationally. The self is who we know ourselves to be in our satisfactions. It knows itself in its

satisfactions and pains. The self is who we think we are and thinking who we are, who we feel ourselves to be and feeling who we are, who we find needs to be corrected, improved and who needs something like wholeness. The self is also a state of needing correction, improvement and wholeness. I am using the word in a way that is closer to *ego* in Freud and Jung, and not at all in Jung's sense of Self. *Self* thus means being an identity and having an identity. The self's being in question and its difference from the pleasure of therapy are not representations. Its being in question and its difference from the pleasure of therapy call for non-representational thought and writing.

2 *The History of Sexuality*, vol. 2, *The Use of Pleasure* (New York: Pantheon Books, 1985), p. 5. Emphasis added.

3 Ibid.

4 The developmental process from early care for self to modern practices of pastoral power is complex and highly differentiated. I must ignore the complications here and provide only a direction for thought about self-burdening.

5 Michel Foucault, *The History of Sexuality*, vol. 3, *The Care of Self* (New York, Pantheon Books, 1986), p. 80.

6 Ibid., p. 40.

7 Foucault, *The Use of Pleasure*, p. 86.

8 Ibid., p. 89.

9 Ibid.

10 Foucault, *The Care of Self*, p. 68.

11 *The Odyssey*, Book X.

12 George Bataille, *Inner Experience* (New York: SUNY Press, 1988), p. 9.

Name index

Abraham, Karl 116
Abraham, Nicolas 185
Adler, Alfred 28, 35, 102, 103, 105, 126n39
Allison, David B. 58
Althusser, Louis 66
Aristophanes 102, 154, 163, 164
Aristotle 5, 11, 34, 102, 144, 181
Armstrong, Robert 36
Artaud, Antonin 137

Balint, Michael 28
Ballard, J.G. 142
Barth, John 163
Baudelaire, Charles 136
Baudrillard, Jean 136, 146
Bergson, Henri 154
Bettelheim, Bruno 3
Binswanger, Ludwig 151
Blake, William 36
Borch-Jacobsen, Mikkel 77
Bosch, Hieronymus 143
Boss, Medard 151, 179
Brecht, Bertolt 88
Brentano, Franz 101, 118
Breuer, Josef 87
Brown, Norman O. 33
Bruel, Carl 121

Cardenal, Ernesto 56
Castoriadis, Cornelius 1
Circe 221–2, 223
Comte, Auguste 97, 101, 102, 103, 109, 124n26, 125n29, 128n65, 131n118
Coover, Robert 45, 51, 53–4

Dali, Salvador 143
Deffand, Mme du 111–12
Delacroix, Eugène 62

Denis, St 111–12, 114–15, 116
Derrida, Jacques 41, 53, 57, 61, 69n1,n12, 97, 151, 153–4, 159–60, 163, 182
Descartes, René 31, 35, 80, 83, 86, 162
Destutt de Tracy, A.-L.-C. 125n29
Devi, Mahasweta 67
Diderot, Denis 14
Didier 24–5
Dilthey, Wilhelm 154
Djebar, Assia 60–2, 67, 68
Durkheim, Emile 33
Dutt, R.C. 50

Eitingon, Max 116
Epictetus 218

Fanon, Frantz 66–8, 72n55, 75n91
Ferenczi, Sándor 102, 112, 115, 116
Feuerbach, Ludwig Andreas 123n18
Fichte, J.G. 81
Ficino, Marsilio 31
Fließ, Wilhelm 118, 121, 123n18, 152
Florence 20–3
Foucault, Michel 30, 52, 205, 210–20, 223
Freud, Ernst 156
Freud, Jakob 109, 117, 118, 119
Freud, Sigmund xi–xiv, 1, 2–5, 10, 15–20, 25–6, 28, 30–3, 37, 39, 42, 49–51, 54–65, 69, 74n75, 77–81, 87, 93–4, 97–131, 135–6, 143–4, 147–8, 151–66, 172, 179, 186–203, 223–4

Garcia Marquez, Gabriel 145
George, Stefan 178
Gibson, J.J. 36
Goethe, J.W. von 119, 120–1, 131n116
Goux, Jean-Joseph 66